Advance Praise for
American Intifada

"For too long, Israel has been the subject of unfair and untrue attacks by politicians, professors, and the press. Whether one agrees or disagrees with all its conclusions, this well-researched, thought-provoking book is an important contribution to understanding and overcoming the phenomenon."

—**Alan Dershowitz**, Professor, Harvard Law School

"Uri Kaufman has written a fascinating, comprehensive study of one of the major issues of our time. It is a significant step toward understanding the emotions, and distortions, surrounding the Middle East."

—**Al D'Amato**, Former United States Senator (R-NY)

"A timely, provocative, and startlingly original explanation of the left's Intifada against the only democracy in the Middle East."

—**Ben Shapiro**, Columnist and Commentator

"In *American Intifada*, Uri Kaufman dissects the ideological betrayal of Israel by Western intellectuals and media, a phenomenon laid bare in the aftermath of Hamas's heinous October 7 attack. This book is both a historical reckoning and a moral challenge, asking why those who champion human rights remain silent—or complicit—when Israel is targeted. A gripping and essential work for understanding the intersection of modern antisemitism and the geopolitics of our time. It reveals how ideology, ignorance, and apathy have converged to distort the moral landscape. Drawing on chilling firsthand accounts and incisive critiques of Western media and politics, Kaufman illuminates the battle for truth amidst the propaganda. This book is a wake-up call—a reminder that the defense of Israel is not just a Jewish cause but a defense of shared democratic values."

—**Malcolm Hoenlein**, Former Executive Vice Chairman of the Conference of Presidents of Major American Jewish Organizations

To Mom

AMERICAN INTIFADA

Israel, the Gaza War,
and the New Antisemitism

URI KAUFMAN

R

A REPUBLIC BOOK

American Intifada:
Israel, the Gaza War, and the New Antisemitism
© 2025 by Uri Kaufman
All Rights Reserved

ISBN: 978-1-64572-104-8
ISBN (eBook): 978-1-64572-112-3

Cover Design by Jim Villaflores

R

Republic Book Publishers
New York, NY
www.republicbookpublishers.com

Published in the United States of America
1 2 3 4 5 6 7 8 9 10

Contents

I.

Strange Bedfellows

"A man with a conviction is a hard man to change."
—LEON FESTINGER[1]

On the morning of October 7, 2023, Alon Davidi was jolted awake by the piercing sound of blaring sirens and exploding rockets. The small Israeli border town of Sderot, where he had been mayor for ten years, was located just a half mile from Gaza. So Davidi and his family were well-schooled in the drill of piling out of bed and running for cover in pajamas. Given that Sderot is a community with more bomb shelters than bus stops, they didn't have far to run.

As mayor, it was Davidi's job to emerge the moment the shelling ceased, make damage assessments, and direct first responders to those in need. There was a familiar but eerie silence that Davidi came to expect after a rocket attack. A fifteen-minute period in which Sderot remained a ghost town, as people stayed in shelters to avoid falling shrapnel. But this time, Davidi emerged to an ear-splitting cacophony of gunfire. His natural instinct was to contact the local police station. He soon learned that officers holed up inside could not come to his aid. They were busy fighting for their lives.[2]

Across southern Israel, Hamas terrorists carried out the largest massacre of Jews in a single day since the Holocaust. An estimated

1

1,163 people were killed, thousands were wounded, and 251 were taken hostage.[3] At least 347 of the dead were young people murdered at a nearby music festival.[4] The mass killings stood out not just in their scale but in their brutality. Palestinians decapitated an Israeli soldier, brought his head to Gaza, and tried to sell it.[5] Some bodies were so charred that they could only be identified as human with a CT scan. Others were found with ash in their lungs, indicating that the victims had been burned alive. One black mass was found to contain two human spines that had fused together, suggesting that the victims were hugging when fuel was poured on them and they were set on fire.[6] An Israeli pathologist later said that "in normal times, murder is carried out very quickly, with a shooting or a stabbing…these were slow, cruel killings, burning people alive, shooting them in a row and then driving cars over them."[7]

Even the Nazis had the good sense to cover up their crimes. The Hamas terrorists enthusiastically posted their atrocities on social media. One was taped calling his parents and bragging that he had just killed ten Jews. His proud parents were recorded praising him.[8] Khalil Shikaki, the most reliable Palestinian pollster, found almost universal support for the attacks among the Palestinian public, which surprised no one.[9] Palestinian and other Arab leaders had long dehumanized Jews, referring to them as "apes and pigs." Senior Hamas official Ghazi Hamad hailed the slaughter on Lebanese television, vowing that the group would continue to launch similar attacks until all of Israel's Jews were exterminated.[10]

* * *

The news of the butchery staggered Israel and, for a brief moment, even its critics. But things soon returned to normal. Or at least what passes for normal when it comes to the Jewish state.

No less than thirty-four different student organizations in Harvard signed a statement on October 10—before Israeli troops had even entered Gaza—saying that they "hold the Israeli regime entirely responsible for all unfolding violence."[11] On October 23, Barack Obama wrote of Palestinians and Israelis that "nobody's hands are

2

clean." What terrible thing had the Israelis done to justify the moral equivalence? Obama said that the "occupation" had made the plight of the Palestinians "unbearable."[12] The trouble, of course, was that there was no occupation. Israel had withdrawn from Gaza almost twenty years before.

And then there was *The New York Times*. A study in Israel analyzed all the articles highlighted during the first seven months of the war in the *Times* daily newsletter Today's Headlines ("Get the best of the Times in your Inbox"). It found that articles sympathetic to Palestinians outnumbered those sympathetic to Israel by a margin of almost five to one. Shockingly, in the first week after the October 7 attack—once again, before Israeli troops entered Gaza—the paper of record split the blame almost evenly, criticizing Hamas in fourteen stories, Israel in twelve, and both in fourteen.[13]

Sympathetic articles are one thing. Worse still was the fact that much of what the *Times* said was patently false. On October 17, prior to the commencement of Israel's ground campaign, an explosion went off in the parking lot of the al-Ahli Hospital in Gaza City. Hamas was quick to blame Israel for the blast and the international press was quick to adopt it as truth. The *New York Times* reported that "the Gaza health ministry said Wednesday that at least 471 people were killed."[14] It would quickly emerge that the explosion was not caused by Israel, but by a homemade Islamic Jihad rocket that had malfunctioned. It also turned out that, although the exact death toll is still in dispute, it was a fraction of the 471 claimed by the "Gaza health ministry." In addition to everything else, it would have been impossible to pull 471 bodies out of the rubble in the short time after the blast and before the "Gaza health ministry" issued its statement. The *Wall Street Journal* quoted an intelligence analyst who put the figure at about fifty.[15] The falsity of the original story and the speed with which it was embraced was so embarrassing that the *Times* issued a rare Editor's Note, acknowledging that its reports "relied too heavily on claims by Hamas" and "left readers with an incorrect impression about...how credible the account was."[16]

So the *Times* wiped the egg off its face, and—like all international media—went right back to relying heavily on claims by the Gaza Health Ministry.

In truth, the Israelis are the best in the world at limiting collateral damage in war, better even than the United States. In 2014, after Israel's Operation Protective Edge, the chairman of the U.S. Joint Chiefs of Staff, General Martin Dempsey, sent a Pentagon team to Israel to learn how the IDF kept civilian casualties so low.[17] After Operation Cast Lead in 2009, British Colonel Richard Kemp said that "the Israel Defense Forces did more to safeguard the rights of civilians in the combat zones than any other army in the history of warfare."[18]

But none of these facts ever seem to register, at least with a certain slice of the body politic. One has only to spend a short time watching the chattering classes on television or reading their columns in newspapers to see a pattern: the more liberal a person's political outlook, the more likely they are to attack Israel with claims that it commits war crimes or violates international law. In the court of public opinion, Israel is a repeat offender and guilty as charged—at least among juries that sit to the left of the aisle.

It is an odd paradox. A visitor from another planet who studied political science and thumbed through an atlas would likely pause at the page dedicated to Israel. "This," our alien friend would jot down, "must be a place admired by the humans known as 'liberals.'"

Israel is the only country in the history of the world to be founded by a labor union. It is the first country to elevate a woman to head of government without her being related by blood or marriage to a king or male politician. Golda Meir's 1969 election as prime minister was the culmination of a long tradition. Women were given the right to vote in Zionist institutions from their inception in the late 1800s. A British suffragette who visited Palestine in 1924—four years before British women received the right to vote—was stunned to learn that a majority of the City Council of Rishon Letzion were women.[19]

Gay rights? Israel elected its first openly gay politician to its national parliament, the Knesset, in 1973.[20,i] Gays have served openly in Israel's military since at least the 1980s. Israeli cities regularly appear on gay travel surveys as among the friendliest in the world.[21] One irony-proof travel writer described Tel Aviv as a "gay Mecca" (apparently unaware how many openly gay people there are in Mecca).

Which brings us to the other side of the paradox. After a little more research, our alien friend would assume that the Arab world is a target-rich environment for progressive fury. When asked what the life expectancy of gays in Palestine is, one demographer answered, "until they are discovered." Gay Palestinians seek asylum in Israel to avoid the fate of people like Ahmad Abu Marhia, who was beheaded in the West Bank.[22] A Palestinian human rights group documented twenty-three "honor killings" of women in the West Bank and Gaza in 2018 alone.[23] But a visit to a college campus would show angry students, mighty in their numbers, shaking their fists, shouting in support of Palestine, demanding sanctions against Israel, and chanting for its destruction ("From the river to the sea, Palestine will soon be free!").

For the first half of Israel's history, it was the other way around. Jerusalem could count on support from liberals and Democrats, while conservatives and Republicans often complained about the "Jewish lobby." Starting sometime in the 1970s, the two sides gradually began trading places. Today, it is progressive Congresswoman Ilhan Omar who complains, "It's all about the Benjamins, baby" (referring to financial support given by Israel's supporters). Meanwhile, Republican Freedom Caucus Chairman Jim Jordan declares, "I stand with our great friend Israel…and look forward to a new

---

[i] America did not elect an openly gay politician to any public office until 1977, when Harvey Milk was elected to serve on the San Francisco Board of Supervisors. As of this writing, no openly gay man has ever been elected to the United States Senate, and only one openly gay woman has been elected to the Senate: Wisconsin's Tammy Baldwin in 2012. Another woman elected in 2018, Senator Kyrsten Sinema of Arizona, describes herself as bisexual.

era of friendship and cooperation with Israel under President-elect Donald Trump."[24]

Why have the two sides traded places on such a high-profile issue?

An oft-repeated explanation has to do with the Jewish state itself. Once a tiny David clinging to the shores of the Mediterranean, it is now a Goliath atop the world of technology.[ii] Liberals support underdogs; conservatives support realpolitik, hence the role reversal.

This theory admittedly goes a long way to explaining the flip on the part of pragmatic Republicans. Years ago, Israel could tug at the heartstrings as the only democracy in the Middle East. But in every material respect, it was a geostrategic charity case with little to offer. Today it is a rising technological power and a crucial ally in cyber warfare and counterterrorism. There is one country, probably more than any other, to whom Washington turns to help stall Iran's nuclear program. That country is Israel.

But what of Democrats? Contrary to popular misconception, liberals are not more likely to fight for underdogs, at least when it comes to foreign policy. After Saddam Hussein invaded Kuwait, it was liberals who were more likely to chant "No blood for oil!" and argue for abandoning Kuwaitis to their fate. Senator Bernie Sanders has long been a prominent voice opposing NATO expansion.[25] More recently, the Congressional Progressive Caucus issued a letter urging the Biden Administration to pressure Ukraine to end the war with Russia.[26]

That liberals would turn their backs on Kuwait is perhaps understandable. It is, after all, an oppressive, oil-rich sheikdom. But Ukraine is a nation with liberal values. The very people in the Congressional Progressive Caucus who signed the letter calling for a cutoff of aid to Ukraine screamed the loudest when the Trump Administration cut off aid to the Palestinians. Why abandon Ukraine but embrace the Palestinians?

[ii] In the decade of the 2000s, Israelis won the most Nobel prizes in the sciences per capita, triple the nation in second place.

The best way to understand the phenomenon is to engage in a simple thought experiment. Let us suppose that every fact related to the Hamas attack on October 7 occurred exactly as described: murders, beheadings, people burned alive, etc. But let's change *one* fact. Let us assume that the people who carried out the terrorist attack were *not* Palestinians. Let us assume that they were Germans of another era or Ukrainians of another era.

In other words, let us assume that they were white people. Not people of color.

In this scenario, you wouldn't expect the Biden Administration to give a multi-billion-dollar aid package to the white supremacist "innocent civilians." But Biden approved billions in aid for Gaza, even as Hamas declared that it would rebuild and attack Israel again. The aid wasn't even conditioned on the release of the eight Americans then being held hostage.[iii] Vice President Kamala Harris insisted that "we cannot conflate Hamas with the Palestinian people."[27]

And now let's take this thought experiment all the way by changing the identities of *all* the parties. In this parallel universe, white supremacists attack an *African country* on October 7, declaring that *blacks* are "apes and pigs." Try to imagine a Republican president sending billions in aid to the white supremacist "innocent civilians," or imagine the vice president arguing that we cannot conflate the white terrorists with the civilians who support them. It would never happen, and liberals would riot if it did. But those same liberals are eager to send billions to Palestinians in Gaza.

In short, what we have is a classic example of cognitive dissonance. First identified by psychologist Leon Festinger in the 1950s, cognitive dissonance describes a well-known human phenomenon: when people are confronted with facts that contradict deeply held beliefs, they usually change the facts, not the beliefs.

---

iii Two of the Americans were filmed in propaganda videos released by Hamas. One, Keith Siegel, wept as he pled for his life. The other, Hersh Goldberg-Polin, was seen with his left arm amputated just below the elbow due to wounds inflicted by Hamas on October 7.

In the worldview of progressives, racism is endemic, and white people oppress people of color. It is through this lens that they see human history; it is this ancient wrong that they wish to right. They, therefore, spring into action and fight for "social justice" the moment they see white people in conflict with people of color.[iv]

This argument admittedly had appeal decades ago in the days of Jim Crow or apartheid. But it has nothing to do with Israel and its conflict with the Palestinians. The differences are as obvious as they are numerous, and they will be explained in more detail below. But taking in these facts requires progressives to hold two conflicting thoughts in their heads at the same time: supporting Israel, despite a worldview that sees white people as oppressors. Better to change the facts than to confront the paradox—better, that is, to come down in support of people of color (i.e., the Palestinians). Overcoming cognitive dissonance is hard work.

This is why *The New York Times* described Gaza as being under Israeli military occupation for years, long after the Israeli army withdrew. This is why Amnesty International described Israel as an apartheid state at a time in which an Arab political party was part of Israel's coalition government. And this is why numerous left-wing media outlets and politicians denied that Hamas terrorists committed rape on October 7, even as those same terrorists admitted on tape that they did.[v][28]

In 2021, Michael Moore weighed in on the Palestinian-Israeli conflict on his podcast. He began by paying homage to the Jewish labor organizers of the 1930s, lawyers who left comfortable lives in New York and moved to Moore's native Flint, Michigan, to take menial jobs in car factories so they could help create the autoworkers'

[iv] Back in the 1980s when I was a college student, I saw a protest against apartheid on campus and politely asked one of the protesters (who happened to be white) why she was so focused on South Africa, when so much of the African continent suffered far worse oppression. She replied in perfect candor that she didn't know why—it was just how she felt.

[v] In between cries of Allahu Akbar, the Hamas terrorists were taped referring to female hostages as *sabaya*, the same term that ISIS terrorists used in reference to Yezidi women, which is widely understood to mean "sex slave."

union. Moore's elegy sounded sincere enough—more than just a cringeworthy attempt to show that he was not an antisemite. But then he turned abruptly to the main topic of the podcast, which was attacking Israel: "The treatment of George Floyd, multiply that by 5 million, 7 million. And there you have the situation in Palestine and Israel...[in a mocking tone, mimicking the Israelis]: 'We have a right to defend ourselves.' Yes, thank you, General Custer, yes you do... You guys are so good at this—Bibi, remember, you're an American; you know how to kill because we're great killers!"[29]

When Michael Moore looks at Palestinians, he sees George Floyd. When he looks at Israelis, he sees General George Custer. And when he looks at Americans, he sees killers.

He is hardly the only one. After the 9/11 attack, leftist social critic Susan Sontag said, "Where is the acknowledgment that this was not a 'cowardly' attack on 'civilization' or 'liberty' or 'humanity' or the 'free world' but an attack on the world's self-proclaimed superpower, undertaken as a consequence of specific American alliances and actions?"[30] Noam Chomsky spoke for many other left-wing intellectuals when he said, "This is certainly a turning point: for the first time in history, the victims are returning the blow to the motherland."[31]

Most American liberals aren't willing to go that far. For one thing, they have a solid understanding of American history. For another, they identify as Americans, so there is at least that backstop against cognitive dissonance. But Israel—the only other country in modern times perceived as "white" and in conflict with what liberals term "people of color"—enjoys neither benefit.[vi,32] For most people, Israel is a Hebrew-speaking Denmark (how many people know anything about the history of Denmark?). And progressives—even many Jewish progressives—empathize first and foremost with people of color. This is the point where cognitive dissonance takes over. This is where the line between fact and fiction begins to blur. The only

---

vi According to Israel's Central Bureau of Statistics, only 32 percent of the country's population is white.

thing left is to change the facts to fit the worldview, to jam the square peg of racial justice into the round hole of the Arab-Israeli conflict.

How they jam that peg into the hole is the subject of this book.

II.

Jimmy Carter—
The Phenomenon in the Flesh

*"To understand a man, you have to know what was
happening in the world when that man
was twenty years old."*

—NAPOLEON BONAPARTE[1]

In 2006, Jimmy Carter released a book about the Palestinian-Israeli conflict: *Palestine: Peace Not Apartheid.*

It is a remarkable document, albeit for all the wrong reasons. A review in the ordinarily sympathetic *New York Times* described it as a "strange little book from a major public figure."[2] When asked for comment, Kenneth Stein, a former executive director of the Carter Center, declined to detail all the inaccuracies he found in the work, replying he was still too busy documenting them all.[3]

Because the misstatements of fact are so numerous and because they appear intermixed as a single mass—not unlike a badly made mudpie—it is best to limit inquiry to only the most egregious examples. Like the Academy Awards, which saves the Best Picture Oscar for last, I shall withhold my overall selection until the end. But in the meantime, let's review the winners in some of the lesser categories. The envelope, please.

In the category of worst misstatement of fact related to an Arab-Israeli war, we have this one: "On June 5, [1967], Israel launched preemptive strikes, moving first against Egypt and Syria, then against Jordan."[4] To say that Israel attacked Jordan (or, for that matter, Syria) in 1967 is not unlike saying that Poland attacked Germany in 1939. The Israelis begged Jordan's King Hussein to stay out of the war through multiple channels, but he decided to attack Israel anyway.[5]

In the category of worst misstatement of fact related to the peace process, we have Carter claiming that the Palestinians were only offered 83 percent of the West Bank in peace talks in 2001, even supplying a map titled "Palestinian Interpretation of Clinton's Proposal."[6] In truth, Israel offered almost the entire West Bank.[7] Top U.S. diplomat Dennis Ross later said that Carter's map was lifted from his memoir without permission and that it was "mislabeled."[8]

And in the category of terrorism, we have Carter supporting the Lebanese extremist group Hezbollah's border demands against Israel. In a report to the Security Council on May 22, 2000, secretary-general Kofi Annan noted that there were no less than ten different Lebanese maps and six Syrian maps that all supported Israel. He and the Security Council rejected Hezbollah's assertion out of hand.[9] Now the U.N. is not exactly known for its pro-Israel sympathies. And Hezbollah's founders murdered hundreds of American troops in the 1983 Marine barracks bombing in Beirut.[10] Carter sided with Hezbollah anyway.[11]

I haven't watched the Academy Awards in years. But back when I did, it was around now that I would turn the channel—I was never interested in who won Best Cinematography in a Japanese Cartoon—and then later check in to find out who won Best Picture. Likewise, I will spare you the numerous lesser categories for misstatements of fact in *Palestine: Peace Not Apartheid*. The best I can say is that if one reads this bewildering little book at a steady pace, one will be rewarded by the fact that it does eventually end.

* * *

Which brings us to the inevitable question of why. Why would someone as smart as Jimmy Carter write a book filled with errors that are not so much egregious as hilarious?[i,12] And why would he say things in interviews down through the years that are, if anything, even worse?[ii,13]

Carter's antics related to Israel are out of character. After leaving the White House, he made his peace with Ronald Reagan and even found a few kind words for Donald Trump. It is only Israel that somehow remained a target for unbending and irrational hostility. Plainly, the feelings that drove him in this regard came from so deep inside that they were impervious to facts or reason.

To understand these feelings, one first must understand the world that produced them.

"My life has been shaped inevitably by the experiences and decisions of my forefathers, and I have learned a lot about my family history." Those are the words that Carter uses to begin his memoir *A Full Life: Reflections at Ninety*.[14] Carter further notes that "even our more recent family history was, to a surprising degree, shaped by violence."[15] The "violence" Carter refers to begins with his great-great-grandfather, who killed a man in a gunfight. It continued with his great-grandfather (a Confederate Army veteran) and grandfather, who were both murdered at various times in gunfights of their own.[16]

It could also have referred to the history of the place where the Carter clan settled and made their fortune. As Carter recounts in his memoir, his family's story in western Georgia began in the early 1800s when his great-great-grandfather, Wiley Carter, "traded for land with an original owner, who won it in a lottery that was held in 1833, after Indians had been forced to leave West Georgia."[17]

---

[i] Some of them really are hilarious. Carter concludes his book on the somber tone that "a baby born during the first Arab-Israeli conflict [in 1948] will be fifty years old next year." As is clear from the date he writes on the bottom of the page, "next year" was 2008. That is sixty years after 1948, not fifty. His asleep-at-the-switch editor was none other than the legendary Alice Mayhew, who rose to become editorial director of Simon & Schuster.

[ii] TV host Chris Matthews once asked Carter if Israel's alleged persecution of the Palestinians was "even worse…than a place like Rwanda," where as many as a million people were murdered. Carter said, "Yes. I think—yes."

Note the passive statement, Indians that "had been forced to leave" (forced by whom?). The unidentified culprit was perhaps the most evil law in American history: the Indian Removal Act of 1830. Upon its passage, the so-called "Five Civilized Tribes" were violently uprooted from their ancestral lands and sent to a wasteland west of the Mississippi. A large percentage died before they got there, succumbing to exposure, disease, or starvation along what was dubbed the "Trail of Tears." I have never been a supporter of any movement to pay reparations for crimes committed over a century ago. But those in favor could be speaking about Carter when they point out that there are people today who still benefit from the fruits of those crimes.

Of course, Carter witnessed none of this. But as a boy, he witnessed something almost as ugly: the American system of Jim Crow.

There were about two hundred people living in the tiny community of Archery, Georgia, where Jimmy Carter was born in October 1924. His was one of only two white families; all the others were African-Americans who had been enslaved, or their immediate descendants. Even at the age of ninety, he could still "recall vividly a seemingly minor incident that has profoundly affected the rest of my life." As he described it, when he was fourteen years old, he approached a gate with some black friends, and they "stepped back to let me go through the opening ahead of them." Young Jimmy hesitated, thinking it might be a practical joke, with perhaps a trip wire planted on the other side. But he eventually learned that "the unearned deference of my black playmates toward me was the result of a cautionary word from their parents that the time had come to conform to the racial distinctions that were strictly observed among adults."[18]

The worst of those social strictures were too painful for Carter to record in his memoir. But they are described in excruciating detail by his biographer.

His father Earl Carter's hero was Georgia Governor Eugene Talmadge, who often cried that the working man had three enemies—and then shouted the "n-word" three times.[19] His mother Lillian Carter

14

was known to have used that word into the 1970s, even telling a *New York Times* reporter in 1977 that marriage between the races was wrong.[20] When Max Schmeling fought his famous rematch with Joe Louis in 1938, Earl Carter placed a radio by the window and turned up the volume so that black tenant farmers could listen outside. Louis went on to knock out Schmeling in the first round, but the blacks dared not utter a peep. A local black man had been lynched in 1910 for celebrating the victory of African-American heavyweight champ Jack Johnson over a white man. Only after silently crossing the railroad tracks and returning to their shacks could they let out a cheer and celebrate through the night.[21]

Carter's first political job was on an all-white, seven-member board of education in rural Georgia. In that capacity, he did everything in his power to thwart Supreme-Court-mandated school integration. He also held up the construction of a new school for black students because its location required white students to walk past them on the same street.[22] He never once met with fellow Georgian Dr. Martin Luther King. In the words of his biographer, he was "scared of being connected to the civil rights movement."[23] In describing the pre-civil rights era, Carter himself said, "apartheid reigned."[24]

Carter got himself elected governor of Georgia by what one observer called "playing the race card," employing a dog-whistle campaign that won him 90 percent of the rural white vote.[25] It was only then that he did a complete about-face and became a champion of civil rights. The sense of shock that befell his supporters is captured perfectly by the title of the chapter in his biography: "He Said Whaaat?"[26]

A cynic might note that Carter experienced his epiphany on the road to Damascus once he was in the governor's mansion and training his sights on the White House. But the plain fact is that he spent not just his White House years but the rest of his life working for the betterment of minorities. He was also embarrassed by the things he had to do early in his political career. When pressed by his biographer on those points, he asked softly, "Are we done talking about this yet?"[27]

There is little doubt that in those difficult years, Carter—like many liberals—formed a worldview that saw white racism as endemic and people of color as perpetual victims. This situation, so familiar to anyone who grew up in the Deep South in the first half of the twentieth century, created a moral imperative to right a fundamental wrong. This cannot be dismissed as mere "virtue signaling." It appears to be a core belief born out of experience—a belief that cuts to the depth of Carter's soul. A perplexed Dennis Ross asked Stuart E. Eizenstat, one of Carter's longest-serving aides, to explain "the hostility that he [Carter] frequently expressed toward the Israelis." Eizenstat, who is Jewish, gave several geostrategic reasons but then added that it was "Carter's regret that he had not played a large role in the civil rights movement.... This moral impulse helped to explain his commitment to human rights—and unquestionably affected his view of Israel and the Palestinians."[28]

It certainly affected what happened between Israel and Egypt in 1978 at Camp David.

* * *

In the early days of the Middle East peace process after the 1967 War, the big word was "linkage." Diplomats from Arab countries refused to even negotiate with Israel, insisting that their dispute with the Jewish state—and all disputes in the Middle East—were "linked" to the conflict with the Palestinians; one could not be solved without the other. Since Palestinians refused even to recognize Israel, all diplomacy was a nonstarter. In July 1967, Jerusalem offered to withdraw from the Sinai Peninsula in return for a peace treaty with Egypt.[iii] The Palestinians refused to negotiate, so Cairo did the same. A stunned U.S. Secretary of State Dean Rusk exclaimed to Egyptian Foreign Minister Mahmoud Riad, "But I got you total Israeli withdrawal from Egyptian territories!"[29]

Anwar Sadat repeated this position in his historic speech to the Knesset in November 1977, saying, "I did not come to you to

---

iii The land-for-peace offer was adopted unanimously by a national unity government that represented 108 out of 120 seats in the Knesset—an all-time record likely to stand.

conclude a separate agreement between Egypt and Israel...it would not be possible to achieve a just and durable peace...in the absence of a just solution to the Palestinian problem."[30] But astute listeners noticed a subtle omission: Sadat avoided his usual reference to the Palestine Liberation Organization (PLO) as an indispensable partner in any negotiation.[31]

Sadat dropped his bombshell four months later, on March 30, 1978, in a meeting with Israeli Defense Minister Ezer Weizmann. He had no interest in a Palestinian state; he was even willing to allow Israeli settlements on the West Bank to remain in place. Weizmann practically fell out of his chair. He later said he was happy Israeli Attorney General Aharon Barak was present to hear it, or no one back in Jerusalem would have believed him.[32]

The chances of any talks failing rise exponentially with the number of issues put on the table. Any sensible mediator will work to shrink a conflict, excluding whatever extraneous disputes he can. This is doubly so in the Middle East, where negotiation is not just the work of the brain, but of the gut and the spleen as well. It should also be noted that, emotion aside, it made no sense for Egypt to negotiate for the Palestinians just three years after declaring the PLO the sole legitimate representative of the Palestinian people. Imagine Ukraine sitting across the table from Russia and insisting that any settlement include disputes related to the former Soviet republic of Georgia.

Yet when it came to the Arab-Israeli peace process, Carter ignored Sadat's signals and, like a car out of alignment, constantly swerved off the path into the oncoming traffic of the Palestinian issue. Perhaps Sadat could live with settlements and without a Palestinian state; Carter could not. Here is how William B. Quandt, a member of Carter's National Security Council, described the situation:

> Sadat focused his comments almost entirely on Sinai, where he insisted on full withdrawal by Israeli forces. He rarely talked in detail about the West Bank or Gaza, preferring to stress general principles such as the nonacquisition of territory by force and the right of the Palestinians to self-determination. He did not

strongly support the American attempt to mobilize opinion behind a freeze on settlements.... Carter was therefore left in the awkward position of appearing to be more pro-Arab than Sadat, a politically vulnerable position, to say the least.[33]

Being more anti-Israel than an Arab leader is certainly "awkward" for any American president. That is why only two presidents have done it (Barack Obama is the other—more on him later). But for an Arab leader to be less anti-Israel than an American president, well, that's not just "awkward"—it's suicidal. On the contrary, Arab leaders need American presidents to give them political cover. The Camp David talks got off on the wrong foot because Sadat ignored all the quiet concessions the parties had traded up to that point and opened the summit by trumpeting extremist positions that included a right of return for Palestinians and Israel giving up its nuclear capability.[34] Then he ran to proudly repeat his demands to the press. The flummoxed Israelis were preparing a salvo in response until they realized it was just political theater. Sadat had merely postured before the Arab world, demonstrating that he hadn't conceded an inch. The stage was thus set to blame any deal on American pressure.[35]

In his memoir, Egyptian Foreign Minister Muhammad Ibrahim Kamel writes that he advised Sadat to go to Camp David because there were only "two possibilities, both good." Either Carter would force Begin to make major concessions to the Palestinians, or the talks would blow up, and the Americans would fault Israel for the failure.[36] The idea that Sadat might give in never even occurred to him.[iv,37] And who could blame him? Prior to the talks, he had been told by Secretary of State Cyrus Vance that Carter sided with Egypt and planned to "sidetrack the Congress so as not to clash with Israel's supporters and address the American people directly on the issue." If that didn't work, he would go to the U.N. Security Council.[38]

---

iv Kamel writes that he only found out about Sadat's secret concession years later when he read Weizmann's memoir, and had he known about it at the time he would have resigned on the spot.

In the end, the Camp David talks deadlocked for almost two weeks over the issue of the Palestinians. But Menachem Begin refused to budge, and to the astonishment of all, Anwar Sadat gave in. Egyptian Foreign Minister Kamel angrily resigned,[39] and some of Sadat's closest friends and allies, like the prominent newspaper editor Muhammad Hassanein Heikal, broke with him as well. But for Carter, it should have been a moment to savor. He had made history. *He had brokered the first Arab-Israeli peace treaty.*

Shockingly, amazingly, Carter couldn't take yes for an answer.

The Camp David Accords, signed on September 17, 1978, were merely a framework agreement. A final peace treaty still had to be hammered out. Carter gave a press conference on September 27, in which he said that Israel had committed to a five-year settlement freeze, all but calling Begin—who insisted he had only agreed to a symbolic three-month freeze—a liar. The trouble was that a week before, Sadat himself had given his own press conference in which he, too, acknowledged that Begin's settlement freeze was only for three months and that it was acceptable.[40] I leave it to the reader to imagine the look on Sadat's face when he found out what Carter had said. Imagine being an Arab leader turning on the television and finding yourself less anti-Israel than the American president who "pressured" you into the Camp David deal.

This pattern continued for all the hair-raising months of negotiations until the final treaty was signed. Carter never stopped trying to tie everything to a resolution of the Palestinian issue. Yasir Arafat made his greatest, and indeed only, contribution to the cause of peace by fortuitously boycotting the talks; had he joined, he could have sabotaged the whole thing. But with Arafat out of the picture, the path to peace was wide open. The prize sat on a silver platter, there for the taking. Moreover, as noted by Quandt, Carter badly needed a political win in early 1979, while "the American electorate would not care much about the details of the agreement."[41] The stage seemed set to make history.

And yet, despite everything, Carter kept returning to the Palestinian issue, raising the prominence of the tail until it grew to wag the dog and even threaten to knock it dead. As a stunned *New York Times* columnist William Safire wrote, "amazingly, it is not Mr. Sadat who has reintroduced the issue that was successfully finessed at Camp David. The heat to write in the loophole comes from Mr. Carter, with his born-again 'comprehensive' scheme."[42]

The story has a mostly happy ending. Begin defied Carter, the Palestinian issue was put on ice, and the two parties signed the first Arab-Israeli peace treaty on the White House lawn on March 26, 1979. I say only "mostly," because it is a flawed agreement in one key respect.

That flaw was the Jewish settlement of Yamit. The Israelis had built it right where the Sinai Peninsula borders Gaza, in the hope of creating an Israeli-held barrier a few miles wide that would prevent smuggling between the impoverished strip and Sinai.

Menachem Begin pleaded with American officials, "emphasizing," as Jimmy Carter put it in his diary, "that the settlements were important as a buffer between Gaza and Egypt."[43] Of course, Anwar Sadat was adamant that Egypt receive every last inch of Sinai, as any leader would. But this is where Carter should have proposed a land swap, with Israel keeping the Yamit salient while giving Egypt a similar amount of land somewhere else in southern Israel. That idea would hardly have been an overreach. Though Syria's Hafez el-Assad and the PLO's Yasser Arafat never concluded peace treaties with Israel, both agreed at one time or another to the principle of land swaps with the Jewish state. Unfortunately, we will never know if Sadat could have been pressured into accepting the idea, because Carter angrily rejected any Israeli presence in Sinai, even one under Egyptian sovereignty.[44]

That blunder casts a shadow over the region to this very day. After Israel withdrew from Gaza in 2005, the Palestinians dug numerous tunnels into Sinai and smuggled a mountain of weapons inside.[v] The soft Gazan soil is perfect for tunneling.[45] Cross-border smuggling

---

[v] According to published reports, some Gazans were forced to work underground against their will, while others were shot when the work was complete to prevent them from telling the tunnel's location.

grew so large that, at one point, gasoline was cheaper in Gaza than in Israel.[46] The illicit commerce enriched many in Egypt—including those who turned a blind eye—and fed an Iranian-funded military industry. Hamas capabilities improved over time, eventually able to produce homemade long-range rockets for just $700 apiece and short-range ones for as little as $150.[47]

Tens of thousands of those rockets would be fired into Israel from Gaza in the twenty-first century. Over three thousand would be fired just in the summer of 2014, during a war that began after Hamas kidnapped and murdered three Israeli teenagers. Another president might have felt a tinge of remorse, seeing the long-term effects of his handiwork.

Carter condemned Israel and called on the world to recognize Hamas.[48]

Carter's hostility was nothing new for Israel. The Israelis agreed to give up three quarters of their land and all their oil to seal the peace treaty with Egypt. But Carter never forgave Menachem Begin for refusing to bend to his will on the Palestinians. Thus, in 1980, he engineered U.N. Security Council Resolution 478, rendering Israel's declaration of Jerusalem as its capital "null and void." Moshe Dayan quipped that the U.N. might as well have declared the Bible null and void as well.[49]

Why on earth did Carter risk torpedoing everything for the Palestinians? Why did he never tire of condemning Israel, no matter the circumstances? Quandt summed it up this way: "Those who knew Carter best sensed that he saw in the Palestinian question parallels with the situation of American blacks."[50]

* * *

But wait, you say. Maybe Carter had it right all along. Maybe there really are parallels between Palestinians and black Americans. Maybe the justice of the Palestinian cause really does crowd out all other considerations. Well, this question brings us to the finale of our awards show. We are now ready to reveal the winner, the passage in Carter's book that snags the trophy as the single most absurd falsehood in *Palestine: Peace Not Apartheid*, a passage so detached from reality that it is worth quoting in its entirety. In describing his first trip to Israel, Carter writes the following:

> I have to admit that, at the time, I equated the ejection of Palestinians from their previous homes within the State of Israel to the forcing of the Lower Creek Indians from the Georgia land where our family farm was now located; they had been moved west to Oklahoma on the 'Trail of Tears' to make room for our white ancestors. In this most recent case, although equally harsh, the taking of land had been ordained by the international community through an official decision of the United Nations.[51]

It is unusual for Carter to get any of his facts right, but this one doesn't even land in the same zip code as the truth.

Unlike Carter's ancestors in Georgia, Jews are as indigenous to Israel as Mayans to Mexico or Italians to Italy. Palestine was not conquered by some foreign nation. Rather, a minority of its people grew to become its majority.

But, say Israel's critics, the Zionists largely originated from Europe. This brings us to the next big difference between white Europeans in the New World and Zionists in Palestine: unlike Christopher Columbus and the Pilgrims—who arrived with their muskets, unannounced and uninvited—the Jews immigrated to Palestine legally. They were invited to come, first by the Ottoman Turks, who were anxious for European know-how and investment, and then by the British, who were given a mandate by the League of Nations to create "a national home for the Jewish people." Not until the campaign against apartheid at the end of the twentieth century did a movement enjoy so broad a consensus among the international community.[vi,52]

---

vi T.E. Lawrence, the champion of the Arab cause and sharp critic of many aspects of British policy after the war, reviewed the record on Palestine and remarked "[I] must put on record my conviction that England is out of the Arab affair with clean hands."

And now for the biggest difference of all. White Europeans in the New World took land from indigenous peoples by *forcing* them out. The Zionists did it by *buying* them out.

The British Balfour Declaration said that "nothing shall be done which may prejudice the civil and religious rights of existing non-Jewish communities."[53] The British took that commitment seriously. So seriously, that when officials arrived in Palestine, they passed the Land Transfer Ordinance of 1920, placing heavy restrictions on Jews even *purchasing* land—restrictions that did not exist under the Ottomans. The law did not last for long. It was quickly taken off the books because of an ensuing outcry—*an outcry that came from the Arabs*. The Jews arrived in Palestine determined to pay whatever it took to buy land. Landowning Arabs had every intention of capitalizing on their desire.[54]

Hundreds of millions of early-twentieth-century dollars were paid to Arab landowners. According to one study, Jews were paying over $1,000 per acre for desert and swampland in Palestine at a time when rich black soil in Iowa was selling for just $110 an acre.[55] I say this without any touch of bitterness. We are all familiar with what makes real estate valuable (location, location, location). If someone thought that malarial swampland in Palestine was worth ten times more than farmland in Iowa, then it was worth ten times more.

Supporters of the Palestinians know all this history, but they have a ready response that is the very battle cry of modern liberalism. The Palestinian spokesman and literary critic Edward Said laid it out in his work *The Question of Palestine*. He spills much ink insisting that Zionist leaders were racists, but supplies little evidence to back it up. Instead, the following figures make cameo appearances: John Stuart Mill, Karl Marx, George Eliot, Georges Clemenceau, Raymond Poincare, John Locke, David Hume, and Joseph Conrad.[56] What do these people have to do with Zionism? Said gives us the answer in his own unique style, one which suggests he received combat pay for each instance in which he sent his readers to the dictionary: "Zionism and European imperialism are epistemologically, hence historically and politically, coterminous in their view of resident natives."[57]

I shall save you a trip to the dictionary and translate that into plain English: Zionists are Europeans. Europeans are racists. Therefore, Zionists are racists. And if Zionists are racists, then the Palestinians must be right.

It is easy to dismiss arguments of this kind as words without sense. But the logic is taken deathly seriously by many, including one James Earl Carter. It led him to believe Yasir Arafat when he told him in 1990 that "the PLO has never advocated the annihilation of Israel."[58] It is that logic that led him to believe Hamas leader Ismail Haniyeh when he said in 2006, "We have no problem with a sovereign Palestinian state over all our lands within the 1967 borders, living in calm."[59] And it is this logic that led him to say of the peace process, despite all the evidence to the contrary, that "it has been encouraging to observe an almost complete absence of violence during those all-too-brief intervals when the prospects for peace and justice gave people hope."[60]

The last assertion is the most laughable of them all. But sadly, Carter was hardly the only president to believe it.

III.

Bill Clinton, George Mitchell, and a Tale of Two Peace Processes

"If this be peace, then let there be war."

—ROBERT MCCARTNEY[1]

Some years need no introduction—their reputations walk before them. Israelis speak of having been born before or after 1948, 1967, or 1973. For a time, people in my hometown of New York City spoke of things that happened before or after 9/11. And in the tight-knit world of diplomats, 1993 is remembered as the great year of optimism. For in that year, not one, but two of the world's most intractable conflicts experienced breakthroughs at almost the same time.

On September 10, 1993, Israeli Prime Minister Yitzhak Rabin announced that his government had engaged in secret negotiations with the Palestine Liberation Organization in Oslo.[i,2] Three days later, Rabin, Foreign Minister Shimon Peres, and PLO leader Yasir Arafat signed a "Declaration of Principles" on the White House lawn. The Israelis agreed to arm Arafat's men and hand over control of

---

[i] The first meeting was technically illegal because the law outlawing contact with the PLO was not repealed until the following month.

25

Gaza and the West Bank city of Jericho. In return, Israel received a vague promise from Arafat to recognize the Jewish state's right to exist. This was a remarkable triumph of hope over experience, given that Arafat had signed sixty-three ceasefire agreements while in Lebanon—his base from 1970 to 1982—and breached every single one of them.[3] Nevertheless, a beaming President Clinton prodded a visibly uncomfortable Rabin to shake hands with Arafat. Rabin was wearing a suit and tie. Arafat was wearing a military uniform.[ii,4]

Just three months later, on December 15, 1993, a similarly unexpected breakthrough held out the hope of ending the intractable conflict in Northern Ireland. Irish Prime Minister Albert Reynolds and British Prime Minister John Major signed the Downing Street Declaration, under which the parties agreed to "seek, along with the Northern Ireland constitutional parties...to build the trust necessary to end past divisions."[5] A three-member panel was appointed to aid the effort headed by former Maine senator George Mitchell.[6]

From the very beginning, the panel issued a set of ironclad rules that became known as the Mitchell Principles. Excerpts are as follows:

> To be eligible to participate in negotiations a party would have to promise to adhere to specific principles of democracy and nonviolence:
>
> The total disarmament of all paramilitary organizations;
>
> To renounce for themselves, and to oppose any efforts by others, to use force, or threaten to use force, to influence the course or the outcome of all-party negotiations;
>
> To agree to abide by the terms of any agreement reached in all-party negotiations and to resort to democratic and exclusively peaceful methods in trying to alter any aspect of that outcome with which they may disagree.[7]

---

ii According to a secret report by Israeli intelligence, Arafat was then at the end of his rope, discredited and out of money due to his support of Saddam Hussein's invasion of Kuwait. The report predicted that within six months the PLO would disband, and a deal could be struck with local Palestinians. If this assessment is true, then the Oslo agreement rescued Arafat from the dustbin of history.

Bill Clinton, George Mitchell, and a Tale of Two Peace Processes

The peace process between Israel and the Palestinians was supposed to be handled in a similar manner. There were no Mitchell
Principles. But the Declaration of Principles signed by Yasir Arafat
in September 1993 contained a side letter in which he agreed, in the
words of Ross, to "renounce terror and other acts of violence."[8] At
the signing ceremony in Washington, a Palestinian leader from the
territories burst into the room of several Israelis and said with tears
in his eyes, "How could you sign a deal with that corrupt liar? Don't
you know that in five years the streets will run red with blood??"[9]

They didn't have to wait that long. Just ten days after the Declaration was signed on the White House lawn, the first Israeli civilian
was murdered while working in an orchard. Another was murdered
four days after that. Then, on October 4—less than a month after
the signing ceremony—a car bomb was set off near a bus filled
with Israeli soldiers. Miraculously, only the Palestinian terrorist
was killed, though thirty Israeli soldiers were wounded. Five more
Israelis would be murdered in October 1993. One of the bodies was
found mutilated.[10]

Nothing was done in response to any of these and other terrorist attacks. But then, on February 25, 1994, an American-Israeli
settler named Baruch Goldstein went into a mosque in the West
Bank city of Hebron with a machine gun and murdered twenty-
nine people.[iii,11] This is when American officials sprang into action.
Dennis Ross writes that "for the next fourteen hours I was literally
never off the phone trying to see what combination of steps might
defuse the situation."[12]

Things went back to normal, or at least what would become
normal during the Oslo peace process. More Israeli Jews were killed
by Palestinian terrorists in 1994 than in any other year in the nation's
history up to that point.[13] Then, 1995 began with a notorious attack
on January 22, in which two Palestinian suicide bombers killed

---

iii Terrorism by Jews against Arabs is exceedingly rare, because Israel prosecutes the
perpetrators and throws them in jail. Another American-Israeli extremist named Jack
Teitel was the only other Jewish terrorist in the decade of the 1990s. Today he is serving a
life sentence for murdering two Arabs.

twenty-one Israelis. The 1994 record was soon overtaken by a new record in 1996. As compared to the seven-year period before Oslo, Palestinian terrorism more than doubled in the seven years after.[14]

Throughout this period, American officials did little or nothing to curb Palestinian terrorism. What's more, *Israeli* officials did little or nothing to curb Palestinian terrorism either.

The Israeli public had the right to expect better. Rabin had campaigned in the 1992 elections promising never to negotiate with the PLO. His security officials were stunned when he not only did so behind their backs, but signed a far-reaching agreement without so much as consulting with them.[15] Incredibly, the only reason that Arafat was forced to include the side letter renouncing terrorism was that *American* officials demanded it. Rabin and Peres never even asked.[iv,16]

Once the bombs started going off, Rabin chose to look the other way. In the words of General Ami Ayalon, who served as head of Israel's counter-terrorism agency, "He [Rabin] never presented Arafat with an ultimatum that if he refused to fight terrorism, there would be no peace process."[17] Rabin even urged Americans not to press Arafat on human rights or corruption.[18]

After an Israeli extremist assassinated Rabin on November 4, 1995, he was replaced by Peres, who was even less inclined to confront Arafat. In the words of General Moshe Ya'alon, the head of Israeli military intelligence at the time, "Peres didn't want to be confused with the facts; he operated based on his vision and thought that his flexibility would change reality."[19] It didn't; predictably, terrorism only got worse. Israeli voters finally had enough. On May 29,

---

iv Oslo also offers a case study for why the framers of the U.S. Constitution wisely required a two thirds majority of the Senate to pass a treaty. The six peace treaties that Israel has signed to date all passed in the Knesset by lopsided majorities, and all succeeded. Oslo, by contrast, passed by a slender majority of 61-50. A 2011 expose by a respected Israeli journalist showed that Rabin probably "encouraged" an Arab legislator to vote yes by giving him dozens of acres of state-owned land. Another crucial treaty, known as Oslo II, passed by an even narrower margin of 61-59. One of the Jewish legislators that voted yes was later convicted of spying for Iran.

1996, they voted Peres out of office. The man they replaced him with was Benjamin "Bibi" Netanyahu.

* * *

While violence raged in Israel, the multiparty talks commenced over the future of Northern Ireland. The extremist political group Sinn Fein was permitted to take part, but not before its ally, the militant Irish Republican Army, declared a ceasefire on August 30, 1994.[20] On February 9, 1996, the IRA broke that ceasefire by setting off a bomb in London that killed two. From that moment, Sinn Fein was excluded from the peace process; the Mitchell Principles were strictly enforced. Mitchell himself writes approvingly that his doctrine "was at center stage."[21]

In June, when talks reconvened, Sinn Fein leader Gerry Adams led a group of fifteen delegates through a throng of supporters and television cameras to the gates of the building that housed the negotiators. He was turned away. There were no less than ten political parties then seated around the table, but Sinn Fein—the most important group on the Irish-republican Catholic side—was the only one left outside. Mitchell's position was as unyielding and unbending as that of the British government: "Until there was a renewal of the IRA cease-fire, Sinn Fein could not participate in the talks."[22]

Mitchell was just as hard on pro-British Protestant radicals. The Ulster Democratic Party was barred from the negotiating table when its military wing took responsibility for a retaliatory killing.[23] Mitchell remembered this as the moment when his effort touched bottom. But he never wavered. "I agreed that they had to go; otherwise there would be no barrier between the talks and the violence on the streets."[24] In this, he received the unflinching support of President Clinton.

The decisive moment came when Ulster Secretary Marjorie "Mighty Mo" Mowlam left her sick bed—she was suffering from brain cancer—and went down to the prison to plead with Protestant radicals to commit to the ceasefire.[25] She left her wig at home and arrived pale and bald. Her dramatic visit had the air of a dying mother arriving to voice her last wish, a wish that not even hardened killers could refuse. That was the icebreaker. The IRA was also convinced to recommit to the nonviolence, the talks resumed, and the Good Friday Peace Agreement was signed on April 10, 1998.

Mowlam succumbed to brain cancer on August 19, 2005.[26] There are a lot of scoundrels in politics. But there are a lot of heroes too.

* * *

Prime Minister Netanyahu assumed office on June 18, 1996, and immediately set out to do the job the Israeli public elected him to do. When forced to choose, Rabin and Peres always made sure the cart was in front of the horse. First, one had to implement the two-state solution, and then Israel would (hopefully) get security. Under Netanyahu, the cart and the horse were put back into their rightful places. First, Israel had to get security, and *then* he would implement the two-state solution. In Netanyahu's words, "One of the key goals in my first term as prime minister was to change the Palestinian perception that 'terrorism pays' to 'terrorism doesn't pay.' I did this by insisting on security and reciprocity."[27]

He was tested almost immediately. On September 24, 1996, Netanyahu gave authorization to unseal the door to a tunnel that ran along the outer rim of Jerusalem's Temple Mount. The door was nowhere near any mosque and opened into the Christian Quarter of the Old City. But Arafat, a human mushroom cloud, ordered his men to go on the attack using the very guns the Israelis had given them as part of the Oslo Accords, ostensibly to fight terrorism.[28] By the time the mini-war ended, seventeen Israelis and about a hundred Palestinians were dead.[29]

Thousands of wars have been fought since mankind became cognizant of territory and the desire to control it—none were started over a door. Admittedly, this wasn't just *any* door, just as the Wailing Wall isn't just *any* wall. But for its American and Israeli champions, the peace process was supposed to be the forum for settling disputes, not the battlefield.

Clinton Administration officials blamed Netanyahu.

They called for a summit where they demanded that Netanyahu make concessions. When he resisted, Clinton went into a dark rage so loud it could be heard in the next room. In the words of Dennis Ross, "Arafat now knew that Bibi was the desperate one."[30] Violence was thus not only tolerated—it was rewarded.

When a semblance of security was eventually restored, Netanyahu advanced the peace process. He agreed to not one but two interim withdrawals—the Hebron Accords and the Wye River Memorandum—but he steadfastly insisted that progress be conditioned on Arafat fighting terrorism. American officials were outraged. After Netanyahu demanded that Arafat arrest thirteen suspected terrorists, Clinton "exploded," according to Ross, who wrote bemusedly that he was "struck by [Netanyahu's] belief that...he was the victim of mistreatment."[31] On another occasion, Ross writes that the Clinton Administration saw Bibi's complaints over a bombing as "an excuse to avoid negotiations" and that Bibi was "killing any prospect of peace."[32]

Meanwhile, the stubborn insistence on that which is most basic in a peace process—namely peace—paid off for ordinary Israelis. During the long, seemingly unending terror campaign that defined the Oslo Peace Process, the lowest loss of life occurred during the premiership of Netanyahu. Only one Israeli died per month on his watch. For Peres, the figures were seven and a half times worse.[33]

The Wye agreement—which required a sizeable withdrawal from West Bank territory by the Israelis—proved Netanyahu's commitment to the peace process, at least while Israeli buses and pizzerias weren't being blown to bits. Signed on October 23, 1998, it caused his right-wing coalition partners to bring down the government and trigger early elections.[34] By now, the Israeli public felt safer and, thus, more willing to take chances for peace. On May 17, 1999, Ehud Barak defeated Netanyahu in a historic landslide. At the time, it was the widest margin ever scored by an Israeli challenger over an incumbent.[35]

The Israeli peace camp was jubilant. One left-wing activist said it was as if they had been freed from a foreign occupation.[36] The great obstacle to peace was removed—now they could finalize a deal with the Palestinians. The cart was finally back in front of the horse.

What happened next was probably inevitable. Barak formed his pro-peace government in July; Palestinian terrorists murdered three Israelis in August.[37] Through it all, Washington pressed the Israelis to continue the peace process and all the interim withdrawals that it entailed.[38] To halt the transfer of territory to the Palestinians and end the talks would "give the terrorists what they wanted." Israel's intelligence service issued a classified report in late 1999 predicting that Arafat would go to war because Jerusalem would be blamed for it one way or the other.[39]

For a brief period during Barak's premiership, it looked like there might be a peace deal between Israel and another of its neighbors, Syria, during which Syrian president Hafez el-Assad prepared his public for the possibility. No such preparation, however, was ever detected on the part of Arafat.[40] He never once gave a speech recognizing Israel's right to exist or renouncing terrorism.[41] To the contrary, he gave a 1994 speech in which he said, "I am not considering it [Oslo] more than the agreement which had been signed between our prophet Muhammad and Qureish," the Arab tribe ruling Mecca with whom the Muslim leader had struck a treaty until he was strong enough to overwhelm them.[42]

Arafat *could* fight terrorists—when he wanted to. After Hamas challenged Arafat and his Fatah group—the group that predominated within his PLO—his gunmen killed thirteen Hamas members and wounded over 150 others in a firefight on November 18, 1994.[43] But when the Israelis demanded that he arrest an arch-Hamas terrorist named Muhammad Deif whose name was a household word throughout the territories, he pretended not to know who the man was.[44] He insisted that Mossad agents were responsible for bombings of Israeli civilians, even as Hamas and Islamic Jihad claimed responsibility.[45]

Although Barak carried out an interim withdrawal and freed four hundred Palestinian prisoners, the violence continued. On May

15, 2000, at the very moment that Barak was in the Knesset fighting to win approval to turn three West Bank villages near Jerusalem over to the Palestinians, Arafat's forces opened fire for no apparent reason.[46] The following day, Marwan Barghouti—the leader of Fatah's armed wing—boasted that his men had fired over six thousand rounds at the Israelis.[47] It was that event, more than any other, that convinced Barak he had to accept Clinton's invitation to Camp David for a make-or-break summit with Arafat. If the talks failed, at least the Israeli public would go to war knowing that all other alternatives had been exhausted.

It was at the summit that the final nail was hammered into the coffin of the Oslo peace process. Ashes to ashes, Camp David to dust. Barak offered a Palestinian state as part of a two-state solution, one that ceded to the PLO all of Gaza, the Arab neighborhoods of East Jerusalem, the Temple Mount, and the equivalent of 92 percent of the West Bank (later sweetened to 97 percent).[48] CIA Director George Tenet was "astounded" by how much Barak offered and asked incredulously, "Why hasn't Arafat accepted this?"[49] As later recounted by Ross, Arafat did not present a single proposal or serious comment in the two weeks that he was at Camp David."[50] Clinton later quipped that the only creative idea Arafat put forth was that the ancient Jewish Temple wasn't really in Jerusalem. Prior to the summit, Clinton had promised the Palestinians that he would not affix blame if the talks blew up.[51] But Barak was so forthcoming and Arafat so unreasonable that he felt compelled to apportion praise and blame all the same.[52]

Then, as now, one of the thorniest issues was that of Palestinian refugees. So this is probably as good a time as any to discuss the "right of return," a Palestinian demand so thoroughly ridiculous it is difficult to know where to start in unpacking it.

By all accounts, it was the Palestinians and their Arab allies that started the 1948 War. Never in the history of the world has there been a "right of return" for aggressors—Poles have a right of return;

Germans do not.[v,53] Even if Palestinians had been on the receiving end of an invasion rather than the perpetrators, never in history has refugee status been handed down from father to son. The vast majority of Palestinians in the year 2000, to say nothing of today, were not refugees. They were the children and grandchildren of refugees. If they are "refugees," then I'm a Polish refugee. Moreover, to the extent that international law ever recognizes a right of return for refugees, it is to the country from which they fled, not the house they lost.[54] Palestinians were offered a right of return, but to Palestine (i.e., the West Bank and Gaza), not the actual houses their ancestors lost in Israel.[vi,55] There are numerous other arguments as well.[vii]

The so-called right of return still became one of the most prominent sticking points. Arafat's Foreign Minister, Farouk Kadoumi, said, "We don't want a state; we want the right of return because it is the winning card to destroy Israel."[56] Another top Fatah official, Sakhar Habash, voiced the same sentiment.

Saudi Arabia's ambassador to Washington, Prince Bandar bin Sultan, told Arafat that if he said no to Barak's proposal, it would not be a tragedy; it would be a crime.[57] In truth, Arafat's decision was even worse than a crime; it was just plain dumb.

It was self-evident from the start that Arafat never intended to make peace with Israel. His goal was to take whatever Jerusalem would give him and then demand more. Indeed, after Arafat died on November 11, 2004, a prominent, London-based Arab journalist named Abdel Bari Atwan said on British television that in July

---

v In 2004, a group of German refugees brought action before the European Court of Human Rights seeking to recover homes they had lost in the aftermath of World War II, when millions of German civilians were expelled from what today is western Poland. The Germans and their lawyers were laughed out of court.

vi Israel proposed numerous plans over the years to try and solve the Palestinian refugee problem, starting in 1949 when David Ben-Gurion offered to resettle 100,000 refugees in Israel in return for a peace treaty. The Arabs rejected that and all the others.

vii Here are a few: (i) only an estimated 20 percent of Palestinians left the borders of what was then Palestine. Most went to the West Bank or Gaza. That means they are not "refugees" under international law, but "internally displaced persons," for whom there is no right of return; (ii) as established in the case of Cyprus, there is no right of return when it upsets the demography of the receiving country; and (iii) 800,000 Jews were thrown out of their homes in the Arab world, creating an exchange of populations.

1994, Arafat told him, "With Allah's help I will turn this agreement into their [the Israelis'] curse...you will yet see the Jews fleeing Palestine...don't breathe a word of this, but always remember what I said."[58]

Despite this, I have always wondered why Arafat didn't take the state that was offered, roll the Israelis back to the '67 boundary, and then continue the war from there. There would never be any shortage of pretexts to justify breaking the treaty, and his many useful idiots in the Western world would inevitably figure out some way to blame Israel.

As it turned out, Arafat did go to war; he just did it without the resources of the state he was offered. A Palestinian minister said that Arafat planned violence from the moment he returned from Camp David.[59] He could have used any pretext, but Arafat chose to go to war over a visit that then-opposition leader Ariel Sharon made to the Temple Mount on September 29, 2000.[60] The Palestinians started shooting at 2 p.m. local time so that it could be broadcast live on American morning television shows. Barak was shockingly measured in his retaliation to this provocation, even after two Israeli soldiers were publicly lynched by a Palestinian mob in front of cameras. He tried to salvage everything with Clinton at a second summit in the Sinai resort of Taba. But Arafat committed national suicide by jumping off the same bridge twice, rejecting a sweetened deal and opting for war instead.

Like the Palestinian minister, Israeli intelligence concluded that Arafat had initiated what became known as the al-Aqsa Intifada. But they questioned whether he intended for it to spin completely out of control, as it tragically did. "Arafat can light the fire," Israel's chief of intelligence said, "but he can't control the height of the flame."[61] That could be said about many of history's pyromaniacs. It would no doubt be confirmed by all those who have tossed lit matches onto ammunition dumps.

Thousands would ultimately die.[viii] But before that, in one of his final acts as president, Clinton formed a fact-finding committee to offer recommendations and investigate how things had gone so hideously wrong.[62] To head the high-profile committee, he needed someone with knowledge, experience, and the gravitas to hold court on the world stage. And so, after careful consideration, he turned to an old friend. He turned to George Mitchell.

The "Mitchell Report," as it is named, was issued on April 30, 2001. No one who read it would believe that it was authored by the same man who had established the Mitchell Principles in Northern Ireland. The report begins by calling on *both sides* to end the violence.[63] But the best was saved for last. Whereas in Northern Ireland, the Mitchell Principles had excluded any party from the talks the moment it committed a single act of violence, in Israel, the world was introduced to a different set of Mitchell Principles: in a land of stabbings, shootings, and suicide bombings, Mitchell called on Israel to immediately resume negotiations.[64] The cart was back in front of the horse.

What was perhaps most striking about the Mitchell Report was how casually it was accepted. Mitchell made no effort in his report to square the principles he had established in one conflict with those he now laid down in the other. Clinton didn't seem to find any contradiction either. It was perfectly natural to exclude Sinn Fein from peace talks the moment the IRA committed a single act of violence—and it was just as natural, apparently, to press Israel to go back to peace talks, even as its buses and cafes were being blown to smithereens.

No two conflicts are identical. But Northern Ireland and Israel-Palestine are about as close of two control groups as one will ever find. Both conflicts started in the 1920s. Both are nationalist struggles over the same territory, with sectarian divisions that go back centuries. Both involve groups deemed terrorist organizations by

---

viii In February 2001, Barak lost an election to Sharon by an even wider margin than the one with which he defeated Netanyahu less than two years before. Your luck can change that fast in the Jewish state.

much of the world. Both involve allies on one side that are said to have a "special relationship" with Washington.

But plainly, some relationships are more special than others. Britain was never asked to suffer a single act of violence, while Israel was pressured to continue making concessions, even as its citizens were being murdered in the hundreds.

In the various histories of the Oslo Peace Process, pro-Palestinian writers focus on the checkpoints Israel set up throughout the territories—as if the checkpoints caused terrorism and not the other way around.[65] Others focus on the slow pace of the negotiations, or the fact that Clinton broke his word and blamed Arafat for the failure of the Camp David summit. But for all commentators who have seen the events as if through a distorting funhouse mirror—Israelis giving up land and wanting war, Palestinians bombing cafes and wanting peace—there has been one unifying theory for the failure of the peace process.

Why did Arafat turn down the two-state solution? Why did he refuse a Palestinian state in all of Gaza, East Jerusalem, and the equivalent of 97 percent of the West Bank? Why did he choose instead to send hundreds of suicide bombers into Israeli buses and pizzerias? The problem was obvious.

The problem was the settlements.

IV.

Thus Spake Obama

"We want to give peace a chance.
But we want to give life a chance first."

—BENJAMIN NETANYAHU[1]

The Bible records that when the Children of Israel entered the land of Canaan, they conquered one town, Jericho, and then made peace with another. But then they faced their greatest challenge. Five Amorite kings formed a coalition and mobilized for war in a place called Gibeon. It was during this battle that the Book of Joshua records one of the most famous episodes of the Old Testament:

> Then Joshua spoke to the Lord…and he said in the sight of Israel: "Sun, stand still [Hebrew: "*dome*"] over Gibeon, and Moon, in the Valley of Aijalon." So the sun stood still, and the moon stopped.[2]

I have recorded the King James translation of the original Hebrew word "*dome*." But that word does not really mean "stand still." The literal translation of the word *dome* is "be silent." Obviously, no one would command the sun to remain silent. But in other contexts, the word *dome* means "stop functioning as usual." The modern Hebrew term for cardiac arrest is *dome lev* ("*lev*" is Hebrew for "heart"). In

38

other words, the best translation of Joshua's commandment is not for the sun to stand still, but rather for it to stop functioning properly.[i]

Or, to put it another way, this was probably one of the first descriptions in history of a solar eclipse.

A total eclipse passed just north of where Joshua stood on July 14, 1406 BCE. This would have created a near-total, or "annular" eclipse, which would have looked exactly as it is described in the Book of Joshua: a portion of the sun shining on the east side facing Gibeon, and the Moon "standing" in front of it on the west side over the Valley of Ayalon. Moreover, the date of the event fits perfectly inside the timeline as presented in the Book of Kings I.[ii,3]

If this is the proper translation of the verse, then it means that the Jews can date their presence in the West Bank, as we know it today, all the way back to July 14, 1406 BCE. From that time, Jews have lived there continuously in an unbroken chain that goes back over 3,400 years. Actually, the term "West Bank" was coined in 1948 as a shortened way of saying "west bank of the Kingdom of Jordan." But that's an insult to Palestinians. So I prefer the real name, which is Judea and Samaria. It was in Judea and Samaria that the Jews built all their great temples. It was in Judea and Samaria that Judah the Maccabee was killed leading his revolt against the Seleucid Greeks. In that entire period of over three millennia, there was only one short, nineteen-year period in which Jews did *not* live in the land we now call the "West Bank."

It was the first nineteen years of the existence of the modern State of Israel.

* * *

In early 1948, the Arab states rejected the U.N. Partition Plan, and their armies mustered for the war that would decide whether there

---

[i] Several verses before, it says that Joshua deliberately attacked in the dark of night, presumably because he wanted the element of surprise.

[ii] The Book of Kings I says that King Solomon built the First Temple in the fourth year of his reign (966 BCE), which was "480 years after the Children of Israel left Egypt" (1446 BCE). This would put Joshua's battle in the year 1406 BCE, the year of the annular eclipse.

would be a Jewish state.[iii,4] No country goes to war with adequate munitions, and the Zionist leadership quickly concluded that the will to defend their homeland outran their means.

Thus, on January 5, 1948, sixty children were evacuated from the Kfar Etzion kibbutz south of Jerusalem and relocated to a Jerusalem monastery. The families listened fervently to wireless reports from the commander of the Etzion settlements who stayed behind. He tried to keep their spirits up by offering upbeat assessments, telling them that soon they would all be coming home. But one day his reports stopped abruptly and everyone knew what had happened. One of the children gathered around the radio was a four-year-old boy named Hanan Porat.[5]

As a teenager, Porat would tell his friends that one day he would return to his home; his friends would tell him that he was out of his mind.[6] Menachem Begin similarly said that one day Jews would return to Judea and Samaria. Members of his political party told him he had to stop talking crazy; he was hurting the party's credibility with voters.[7]

But then, in 1966, a group of seven young men seized power in Syria and launched a terror campaign against Israel. One of the seven was a man in his thirties named Salah al-Jundi, whom the East German Stasi described as a psychopath.[8] Israeli retaliation ramped up with each attack, as did alarm in Moscow. To scare their clients into restraint, the Soviets warned the Syrians, falsely, that the Israeli army had mobilized for a full-blown invasion. This lie had the opposite effect, causing Syria, Egypt, and Jordan to mobilize to meet the imagined threat. Thus began a crisis in May 1967 that finally boiled over that June into the Six Day War.

---

iii Arab war goals were laid out by Arab League Secretary Azzam Pasha in a newspaper interview: "This will be a war of extermination and a momentous massacre which will be spoken of like Mongolian massacres and the Crusades." The leader of the Palestinians, Haj Amin al-Husseini, spent WWII in Berlin making propaganda broadcasts for Hitler. In his own words, "our fundamental condition for cooperating with German was a free hand to eradicate every last Jew from Palestine and the Arab world... The answer I got was 'the Jews are yours.'" Husseini sent his nephew to the Sachsenhausen concentration camp on a fact-finding mission.

All of Israel's plans depended on keeping Jordan out of the war, since most of Israel's air bases were within range of Jordanian artillery. But in Amman, King Hussein ignored Jerusalem's pleas for restraint and attacked anyway. Three days later, Israeli soldiers were praying at the Western Wall. It was the first time the city was united under Jewish control since 63 BCE.

One of the soldiers swaying in prayer was Hanan Porat. He was there when they liberated the Western Wall, and there two days later when they fought their way up the Golan Heights. As they went into battle, he told a friend that if he survived, he was going to return to the home he had lost nineteen years before.[9]

It was not an unrealistic expectation. Though hard to believe now, there was a time way back in the summer of 1967 when it was widely accepted that Israel had legitimate claims on at least a portion of Judea and Samaria. The OPEC oil cartel had not yet acquired a chokehold on the global economy, and the West had not yet acquired its heightened sensitivity to the claims of "people of color." In this world, the Arab invasions in 1948 and 1967 were the violations of international law. Israel's fighting back was justified.

Moreover, the "West Bank" was not occupied territory, because the Fourth Geneva Convention states that this appellation only applies to land belonging to a "High Contracting Party"[10]—a fancy way of saying that to be "occupied" under international law, the land in question must belong to another country. The "West Bank" did not belong to Jordan, because Jordan had acquired it in 1948 in an aggressive war.[iv] It didn't belong to the Palestinians, since they had rejected the 1947 Partition Plan and never assumed sovereignty. In fact, the last time the international community *had* agreed upon sovereignty was at the San Remo Conference in 1920, when Britain received a League of Nations Mandate to create a Jewish state. Legal observers thus pointed out that the default position was that land

---

iv The 1949 General Armistice Agreement between the two sides even said that "the Armistice Demarcation Lines…are agreed upon by the Parties without prejudice to future territorial settlements or boundary lines or to claims of either Party relating thereto." (Article VI, Par. 9)

in the West Bank belonged to the Jews, not the Arabs. It seemed equally obvious that bloodshed on the battlefield had to be compensated, if only with homes lost in 1948.

It is for all these reasons that U.N. Security Council 242 passed unanimously on November 22, 1967. It stated that Israel was merely required to withdraw from "territories" it had captured, but not "all territories" or even "the territories."[11] The phraseology was deliberate. The door was left wide open to claims by people like Hanan Porat.

Porat founded a settler movement called Gush Emunim, or "Bloc of the Faithful." The movement encountered resistance from the Israeli government at first, but gradually the settlers wore the government down, using civil disobedience as their weapon. They were, after all, returning to villages lost in 1948. Eventually, the Israeli public would no longer tolerate photos and television reports of soldiers carrying settlers out of their homes. Over the years, the settlements expanded.

A lot more thought went into settlement building than one might realize from reading American newspapers. Early on, the rule was established that Palestinian property rights had to be respected, so all settlements were thus built on either state-owned land or, in rare cases, land purchased from Palestinians (at exorbitant prices). Germans old enough to remember the aftermath of World War II, when millions were driven from their land by the Allies, could only look on with envy. More importantly, the vast majority of settlements were clustered on a tiny sliver of land that hugged the old 1967 boundary. This sliver, comprising just 7 percent of the West Bank, was called the *Kav Hatefer*, or the "Seam Line." Actually, the Hebrew word "*tefer*" means a "stitch," as in a stitch sewed with a needle and thread. One had only to look at a map of the settlements to understand the reason for the name.

Settlement activity exploded during the years of the Oslo peace process. The number of settlers grew from 115,700 in 1993 to 176,973 in 1999, an increase of over 50 percent.[12] Paradoxically, the slowest rate of growth occurred under Netanyahu and the highest under Barak's left-wing Labor government.[13] This is because, as terrorism mounted, Barak needed political support from anywhere he could get it. To heap irony onto the paradox, it was the *settlers* who agreed to rescue him—but only if Barak promised to build more settlements. In picturing the meeting between the two sides, I always imagined two guys in a bar making a bet. Barak wagered that he could get to the two-state solution and thus dismantle the settlements. The settlers laughed at him, wagering that the Palestinians would never make peace, and used their hoped-for intransigence as an opportunity to build more settlements.[14] Such are the strange workings of Israel's political system.

It is worth pointing out that Israel was within its rights to build settlements under all of the Oslo agreements. Palestinian legislator Hanan Ashrawi excoriated Arafat and the Palestinian leadership for agreeing to this, but the logic was unassailable.[15] Even if one accepted the notion that Arabs could live as a minority in Israel while Jews had to be ethnically cleansed from Palestine, the simple fact was that settlements built today could always be removed tomorrow.

And so it was at Camp David. Barak offered to withdraw from Gaza and the Arab neighborhoods of Jerusalem. He also offered to dismantle the settlements located *outside* the Seam Line. But he demanded to keep the settlements *inside* the Seam Line; that is to say, the majority of the settlements which were located inside the 7 percent of the West Bank that hugged the old '67 boundary. In return, he offered to give the Palestinians a swap of a similar amount of land inside pre-1967 Israel.[16] The ubiquitous George Mitchell, who later served as Middle East envoy under President Obama, estimated the number of settlers outside the Seam Line in the year 2000 at 45,000. Removing them would not have been easy. But as of this writing, Israel has dismantled forty-nine settlements and evacuated over 10,000 people, all without a single death or injury.[17] Moreover, in thinking about these things I always apply what I call the "de Gaulle Rule": if France could withdraw from Algeria, then anyone can withdraw from anyplace else.

Arafat accepted the idea of land swaps before blowing up the talks over other issues. This was not because he experienced an uncharacteristic spasm of moderation. It was because he wanted to acquire land in the heart of pre-1967 Israel to enable him to build a land bridge connecting the West Bank and Gaza.[18] The two sides never agreed on which land, or even how much land to swap. But at least a precedent was set: the Palestinians would one day get to build a connector between Gaza and the West Bank, and Israel would one day maintain control over at least some of the settlements.

* * *

The George W. Bush years began not much differently from the Clinton years, with the cart hitched firmly in front of the horse. Bombings and shootings raged through Israel as never before. The Bush Administration looked to Israel to make concessions. Prime Minister Ariel Sharon demanded just seven days of quiet before returning to the negotiating table. This was deemed an unreasonable request.[v,19]

But then two things happened. One was 9/11. The other was that on January 3, 2002, Israeli commandos captured a ship called the *Karine A* carrying tons of weapons being smuggled to the Palestinians from Iran. The Israelis maximized Arafat's embarrassment by publicizing the event while he met with American Middle East envoy General Anthony Zinni.[20]

It all resulted in a new initiative that became known as the Roadmap for Peace. Bush's Roadmap was not so much a peace plan, as a timeline for carrying out a peace plan. What made it revolutionary was this: the first step of the Roadmap was ending Palestinian terrorism; the last step would be the two-state solution. Israeli officials were elated—they would no longer be expected to negotiate under fire. The horse was back in front of the cart.[21]

Then Prime Minister Sharon went one better and offered to withdraw from the Gaza Strip. In return, he was rewarded with an

---

[v] Ehud Olmert, who served as Ariel Sharon's Finance Minister, writes that he tried to gently explain to top Bush official Condoleezza Rice that what was happening in Israel bore no relationship to what she experienced growing up as an African-American in Montgomery, Alabama in the 1950s.

April 14, 2004, letter from the White House,[22] in which President Bush declared that "it is unrealistic to expect that the outcome of final status negotiations will be a full and complete return to the armistice lines of 1949." Bush made it clear that he expected land swaps. But for the first time, an American president ratified what the parties themselves had quietly agreed upon: that at least some of the settlements would remain in Israeli hands.[23] Even the Palestinians quietly acceded to the idea of settlement building, as long as it was limited to inside what now became known as the "settlement blocs." It was an elegant compromise that served both parties.

Then, on January 20, 2009, Barack Obama was sworn in as the forty-fourth President of the United States.

In deciding how to proceed, Obama decided to put not just the cart back in front of the horse, but the settlements as well. Of the Palestinians, he demanded that they take concrete steps to end "incitements to violence"—but not the violence itself.[24] Mitchell was brought in once again as Special Envoy for Middle East Peace. And he backed up his boss, arriving like a chef to serve his specialty: the Mitchell Principles. Unfortunately for Jerusalem, he served the Israeli version—that is, demanding negotiations *with* violence still going on—rather than the Irish version: no negotiations unless violence stopped.

But even this was not enough for President Obama. The Israelis, he believed, not only had to take an exit ramp off the Roadmap and go back to the negotiating table while under fire. They also had to *make concessions to the Palestinians* to win the privilege of engaging in peace talks at all. Thus, in one of his first acts as president, Obama declared that *all* settlement building had to cease everywhere, including Jerusalem.[25] This was a position that was even more anti-Israel than that of the Palestinians. Of course, the Palestinians cannot be less anti-Israel than Washington. So Palestinian leader Mahmoud Abbas reversed course and said that he would not return to negotiations without a moratorium on *all* settlement construction, even in Jerusalem and the settlement blocs.[26] In short, Obama put back into play the only item the parties had agreed upon already. Netanyahu told a reporter that, as he left a meeting in the Oval Office, Obama had said to him, "I come from Chicago where I had to deal with tough opponents." Then he gestured with his hand as if slitting someone's throat.[vi,27]

Let us pause here and engage in another thought experiment. Suppose that the invaders of 1948 were not Jordanians and Palestinians but Germans. Suppose it was they who ethnically cleansed Jews out of Judea and Samaria. And suppose they invaded a second time in 1967—again, for the stated purpose of committing genocide against Jews—only this time they lost, and the very Jews who were driven out in 1948 argued to return to their homes. Do you really think that Obama would side with those German white supremacists? Do you really think he would insist that the ethnic cleansing of 1948 by Germany would morally and ethically deserve to be history's verdict? But here the attackers were not Germans; they were Arabs, who, in this new world of intersectionality, were deemed "people of color."

In actuality, Obama was overheard snapping, "If we can't condemn settlements, we might as well go home!"[vii,28]

On some level, Obama must have realized how extreme a policy shift his antics represented. He justified the decision in his memoirs by saying, "I thought it was reasonable to ask the stronger party to take a bigger first step in the direction of peace."[29] But rather than illuminate his reasoning, he reached for what would become a familiar dog whistle of his and subsequent Democratic administrations. He complained of the sharp domestic reaction he received—and by this, he meant the Jewish American response. The episode, he writes, "remind[ed] me that normal policy differences with an Israeli prime minister...exacted a domestic political cost that simply didn't exist when I dealt with the United Kingdom, Germany, France, Japan,

---

vi Left to his own devices, Obama would probably have gone even further. Obama's right-hand man David Axelrod writes in his memoir that his boss "had pulled his punches with Netanyahu to avoid antagonizing elements of the American Jewish community."

vii Jimmy Carter described territorial compromise as "an unacceptable modification" to "a system of apartheid."

Canada, or any of our other closest allies."[30] Incidentally, to get around *this* problem, Obama reached out to German Chancellor Angela Merkel (as we all know, there aren't many Jews *there*). He asked her to cool her ordinarily warm relations with Israel and confront Netanyahu publicly.[31]

The settlement freeze Obama imposed lasted for ten months. Abbas refused to negotiate for eight of them.[32] He then agreed to meet just as the freeze was coming to an end. But the talks predictably went nowhere—so Obama pressed for a two-month extension of the settlement freeze.[33] The diplomatic (non)effort was put on hold by the outbreak of the Arab Spring uprisings in early 2011, Abbas's invitation to Hamas to join his government in May 2011, and then by the American presidential elections.[34] But the precedent was set. Israel was heretofore required by Obama to pay for the privilege of negotiating.

The pressure returned in 2013. After Obama won reelection, he appointed John Kerry secretary of state. Israel once again was instructed to make a major concession before the talks began. But this time, the Obama Administration relented on its demand for a settlement freeze, which by now was politically impossible for Netanyahu. Instead, Israel could satisfy Obama's inexplicable demand for an initial concession by freeing ninety convicted terrorists.[35] It had come to this: under Bush, the precondition to talks was that Palestinians arrest terrorists; under Obama, the precondition was that Israel free them.

Obama's demand was as shocking as it was unprecedented. The freeing of prisoners, when it happens, is always done at the tail end of the process, as in the case of Northern Ireland, where it did not occur until the signing of the Good Friday Agreement. British Prime Minister Tony Blair said that seeing IRA murderers walk free was "very hard to stomach."[36] One can only imagine the effect on his stomach, to say nothing of his blood pressure, if Washington had demanded that he free those killers *first*, and merely for the privilege of negotiating with the IRA.

Plainly, Obama did not condone Palestinian violence or terrorism. He even helped Netanyahu combat rocket fire from Gaza with a special appropriation of $225 million for Israel's Iron Dome antimissile system.[37] But he backed the Palestinians in ways that were virtually certain to lead to more terrorism and violence. Meanwhile, the Israelis supported Kerry's 2014 peace initiative, while the Palestinians refused to even submit a response.[38] Yet this did not prevent Obama from taking a parting shot at the Israelis while he was a lame duck, engineering a 2016 U.N. Security Council resolution that, taken at face value, would require Israel to give up the Western Wall.

Obama has always been guarded in describing his motives, but occasionally they have slipped out. During his eulogy of Shimon Peres on September 30, 2016, Obama claimed that Peres had said, "The Jewish people weren't born to rule another people; we are against slaves and masters."[39] Obama's recollection seems to have been driven more by Freudian psychology than anything he ever might have heard. Peres made many statements over the years on every subject under the sun—but "slaves and masters"? No one ever remembered him saying anything about that. And why would he? Palestinians have never been enslaved by Israel or anyone else.

An even clearer picture emerges from an episode described by Obama's admiring aide, Ben Rhodes. At a meeting in Ramallah that Obama held with Palestinian high school students, one teenager (in Rhodes' words) "built up to a line that he had clearly practiced." The young man stated, "Mr. President, we are treated the same way the black people were treated in your country." The young man allowed a pregnant silence to fall upon the room before adding that this was "funded by your government, Mr. President."

As Rhodes tells it, "Obama looked drained. He had no good answer for the kid, so he didn't bother faking it." He offered words of support, saying that "he hoped young Palestinians could get a higher profile in the United States." Then, on the flight back, he told Rhodes, "It took a lot of guts for [the young man] to do that."[40] The well-prepped young man clearly knew which buttons to push when dealing with an African-American president. He did not need any "guts" to pretend that Israel had a history of slavery and Jim Crow. What he needed was a president suffering from cognitive dissonance.

* * *

The election of Donald Trump to the presidency in 2016 left the pundits and the experts stumbling for answers. How could the American people have issued such a stern repudiation of the Obama years? Or, as filmmaker Michael Moore put it: *"How the fuck did this happen?"*

Some pointed to the American people's loss of faith in institutions following 9/11 and the 2008 financial crisis. This is an interpretation that found much favor among the liberal establishment; after all, both bad events had occurred under a Republican. The trouble with this theory is that Trump was elected in the United States of America, where memories are short and the news cycle is measured in hours. During the Trump-Clinton campaign, I don't remember anyone talking about 2008, let alone 9/11. I don't remember any crisis of faith in institutions either, except maybe for distrust and contempt for the media. But even the media's fall from grace wasn't any different in 2016 than it was in 2006, 1996, or any other year since the advent of the internet and cable news.

I'm not smart enough to know why Trump won in 2016, just as I don't know why Biden won in 2020 or why Winston Churchill lost in 1945. John McCain once said that winning any election is catching lightning in a bottle. But one commentary that stood out for me came from none other than Barack Hussein Obama. In a despondent moment, he said to his aide Ben Rhodes, "Maybe people just want to fall back into their tribe."[41]

For supporters of Israel who voted for Trump, this is arguably true. But it should be noted that they only did so because, at least when it came to the Palestinians, Obama had already been engaged in tribal identity politics and comparisons for eight long years.

V.

Cognitive Dissonance:
The Tragedy of the Israeli Left

"Power corrupts. Lack of power corrupts absolutely."
—THOMAS HUGHES[1]

In 1954, a team of psychologists studied a cult led by a suburban housewife named Marian Keech, who claimed to have learned from alien beings that a catastrophic flood would destroy the world on December 21 of that year.[2] She must have been awfully charismatic, because her followers believed her bizarre declarations so completely that they quit jobs, sold possessions, and assembled on December 20 in the expectation of being rescued by a flying saucer.

But, as described in the classic psychology work *When Prophecy Fails*, after the flood and the flying saucer never arrived, the members of the cult did not abandon their beliefs. Instead, they offered elaborate explanations for why Keech's predictions had failed to materialize. Many doubled down and became even more committed to the prophecy than before.[3]

The psychologists, led by Dr. Leon Festinger, concluded that when people have deeply held beliefs, and then facts contradict those beliefs, people change the facts, not the beliefs. He dubbed

50

this phenomenon "cognitive dissonance."[4] The first key condition for cognitive dissonance is a large, irreversible sacrifice made by the individual in furtherance of a belief. The second is a social group of like-minded adherents who are there to offer emotional support—and post-mortem spin—when the belief is proven false.[5]

There is perhaps no field of human endeavor more susceptible to cognitive dissonance than government policy. It was this phenomenon that Hans Christian Andersen mocked in his satirical classic *The Emperor's New Clothes*. Everyone knows the tale. A king is convinced by a pair of con artists that they can dress him in the most beautiful garments, but garments that can only be seen by intelligent people. The ruse works, fooling not just the king but his advisors as well—that is, until a child cries out that the emperor is marching naked through town. In many retellings of the tale, including the one I read when I was a child, the con artists are arrested and the story has a happy ending. But in the original satirical version, the naked king continues walking through town, unable to acknowledge that he was taken in, all the while being trailed by his sycophantic ministers carrying his imaginary cape behind him.

A more serious description of cognitive dissonance in government is discussed in historian Barbara W. Tuchman's classic work, *The March of Folly*. The first sentence pretty much captures the essence of her argument: "A phenomenon noticeable throughout history regardless of place or period is the pursuit by governments of policies contrary to their own interest."[6] Simply put, no one in politics ever admits that they made a mistake. Egos are inflated, attention is high, and investments are large. There will always be like-minded politicians and intellectuals to offer support, even when the foolishness of a policy is self-evident. Rather than shift course when faced with the consequences of a failed policy, most public figures double down. Tuchman concludes that "wisdom in government is still an arrow that remains rarely used in the human quiver." One example Tuchman brings as the *opposite* of the trend—"the rarest kind of reversal," in her words—was Anwar Sadat's abandonment of war in favor of peace.[7]

Israeli left-wing ministers during the 1990s and 2000s were models of cognitive dissonance. The head of the Palestinian counter-terrorism force, Jibril Rajoub, caused something of a stir in June 1994 when, immediately after taking command in Jericho, he told an Israeli reporter that "those who are opposed to the deal with Israel may continue their armed struggle." But shortly after this, the leader of the Israeli peace camp, Minister of the Environment Yossi Sarid, told a reporter that "the early signs of the performance of the Palestinian Police Force are very encouraging...we have no reason to complain."[8]

By the early 2000s, the peace process was gone, the al-Aqsa Intifada raged, and Israel experienced the worst urban terrorism since the 1948 War. Every rosy prophecy for what Shimon Peres called "The New Middle East" had turned out to be wrong.[i,9] In the ten years following the signing of the Oslo Accords on the White House lawn, the Palestinians sent 250 suicide bombers.[10] In March 2002, a suicide bomb went off every other day. The head of Palestinian Intelligence in the West Bank, Tawfik Tirawi, told an Israeli reporter in 2003, "We arrested people involved in attacks against Israel, and then we freed them, and then we arrested them again and freed them again. The Israelis said that our prisons were a revolving door and they were right."[11]

A retired general who had headed Israel's fabled Military Intelligence predicted in 1993 that "the Palestinians would never risk losing what they would gain in the peace process." Estimates ran to 30 percent annual growth for the Palestinian economy. But by 2004, terrorism had grown so bad that Israel had to close the Erez Industrial Park, which was founded along the border with Gaza in 1970 to give jobs to impoverished Palestinian workers. Not only had the economy made no gains, what was already in place before Oslo was lost.[12]

---

[i] In October 1993, Peres said that he was not motivated by "Israel's narrow interest, but rather by Israel's broader interest, which is 'the Greater Middle East interest.'"

Cognitive Dissonance: The Tragedy of the Israeli Left

This represented something that almost never happens in public life: a political ideology put into practice and then proven completely wrong. Israel had handed over territory to its enemies, asking only that its right to exist be recognized at some point in the future (it never was). It had given peace a chance by removing Netanyahu from office and electing Barak. It had offered to divide its capital, hand over the holiest site in Judaism, and retreat to the pre-'67 boundary (albeit with minor land swaps).

Then, after Israel did all that, the Palestinians rejected the offer, went to war, and refused to even put forward terms for peace.

For the Israeli peace camp, these were the times that tried men's souls. How had things gone so hideously wrong? How had the prophecy of peace vanished in a mushroom cloud of violence? Yossi Sarid, long a leader of Israel's peace movement, sat down for an interview in 2002 to discuss these very questions. When asked if Oslo was a mistake, he gave the following answer: "I don't see any cardinal mistakes in the Oslo agreement. No agreement is perfect, but there were no big blunders."

The interviewer pressed him. Thousands were dying. Surely *some* mistakes were made. Wasn't there something that could have been done differently? Sarid answered, "The only mistake with the Oslo Accord was that it left the settlements in place."

To his credit, Sarid at least cut off ties with Arafat because "there is no relationship between what Arafat says to me and what he actually does."[13] Newspaper editor and Member of Knesset Uri Avnery, on the other hand, never wavered in his belief in the correctness of his cause. After Arafat died, Avnery compared the terrorist leader to, of all people, Moses.

> There is a great similarity [between Arafat's death] and the death of Moses, who removed a people from slavery and led its march to freedom for 40 years, almost exactly like Arafat. There is also a similarity in the fact that Arafat too reached the gate of the Promised Land, saw it from afar but did not enter it.... [He was] a giant.[14]

Avnery went on to describe Arafat as "a very gentle person and a very warm person filled with empathy." How, then, had the Camp David summit failed? Avnery: "It is Ehud Barak who bears that responsibility. Barak is the arch-idiot of the Israeli-Palestinian conflict."[15]

Another common refrain was that if only Israeli Prime Minister Yitzhak Rabin had not been assassinated in 1995, there would have been peace—a theory that gained some traction when it was adopted by Bill and Hillary Clinton.[16] If anything, the opposite is true. All agreed that Rabin's assassination was a despicable crime—the Israeli public was so stunned that traffic fatalities dropped.[17] But his assassination turbo-charged the peace process. Prior to his murder, Rabin was sinking in the polls, as was support for the peace process, due to all the terrorism happening under his watch.[18] After the assassination, the Israeli right was discredited—accused of somehow "inciting" the assassin—and the public got behind the peace process as never before.

But Rabin's own ministers later acknowledged that even if he had lived, the outcome would have been the same.[19] I would never suggest that the assassination was a "good" thing, but the fact is that once Rabin was no longer in power, those that came after him were far more willing to make concessions to the Palestinians. In the final speech that he gave in the Knesset, just a month before he was murdered, Rabin said that he would never agree to a full-fledged Palestinian state.[20] His right-hand man, Eitan Haber, said that Rabin never intended to offer Arafat more than 60-70 percent of the West Bank.[21] Another minister said that if Rabin knew how much Barak had offered he would flip in his grave.[22] The idea that "personal chemistry" would have gotten a deal over the finish line is ridiculous; Rabin couldn't even get Arafat to fight terrorism. He certainly couldn't have gotten him to give up the right of return.

To be sure, there were Israelis who had the courage to acknowledge that they had made a mistake supporting Oslo. Amnon Dankner, the editor of one of Israel's largest newspapers, said, "The question of why so many intelligent and patriotic people chose to fool themselves bothers me terribly because I was one of them."[23] Nevertheless, many supporters of Oslo could not bring themselves to accept that they had wasted their adult lives to fight for a wrong-headed cause.[ii] A typical example is Peace Now Knesset member Tzali Reshef, who admitted that everything was lost and his life's project ruined—but that he'd still been right all along.

> It's a hard thing when you devote 25 years of your life to a project and then see it collapse so terribly. It is also difficult on a personal level. But I will not say that my entire conceptual world has been undermined. I don't think we were fundamentally wrong.[24]

In America as in Israel, cognitive dissonance hangs heavy in the air. But the smog that distorts the horizon is comprised of a different set of contaminants. Liberal Israelis are driven by their revulsion of war; liberal Americans are driven largely by their revulsion of racism. Although the origins are different, both share the same set of delusions contrary to all evidence. Both agree that the real problem is the settlements. Both agree that Israel should immediately implement the two-state solution, even as the Palestinians reject it. And both agree that the obstacle to everything is Prime Minister Benjamin Netanyahu.

I've long been a fan of Netanyahu, or "Bibi" as he is known. Let me give just one reason. Since 2003, Bibi has overseen the Israeli economy for all but four years, either as prime minister, or as finance minister under Ariel Sharon. In that time, Israel's GDP has grown from $131 billion to $564 billion.[25] That works out to a growth rate of 8 percent per year, every year for twenty years in a row. Admittedly, there is plenty of credit to go around. But if you had to pick one person, you would have to pick Bibi: the guy who finally convinced the Israeli people that socialism and the Jewish brain don't make for

---

ii It must be noted that Oslo did yield some limited benefit. If it hadn't been for Oslo, King Hussein wouldn't have felt his status as custodian of the Temple Mount threatened and wouldn't have signed a peace treaty with Israel in 1994. But the border between the two countries had already been quiet for decades.

a profitable partnership. Peres, the last of Israel's utopian socialist founders, derided everything Bibi did as "piggish capitalism." But selling off state-owned companies, breaking up monopolies, and restructuring the tax system turned Israel into one of the wealthiest countries in the world.

But what about the peace process? Before delving into that, it is important to get a little background on the blood sport of politics as practiced in the Jewish state. During the debate on the Camp David peace treaty in 1979, a prominent politician launched a ferocious attack from the floor of the Knesset. The proposed treaty meant giving up defensible borders, removing vital air bases, and, worst of all, dismantling settlements. The government had acted in secret. The government was incompetent. The deal was dangerous. The politician sat down. Then he voted for the treaty. That politician's name was Shimon Peres, foreign minister and architect of the Oslo Accords.[26]

You can't take the politics out of politics. This is doubly so in Israel, where the electoral system is structured to reward radicalism, so the art of going low is regularly taken to new heights. It is for this reason that I always judge politicians not by their words, but by their deeds.

Benjamin Netanyahu has served as prime minister longer than anyone in Israeli history. In the 1990s, he agreed to two different withdrawals, the Hebron Accord and the Wye River Memorandum. But he never actually came out and said that he would support a Palestinian state. The political gymnastics continued into the 2000s. In his Roadmap for Peace, Bush agreed that security for Israel had to come first. But the price he extracted in exchange was that Israel had to commit to the creation of a Palestinian state once security was established. This was extremely controversial in Israel at a time in which bombs were going off every week. But it passed in a narrow 7-5 vote—the first time the government of the State of Israel voted to create a Palestinian state. Netanyahu abstained.[27] Later, Sharon announced his plan to dismantle every settlement in the Gaza Strip and withdraw. Netanyahu voted for it six times. But then, when it was about to be implemented, he resigned in protest.

In a speech on June 14, 2009, Netanyahu finally brought word and deed into alignment. He declared that in return for security, and Palestinian recognition of Israel as a Jewish state, he would agree to the establishment of a "Palestinian state alongside the Jewish state."[28] The speech drew barely a yawn in Israel, because it merely confirmed where everybody knew he stood already.

In dealing with the Obama Administration, which demanded commitments on withdrawal, Netanyahu first wanted commitments on security. "When I asked the Israelis to discuss territory," said Mitchell. "I again was told that the U.S.-Israel security dialogue had to be concluded first."[29] But in the echo chamber between the Israeli left and the American left, this was always held up as proof that Netanyahu was opposed to the two-state solution. Why was there no peace in the Middle East? Why, Benjamin Netanyahu's intransigence, of course. Meanwhile, the steady drumbeat of Palestinian suicide bombers slaughtering innocent Israelis, time and time again, was ignored as thoroughly as the emperor's lack of clothes.

The insistence on security was hardly the reason for the failure of the two-state solution. But it was the reason Netanyahu won so many elections (the booming economy didn't hurt either). What Abraham Lincoln once said is as true today as it was in the 1860s: you can only fool some of the people some of the time. Left-wing Israeli politicians could fool themselves. The Israeli public was another story. Eventually, all the cognitive dissonance became too much for the Israeli public. In the most recent election, the once mighty Labor Party—which founded the State of Israel and dominated its politics for almost thirty years—barely made it into the Knesset, winning the minimum four out of a possible 120 seats. The far-left Meretz Party did even worse—it could not achieve any representation in the Knesset at all.

But the Israeli left lives on in international media and in academic journals. Whenever someone needs a quote attacking Israel, or supporting some strange revision of history, there will always be a former-Israeli-politician, former-general, or former-something-else willing to step up to the microphone.

And then there is the leftist Israeli newspaper *Ha'aretz*, a once proud news organization that went off the rails after the Camp David summit failed in 2000.[iii,30] For critics of Israel, its pages are the gift that keeps on giving. One prime example: a 2005 story by one of the most radical *Ha'aretz* journalists, Gideon Levy, reported that a Palestinian was sadistically killed by Israeli soldiers, who supposedly tied him to a donkey that dragged him across the ground. A rival newspaper fact-checked the story and showed that it was false; no such crime had been committed. In fact, no crime had been committed at all—the whole thing was based on an unsubstantiated rumor. In a normal country, that sort of thing spells the end of a reporter's career. But turn on Israel's Channel 13—the equivalent of America's MSNBC—and until recently, you would still see Levy almost every night, screaming, shouting, and waving his hands. Levy is often described in the international press as "courageous." He is a darling of Western media and academia and is possibly the most famous Israeli journalist in the world.[31] Almost everyone in Israel knows him as a figure of ridicule.

However, many of the usual suspects in the cognitive dissonance crowd are actually serious people, like retired general Ami Ayalon. Ayalon is an authentic hero, having served as commander of the Israeli Navy, and one of only forty people in history to win the Medal of Valor, Israel's highest military honor. But he is also a left-wing extremist and a firm believer in the Cult of Peace that accompanied the Oslo Accords. He, of course, at least partly blamed the failure of Oslo on the settlements, saying that terrorism spiraled during the al-Aqsa Intifada because "the way that we [Israelis] are fighting has stolen any hope from the Palestinians that they will be freed from us."[32] This is one of those moments in which you have to hold two conflicting thoughts in your head at the same time. It is possible to

---

iii On October 31, 2024, a year after the October 7, 2023 attack, *Ha'aretz* publisher Amos Schocken referred to Palestinian terrorists as "freedom fighters" and called for sanctions against Israel.

be an authentic hero and still a left-wing extremist, impervious to facts. It is likewise possible to be very patriotic and very smart and still suffer from cognitive dissonance.

Like Ayalon, Peres did truly great things for Israel. An Israeli reporter once joked that in a thousand years, historians will assume that "Shimon Peres" was the name of a government position, not a person, because it was impossible for a single human being to have held so many jobs.[33] He was at the center of his nation's affairs for almost seventy years. I would have loved to have been a fly on the wall in 1953, to witness a thirty-year-old Peres walk into Ben-Gurion's office, at a time when only three superpowers had the atomic bomb, and explain how he could deliver one for tiny, impoverished Israel. I would have loved to witness him as defense minister in 1976, engineering the Entebbe rescue operation. What I enjoyed far less was reading about Peres during government deliberations in March 2002, after a suicide bomber had killed thirty people. In that meeting, he opposed a military response, turned to ministers who demanded action, and said, "You are destroying my life's work!" But when I read it, I didn't feel anger—I felt pity.

I feel no such pity for American journalists and intellectuals who have turned Netanyahu into the man who is, hands down and beyond rational debate, the most unfairly maligned politician on the face of the earth. A *New Yorker* piece on the neoconservatives that led America into the disastrous 2003 Iraq War went down the Washington cast of characters. But ultimately, it declared that Netanyahu was "worse than all of them."[34] Seriously?

But I save my greatest antipathy for those who act on those biases and attempt to translate them into policy. I save it for lobbyists. I save it for J Street.

VI.

The Anti-Israel Advocacy
Group J Street

*"The worst thing for a brand is to have a kind of false
part out there as to who they are."*
—LEE CLOW (Advertising Executive)[1]

On April 15, 2008, a political consultant named Jeremy Ben-Ami founded a lobbying organization that he named J Street. Washington, D.C., is laid out along a grid of alphabetically named streets that skip over the letter "J." Ben-Ami thus named his advocacy group after the missing street, hoping to lobby on behalf of a supposedly missing voice, one that believes in a more "evenhanded" approach between Israelis and Palestinians.[2] The first time I heard this explanation for the name "J Street," I have to admit I was puzzled. The Palestinian voice, missing in Washington? Does this guy watch television?

Prior to adding his voice to the chorus of those attacking Israel, Ben-Ami made a name for himself working for Democratic political candidates. All had lost because all were positioned at the most liberal extreme of the political spectrum. Losing an election is no fun. But of all the defeats, there was one incident that most stood out for Ben-Ami. He writes that he was "furious" at the way his client Howard Dean had been made to "sweat and suffer" in the 2004 presidential primaries over remarks that had broken the "rules." Dean had gotten into trouble by, among other things, referring to members of Hamas as "soldiers" rather than "terrorists."[i,3] I suppose in a way Ben-Ami has a point. After all, *The New York Times* called the terrorists who murdered Israeli athletes at the 1972 Munich Olympics "commandos," and nobody thought anything of it.[4] But more on that later.

Ben-Ami was, and is, ambitious. J Street's mission is nothing less than "changing the dynamics of American politics when it comes to Israel and the Middle East."[5] He wants "a voice in the American political debate that reflects the progressive and liberal tendencies of [the Jewish] community,"[6] a voice reflecting the "same values" of "justice and equality for all" that Jews fought so hard to achieve in the United States.[7] The quotes above are all taken from Ben-Ami's memoir, *A New Voice for Israel: Fighting for the Survival of the Jewish Nation*. One expects the title to end, "And you're welcome!"

Before taking a deep dive into J Street, it pays to linger for a moment on the memoir's subtitle. Why exactly is the survival of the Jewish nation at risk? The answer, as Ben-Ami and so many other like-minded individuals remind us, is demography. One day, he warns, Jews will be a minority in the land "between the Jordan River and the Mediterranean Sea."[8] Man the lifeboats!

To be sure, back in the 1980s the demographic problem was all anyone talked about. Arabs in pre-1967 Israel had a much higher birth rate than their Jewish counterparts. It was this fear that stoked the rise of the radical American-Israeli rabbi Meir Kahane, who advocated the transfer of Arabs out of the historic Land of Israel. But the fear turned out to be misplaced. It is said that even a busted

---

i Dean apologized for the gaffe and the apology was accepted. But not long before Dean got into trouble, Republican Senate Majority Leader Trent Lott praised former segregationist Senator Strom Thurmond at Thurmond's hundredth birthday. The praise was likewise deemed a breach of the rules. But Lott's apologies were *not* accepted and he lost his career.

clock is right twice a day, and the same can be said for Israeli opti-
mists. On this issue, all their wildest, rosiest, craziest predictions
came true. The Soviet Union collapsed, over a million Jews immigrated to Israel, and the birth rate of Jews eventually overtook that
of Arabs. Practically overnight, the demographic problem was stood
on its head.

So to create his desired perilous demographic problem, Ben-
Ami counts all the people between the river and the sea. That
includes Gaza.[9] Once upon a time that position might have been
legitimate. But by the time Ben-Ami wrote his book, Israel had dismantled every settlement and withdrawn from Gaza. Israel had even
helped establish a Palestinian government there in accordance with
its Oslo treaty obligations. Nevertheless, Ben-Ami still views Gaza as
somehow being part of Israel—in other words, as under occupation.
(More on this later, when I get around to talking about the newspaper that refers to Palestinian terrorists as commandos.)

What is true of Gaza is also true of the West Bank. Although
Israel didn't withdraw all the way back to the '67 boundary in the
West Bank under Oslo II, signed in September 1995, it withdrew
from enough territory to allow over 90 percent of Palestinians to live
under their own government. Oslo II runs to almost two hundred
pages and is arguably the most complicated treaty that the State of
Israel has ever signed. It covers every aspect of Palestinian governance, stating that the "West Bank and Gaza Strip...will come under
the jurisdiction of the Palestinian Council,"[10] and that "neither side
shall initiate or take any step that will change the status of the West
Bank and the Gaza Strip."[11] To become citizens of Israel, West Bank
(and Gazan) Palestinians would have to tear that up, and the other
six Oslo treaties they signed. But Ben-Ami counts them in the
demographic problem anyway. Viewing treaties as scraps of paper
to be torn up at Israel's expense is a strange position, to put it mildly,
for someone who claims to be "pro-Israel, pro-peace."

Of course, there is nothing strange about this in anti-Israel cir-
cles, where Israel is wrong no matter what it does. As demonstrated
by Gaza Disengagement, Israel can dismantle every settlement and

pull back to the '67 boundary and help establish a local Palestinian government in accordance with a treaty. But as far as they and Ben-Ami are concerned, nothing has changed. The Israelis might be completely gone from Gaza, but the occupation and demographic problem live on. Somehow Israel is always the bad guy. And that tells you pretty much everything you need to know about Jeremy Ben-Ami.

It also tells you everything you need to know about J Street. The surest way to predict how this organization will come down on an issue is not human rights, self-determination, or even the achievement of peace. The surest way to predict is to ask a very simple question: Is it bad for Israel? If it is, then J Street will usually get behind it. The same is true in reverse. If something is good for Israel, J Street will almost always oppose it.[ii,12]

The Golan Heights is a perfect example.

Had the Syrians accepted a ceasefire offer on June 8, 1967, they would have emerged unscathed, and the conflict we know today as the Six Day War would be known as the Four Day War. Instead, they foolishly turned the offer down, and thirty-six hours later, the Israelis had conquered the Golan Heights. The Golan's Syrian population was saturated with government propaganda about the barbaric intentions of the Jews, so the vast majority fled in a panic. But some six thousand members of the Druze sect remained behind. Their kinsmen from Israel told them they had nothing to worry about.

Israel has long enjoyed a special relationship with the Druze, which is an offshoot of Shia Islam. The Druze are the living embodiment of the coexistence envisioned by Israel's Zionist founders. They serve in combat units of the Israeli army in numbers far exceeding their percentage of the population. They even vote right of center, with many of them casting their ballots for Likud. It took a generation, or maybe a generation and a half. But eventually the Druze on

---

ii Another concern for J Street is racism. In 2016 it said, "we have deep respect for the mission and the work of the Movement for Black Lives, and deep admiration for their achievements in moving the ongoing crisis of racism and racist violence to the center of our national conversation."

the Golan Heights joined that special relationship. It's partly because they were treated well by Israel and partly because they never harbored any genocidal intentions towards the Jews. But mostly it's because they like living well.

The Assad regime in Damascus wanted to maintain ties with the Druze community and gave its young people free education in Syrian universities. Remarkably, Israel allowed these young people to travel to an enemy country to become educated (and to some degree indoctrinated). It resulted in the Golan Druze trading stereotypes with their Jewish neighbors living in nearby settlements: in the Golan Heights, the Druze are the doctors, dentists, and accountants, while the Jews are the farmers and cattle ranchers.

All this education and coexistence have transformed the Druze from one of the poorest people on earth, literally, to one of the wealthiest. They are a very secretive, insular clan, so getting a good read on public sentiment is not easy. I paid a pollster in the early 2000s to see whether they preferred returning to Syrian rule. He warned me that others had tried and failed, but thought we might be able to coax an answer if we buried the question among a hundred others. After spending a week on the project, he threw up his hands and confessed that the locals saw right through it—no one would answer anything. Nevertheless, practically all observers agree today that the desire to remain under Israeli sovereignty is near universal. After the Syrian civil war broke out in 2011, I was traveling in the Golan Heights and asked a young man if he wanted the Golan returned to Syria. His answer, to say nothing of the look on his face, made it clear that he wanted to live in Syria about as much as I did.

For years, the Druze lived in fear of exactly that. There is anecdotal evidence that whenever it looked like such a land-for-peace deal might happen, real estate sales spiked in northern Israel, driven by Druze anxious to flee. But in 2019, President Trump finally put the issue to rest by recognizing Israeli sovereignty over the Golan Heights, which served three vital American interests: it enhanced Israeli security at the expense of Bashar al-Assad, one of the most brutal, pro-Putin, pro-Iranian dictators on earth; it enhanced the cause of human rights—starting in 1981, Druze were offered full citizenship in Israel's democracy; and it enhanced the cause of self-determination—this, after all, is what most locals wanted. Apart from perfunctory expressions of regret, it was met with barely a peep of protest in the Arab world. Well, that's not completely accurate. Assad was outraged. So was the terrorist group Hezbollah. So were the Palestinians.

No surprise, J Street opposed it too, accusing Trump of "playing dangerous partisan games with U.S. foreign policy," and deriding the decision as a "needlessly provocative move that violates international law."[13] Actually, Trump's recognition was fully in keeping with international law. Israel had won the plateau in a war of defense after Syria attacked Israel, and U.N. Security Council Resolution 242—passed in the fall of 1967—left the door open to just this sort of border adjustment. Most compelling of all were the humanitarian considerations. Trump's declaration was issued during the Syrian Civil War, one of the most destructive conflicts of the twenty-first century. Imagine living your life knowing that at any moment some diplomats far away might move the border and leave you and your family inside Syria. As the Druze on the Golan Heights were breathing a sigh of relief, their relatives in Syria were being smuggled to Lebanon or hidden in basements to avoid being drafted into Assad's army.[14]

J Street prides itself on supporting self-determination—but only, it seems, in the case of the Palestinians. In the case of the Druze, it believes that honoring their desire for self-determination is a violation of international law. It is hardly what you would expect from an organization that insists it is "pro-Israel." But it is exactly what you would expect from an organization that is the opposite.

You could say the same about pretty much everything else J Street touches. Right after J Street came into existence, war broke out between Israel and Hamas. The Israelis wanted time to root out the Hamas terror cells firing rockets into Israeli cities. Hamas wanted a ceasefire. J Street called for a ceasefire. This caused Morton Klein, the president of the Zionist Organization of America, to say that "J Street is anti-Israel. Not simply extremist leftwing."[15]

In 2011, J Street tried to persuade the Obama Administration to allow a U.N. Security Council resolution condemning Israel to pass. The lopsided resolution was so bad that Obama ignored the advice and vetoed it anyway. But as a result of the episode, liberal congressman Gary Ackerman broke off ties with J Street, saying that the organization was "so open-minded about what constitutes support for Israel that its brains have fallen out."[16]

And then there was the issue of the American embassy. Back in 1995, Congress passed the Jerusalem Embassy Act by a huge bipartisan majority, requiring the U.S. to move its embassy to Jerusalem. But it gave the president a waiver to suspend the move "if he determines and reports to the Congress that a suspension is necessary to protect the national security interests of the United States."[17] Now that's a pretty high bar—protecting national security. But for years, people made the argument anyway, predicting that violence would break out and U.S. embassy personnel would have to be evacuated from Arab capitals, were the embassy to be moved. Then came Donald Trump. Call him crazy. Call him irresponsible. But he moved the embassy and…nothing happened. No violence. No evacuations. No harm to national security. Bupkis.

You would think that a "pro-Israel" group would be in favor of giving Israel the same right as North Korea or Syria—the right to declare the location of its capital. You would think that a "pro-peace" group would want to reward Israel for consistently supporting the two-state solution, and maybe even put a little pressure on the Palestinians for their intransigence. (I say "a little" because the embassy was moved to West Jerusalem, which everyone agrees will remain in Israeli hands, not East Jerusalem, which is in dispute.) Additionally, Trump's announcement was accompanied by his statement that no final status issues were affected by the decision. The embassy could open for business in West Jerusalem, and a Palestinian capital could still be declared one day in East Jerusalem.

So J Street condemned it as a "highly provocative and counter-productive step."[18]

The items above are revealing, but none of them relate directly to the peace process. That's where the rubber hits the road, and where we might look to J Street to be that voice for "pro-Israel, pro-peace Americans." Or at least pro-peace Americans—J Street being what it is, I would settle for just one and call it even. An organization that could get its arms around just the "peace" half of the moniker would warmly embrace *any* peace treaty between Israel and its neighbors. It would praise that effort and work to see it expanded to include even more neighbors. In other words, it would look at how J Street reacted when Israel signed the Abraham Accords. And then it would do the opposite.

First, a little background. We've all heard the old saying "the show must go on"—it's the same in diplomacy. So after the Camp David summit blew up (figuratively and literally), people wondered what would become of the peace process. Some said that peace had to be "inside out," meaning that no progress could be made unless a solution was found to the Israeli-Palestinian conflict. Others said that it could be "outside in," meaning that the focus should shift to Arab countries that might be willing to ignore the Palestinians, and sign a peace treaty with Israel without regard to the Palestinian issue.

The "inside out" view of the world was put forth by President Obama's secretary of state, John Kerry, in a December 2016 speech:

> There will be no separate peace between Israel and the Arab world.
> I want to make that very clear to all of you. I've heard several prominent politicians in Israel sometimes saying "Well, the Arab world is in a different place now, we just have to reach out to them"....
> No, no, no and no.... There will be no advance and separate peace with the Arab world without the Palestinian process and Palestinian peace.[19]

In 2020, President Trump, his son-in-law/advisor Jared Kushner, and U.S. Ambassador to Israel David Friedman took the inside-out theory and turned it upside down. That was the year they brokered the Abraham Accords, which saw four Arab countries—the United Arab Emirates, Bahrain, Morocco, and Sudan—sign peace treaties with Israel. Fittingly, there was one Arab country for each of John Kerry's four "nos." (There was even a fifth country to go with his word "and," because a European Muslim country, Kosovo, signed a peace treaty with Israel as well.[20])

Prophecy is a lost art (or, to paraphrase Yogi Berra, it's hard to make predictions, especially about the future). People get things wrong all the time. But predictions tell us a great deal about the prognosticator. People don't just predict what they *think* will happen. They often predict what they *want* to happen. A Hollywood movie producer famously predicted that television would be a passing fad.[21] Western Union said the same about the telephone.[22] You get the idea.

Now, if you are the sort of person that wants to fight for the Palestinians—which is to say, if you are John Kerry—then you want to empower them. You want to pretend they possess magical veto powers over the wider peace process. You want to believe in the inside-out theory and proclaim "four nos." And you want to insert the Palestinians back *into* the process rather than leave them on the sidelines. You want to do this, even though the Palestinians have rejected every compromise proposed since 1937.[iii,23] Even though inserting the Palestinians makes it harder to reach additional peace treaties, not easier.

What Kerry said is exactly what J Street said as well. Only J Street didn't just predict it; J Street said it *after* the treaties had been completed. When asked for comment by *The New York Times*, Ben-Ami played down the Abraham Accords, saying, "It's not conflict resolution, and it's not peace—this is a business deal…it shouldn't be overplayed as resolving a core conflict for Israel and its neighbors."[24] It is difficult to see how anyone with even a passing familiarity with

---

iii In 1940, Palestinian leader Amin al-Husseini rejected the British White Paper, even though it abrogated all of London's commitments to the Jews and offered a Palestinian state on 100 *percent of the land between the river and the sea.* In 1944 Husseini launched Operation Atlas, a plan to kill Tel Aviv's 150,000 Jews by poisoning their water supply. The Palestinian commander of the operation was Abu Ali Hassan Salameh, father of the man who masterminded the massacre of Israeli athletes at the Munich Olympics in 1972.

the Arab-Israeli conflict could have said something so head-smack-ingly stupid. In the first seventy-two years of Israel's existence, it achieved peace with only two Arab countries. In the space of just four months in 2020, Israel signed twice that number of peace trea-ties. And unlike Egypt and Jordan, the UAE made it clear that this was not going to be "cold peace," but real peace that included cul-tural ties, tourism, and trade. It signed the Arab world's very first free trade agreement with Israel.[25] Trade is now measured in the bil-lions. This is what Ben-Ami derides as "any old business deal."

A "pro-Israel, pro-peace" organization would be expected to pop champagne and dance in the streets, especially since other Arab countries like Saudi Arabia and Oman dropped hints that they, too, were prepared to sign peace treaties. J Street kept the champagne on ice and held a policy symposium. In its own words, "Participants who were critical of the Abraham Accords made strong arguments, noting that key parties who brought them about…did not do so with Palestinians' interests at heart. These are important concerns." The organization then made ten policy recommendations, which began with "Make Palestinians a full and equal partner" and con-tinued with "leverage normalization moves by Arab states to secure benefits for Palestinians." And then there was the *coup de grace*: link-age. Remember Jimmy Carter's "linkage" that nearly sank the Camp David peace treaty with Egypt? J Street thinks that's a good idea, and suggested, "appoint[ing] a US Special Envoy to work on…linkages with the Israeli-Palestinian issue."[26]

J Street meant every word of it. In the middle of 2023, Saudi Arabia negotiated terms of a hoped-for peace treaty with Israel through the Biden Administration. *The Washington Post* reported, as did others, that the Saudis merely wanted "sweeteners of some kind for the Palestinians so that Saudi authorities could say to their own people…that they are still fighting for the Palestinian cause."[27] A peace treaty between Israel and the most important Arab coun-try—not just the wealthiest, but the guardians of the holy Muslim shrines at Mecca and Medina—would be a paradigm shift, on par with the peace treaty signed with Egypt.

So J Street issued a policy paper that declared the negotiations an "opportunity to advance...Palestinian interests." It then set forth a long list of major concessions to the Palestinians that the U.S. and Saudi Arabia should seek to secure (settlement freeze, transfer of territory to the Palestinians, etc.).[28]

It beggars the imagination that a "pro-Israel, pro-peace" organization would advocate for any of this. But of course, J Street is neither of these things. It is a pro-Palestinian lobbying group, one that—like many others crowded into Washington's alphabetical street grid—is anxious to advance Palestinian interests, even if that means sacrificing further peace treaties. Like other pro-Palestinian lobbying groups, it argues that Washington should pressure Israel to change the policies of its democratically elected government.[29] I loathe Israel's outrageous judicial system—which is a textbook case of white minority rule (albeit a liberal variant)—but I would never want Washington to withhold arms or aid to pressure Israel to change it. Israel is not a banana republic and those of us who live in America have no business interfering with its democratic process.

J Street even wants Washington to dictate war policy to Israel. On February 15, 2024, during the fiercest Hamas war yet—this one sparked by its brutal massacre of some 1,200 Israelis the previous October—J Street called on the Biden Administration to "bring immediate and effective pressure to bear to deter Prime Minister Netanyahu" from launching an offensive in southern Gaza to free Israeli hostages.[30] None of the truly pro-Israel lobbying groups would contemplate doing anything like this.

Of course, J Street has the right to advocate for any position it wants. The problem is not that it echoes the views of other anti-Israel advocates crowded into Washington's alphabet grid. The problem is a lack of truth in advertising. J Street's constant insistence that it is "pro-Israel" is about as truthful as the tobacco companies using healthy-looking cowboys to market cigarettes. J Street could just come out and say, "We view our mission as advocating for the Palestinian cause in American politics." But if they did that, they couldn't play their central role in Washington, which is to give political cover to liberals when they stick it to Israel.

I often wonder if J Street is doing the Palestinians any favors. You see, J Street has indeed realized Ben-Ami's goal of "changing the dynamics of American politics when it comes to Israel and the Middle East." But not in the way that it intended. The pro-Israel community has watched J Street, and others like it, and has become not just energized but weaponized.

In my lifetime, I have looked on with awe as the mainstream pro-Israel lobbying group, AIPAC, has grown exponentially. AIPAC's main annual event is its Washington Policy Conference, which I attended for the first time in 2005, as one of perhaps a thousand participants. The most recent Policy Conference in 2020 had almost twenty thousand attendees. It was suspended during Covid and has remained suspended because AIPAC cannot find a venue big enough to accommodate all that want to attend.

More importantly, AIPAC and other mainstream supporters of Israel have grown more militant. AIPAC long avoided partisan politics. But in recent years, it has dived headfirst into the political fray as a major source of funding for candidates. In 2023 it raised $73 million, while its political action committee—although limited to small donations—raised a record $21 million.[31] In 2022, it targeted anti-Israel candidates in seven races. It picked off each and every one.

Ben-Ami witnessed this and saw a familiar culprit—AIPAC was racist. Here is what he told *The New York Times*: "There seems to be something particularly on the line for some parts of the Jewish community when women of color speak out."[32] Now, in some cases AIPAC indeed targeted anti-Israel black women and Hispanics. But it also supported pro-Israel black women and Hispanics. And in one race, it helped depose incumbent congressman Andy Levin who is white, male, and Jewish. In ridding America of anti-Israel advocates, AIPAC is an equal opportunity (un)employer.

In J Street's defense, I will say this: as pro-Palestinian groups go, it is probably the most moderate. It praises those that call Israel an apartheid state, but stops short of calling Israel an apartheid state itself.[33] It supports many groups who call for boycotting Israel, but stops short of calling for a boycott of Israel itself.[34] Other pro-Palestinian groups are far more radical, but they don't call themselves "pro-Israel." They legitimize their support for Palestinian rejectionism with a different kind of branding.

They call themselves "human rights groups."

VII.

Human Rights and Human Wrongs

"Starvation is a legitimate method of warfare."
—SECTION 5.20 OF THE U.S. DEPARTMENT OF DEFENSE
LAW OF WAR MANUAL (2015)[1]

Until recently, the most prominent critic of Vladimir Putin—and not coincidentally, the most courageous—was a jailed lawyer named Alexei Navalny. Navalny had long stood out in Russia as a passionate advocate for democracy and a crusader against corruption. Navalny was prominent in another notable way: he was big, strong, and seemingly unkillable, having avoided the fate of other Putin critics by surviving an August 2020 poisoning attempt. The poisoning was tied directly to Russia's FSB intelligence agency; Navalny got a member of its elite toxins unit to incriminate himself on tape by calling him on the phone and impersonating a fellow FSB agent.[2] Nevertheless, following a month-long recovery in a Berlin hospital, Navalny got right back on a plane and headed straight to Moscow to continue his work opposing the Putin regime.[3] As expected, he was arrested in the airport and sent to a hellish Russian penal colony located north of the Arctic Circle.[4]

Navalny died in Russian custody. His mother was told that he had died of "sudden death syndrome."[5] It was sudden, all right.

Navalny was seen on film the night before, looking perfectly healthy. But strictly speaking, he died of natural causes—natural, that is, to the life he chose, fighting for democracy in Russia. The only thing unnatural about this courageous man was how long he survived.

When Navalny was first arrested, Amnesty International labeled him a "Prisoner of Conscience"—its highest designation.[6] As Amnesty works "for the immediate and unconditional release of all prisoners of conscience,"[7] the declaration was meant to mobilize Amnesty's ten million activists around the world in the cause of obtaining Navalny's freedom.

But this time an outcry went up. Amnesty was, in its own words, "bombarded" with complaints. Navalny was accused of having made remarks hurtful to homosexuals over ten years before.[8] Amnesty decided, in its own words, to "re-examine the case," not unlike a group of prosecutors, and to "conduct a thorough review of the evidence base." At the conclusion of its investigation, Amnesty determined that "we had made a mistake in our initial determination." Navalny had indeed made the comments. So Amnesty stripped him of his designation. It would no longer work to free him from jail. He was not a Prisoner of Conscience after all.[9]

Amnesty defines its core values as including "international solidarity," "effective action for the individual victim," and "democracy and human rights."[10] Navalny never did anything to harm homosexuals or deprive them of their human rights, nor did he advocate depriving them of their rights if he ever came to power. Navalny merely made hurtful comments about gay people, and those many years before. So the choice was not between advancing two different versions of human rights. The choice was between advancing democracy or advancing progressive values through cancel culture. Although fighting for progressive talking points does not appear on Amnesty's list of core values, plainly this was so in the Navalny case—at least until Amnesty was forced to reverse itself several months later after yet another outcry.

Amnesty is a prominent player in what has become a growth industry: the non-governmental "human rights" organizations, or

NGOs for short. These organizations arose after the Holocaust to expose government abuse and, it was hoped, prevent other catastrophes from occurring in the future. (Not surprisingly, many of the most prominent early organizations were founded by Jews.) In 1948 there were sixty-nine NGOs consulting the United Nations. By the end of the twentieth century, there were more than two thousand.[11]

There are no watchdogs watching all these watchdogs, so there is no accountability. What's more, the NGOs control enormous resources. Amnesty alone raised $462 million just in the year 2022.[12] While Amnesty claims it receives most of its donations from small donors,[13] Human Rights Watch (HRW), another large player on the global stage, received $100 million from the Hungarian-American progressive billionaire George Soros in 2010.[14] HRW also secretly took millions of dollars from Qatar—an autocratic emirate that hosted the Hamas leadership—as well as $470,000 from a Saudi billionaire that HRW itself criticized for abuses in one of his companies. Saudis, billionaires, and especially Saudi billionaires are not exactly known for financing those who attack them. Knowing the degree to which the Saudis are committed to the cause of human rights—which is zero, nada, nothing— the thought of this being hush money might never have crossed my mind, had not HRW declared taking the $470,000 "a deeply regrettable decision" after it was outed.[15] You think?

In the years following the Vietnam War, the NGOs tacked sharply to the left. The Navalny case is just one small example.[16] Princeton University professor Richard Falk is another. He has served on the boards of Amnesty International, HRW, and the UN Human Rights Council. In 1979, he penned an infamous op-ed in *The New York Times* entitled "Trusting Khomeini" that described the Ayatollah's movement as "largely non-violent." In the Iranian revolution, Falk saw "hopeful signs, including the character and role of Ayatollah Khomeini."[17]

When Khomeini came to power in 1979, the cleric was almost eighty years old. He had a long record of speeches and fatwas. It is said that when the leader of the Shiite faith, Grand Ayatollah Hossein Borujerdi, was on his deathbed in 1962, he said, "Follow anyone you like except Khomeini, for following Khomeini will leave you knee-deep in blood."[18] Anwar Sadat called Khomeini a lunatic. Falk's man-love for Khomeini ignored the Ayatollah's well-earned reputation as a violent fanatic eager to do war with the West. But the warm words fit into Falk's pattern of deep hostility towards Israel and the United States—a hostility he brought to all the organizations he helped lead.

Being positioned on the outermost extreme of any political ideology will typically limit your reach to a narrow segment of the public. But the NGOs have credibility among the wider public because they enjoy the halo effect showered upon defenders of "human rights." The branding is exquisite. If you criticize them, you are on the defensive before you open your mouth. You are opposing "human rights," are you not?

Thus we come to perhaps the favorite target of the NGOs, which is the State of Israel. HRW's current head, Ken Roth, is one of those people who reminds me of an old joke: he's Jewish, but only on his parents' side. He has been described by the director of the NGO UN Watch as someone who "wakes up every day thinking about how he can turn the knife and twist it against Israel."[19] Robert Bernstein, the founder of HRW and its chairman for twenty years, penned an op-ed after he stepped down in which he said, "I must do something that I never anticipated: I must join the group's [HRW's] critics," because the organization was "helping those who wish to turn Israel into a pariah state."[20]

HRW had a lot of help. Global NGOs draw heavily upon Israeli NGOs operating on the ground.[21] For reasons I cannot explain, Israel allows foreigners, and even foreign governments, to fund activists whose sole motivation is to malign it. A 2018 study revealed that thirty-nine Israeli NGOs received $100 million from the European Union and Western European governments over the course of the previous five years. In the words of the study's author, "all 39…stridently oppose the government's policies regarding the West Bank, and a number promote allegations of 'war crimes.'"[22] These Israeli "human rights" organizations don't always let themselves get confused by the facts; for example, the Israeli group Shovrim Shtika ("Breaking Silence") has been shown on at least three occasions to have made charges that were patently false.[23]

It is likely that the Biden Administration operated based on the information fed to it by the NGOs, because during the Gaza War the president issued an executive order placing sanctions on West Bank settlers it said had committed violence against Palestinians.[24] Israeli police said that they had never even heard of 80 percent of the people that were sanctioned. "We have no idea where they are getting their information," a senior police official told a reporter.[25]

The local NGOs also help promote the idea that Israel is an apartheid state.[26] In 2022, Amnesty International issued a 280-page report that concluded that Israel "has perpetrated the international wrong of apartheid, as a human rights violation and a violation of public international law."[27]

What is most notable about the Amnesty report is not so much that it ignores history—not, in other words, that it ignores the fact that Israeli Arabs have the right to vote and have always had the right to vote, or even the fact that Israel never engaged in the vote-suppressing shenanigans that were used in places like the Jim Crow South (Israel has never had a poll tax, for example). The Israeli system also does not have districts, so there has never been any gerrymandering; on the contrary, the unruly Israeli system of one-man-one-vote with no districts gives voice to every corner of society. For most of Israel's history, a party only needed 1 percent of the vote nationally to get into the Knesset (today the figure is 3.25 percent). So minorities are not disenfranchised—they are turbocharged, usually given the role of kingmaker. Amnesty's report ignored all this, as well as the hundreds of Arab figures who have served as mayors, judges, and of course, members of Knesset.

What makes the Amnesty report so striking is its timing. When Amnesty issued its report, not only were Arabs voting, not only were they represented in the Knesset in numbers that roughly corresponded to their percentage of the electorate, not only were they represented on Israel's Supreme Court and as the mayors of every Arab town in the country, *they were then members of Israel's governing coalition.*

An Arab party carrying the innocent-sounding name "United Arab List"—it's actually Israel's Islamist party—only got about 4 percent of the vote. But that was enough in Israel's system to position it as kingmaker. It was courted by both sides, including Likud, then headed by Benjamin Netanyahu. However, the Arab party chose to throw its support to the diverse coalition headed by Naftali Bennet. It thus won a $9 billion government aid package for Arab Israeli towns and cities. I don't fault the party, of course—this is exactly how democracy is supposed to work. The point is that $9 billion is a lot of scratch in a country as small as Israel. I doubt there is another country on earth where you can leverage just 4 percent of the vote into something that big. Israel the apartheid state? It's more like an apartheid state in reverse.

You can tell a lot about a country from its political system. In Britain we see a nation steeped in tradition that slowly morphed into a parliamentary democracy. In America, we find the Electoral College, an unusual institution that, as of this writing, has handed the presidency to the loser of the popular vote almost 10 percent of the time. We also find a Senate where 40 percent of the seats are granted to just 10 percent of the population, at least partly enacted to empower southern plantation owners and keep them from seceding (it worked for seventy-two years).

Israel's political system looks like something assembled at gunpoint. That's because David Ben-Gurion slapped it together with two guys you never heard of on a single afternoon in 1948. Students of political science have long sought out an Israeli version of the Federalist Papers. No such document exists. Ben-Gurion probably didn't even have a stenographer present; there are no minutes of what the three men discussed.[28] We therefore don't know if Ben-Gurion intended to create a system that empowered minorities, or if it happened because he didn't think it through.

What we do know is that the people of Israel are content to leave things the way they are. Ben-Gurion himself tried to change the system in the 1950s, to raise the minimum threshold to get into the Knesset from 1 percent of the vote to 10 percent. He was shot down.

In a recent poll, only 1 percent of Israelis thought the system should be changed (the poll's margin of error was 4 percent).[29] In short, the Israeli public is content to give minorities political power that allows them to punch way above their weight.

The Israeli public has also shown a tolerance for Arab radicalism that is nothing short of astonishing. At the beginning of World War II, the British arrested fascist Member of Parliament Oswald Mosley and kept him behind bars until 1943. In the same period, the United States infamously herded Japanese Americans into detention camps. In Israel, the nation that has not known a day of peace in its history, politics resembles Chicago's mob wars of the 1920s: the rules are there ain't no rules.

Supporters of al-Qaeda have been permitted to serve in Israel's Knesset. Remember the United Arab List party I mentioned above, the one that got $9 billion as a member of the ruling government? Well, back in 2002, it had a member of Knesset named Muhammad Kana'an, who said, after the 9/11 attack, "A blessing upon you Bin Laden, we all salute you."

The Chairman of the Arab-Israeli HADASH Party, Muhammad Baraka, attended a 2002 student rally in which a Palestinian university president cried, "We will flood Israeli streets with blood!"[30] The cry brought the cheering crowd to its feet. Baraka was filmed cheering with everyone else.

And then there is Azmi Bishara, the head of the Arab-Israeli BALAD party. He was caught during the 2006 Second Lebanon War passing secrets to the Lebanese terrorist group Hezbollah, with whom Israel was then at war. In another time and place, a senior lawmaker caught passing secrets to the enemy in time of war would be handed a bullet and a Luger and asked to do the graceful thing. But Israeli authorities decided it would be best for all involved if Bishara were permitted to flee the country. He lives in comfortable exile in Qatar to this day.[31] A political party could play out its fate in a thousand countries where a scandal of this magnitude would take it down, and only one where it wouldn't. But that one is the State of Israel. In the election immediately after Bishara was caught passing secrets to Hezbollah, his BALAD party got the most votes in its history.[32] Such are the workings of Israel's evil system of apartheid.

But what of the Palestinians in the territories? Aren't they living in an apartheid state? Here Amnesty's analysis is, if anything, even more detached from reality.

The Arabic-speaking Druze who live in the Golan Heights have the right to vote. As we have seen before, civilian law was applied to them over forty years prior to the issuance of Amnesty's report. Ironically, it is only *because* they are under Israeli sovereignty—under what Amnesty calls "apartheid"—that they have the right to vote, or any human rights at all.

Gaza? From Israel's perspective, it is a foreign country. Israel withdrew completely from Gaza over fifteen years before Amnesty issued its report. Gaza also had its own government, elected via the well-known system of one man/one vote/one time. Amnesty might just as well have claimed that Egyptians or Jordanians live in apartheid states, because they don't have the right to vote in Israel either. The nastiest thing you can say is that after Hamas assumed power in 2007, Israel placed restrictions on wartime material that could travel into Gaza through Israel, as every nation at war does.

The West Bank? There Palestinians live under their own government, in accordance with the Oslo treaties they signed. After Arafat died in November 2004, the Israelis managed elections for the Palestinian Authority, in accordance with their Oslo treaty obligations. The winner of those elections was Arafat's longtime deputy Mahmoud Abbas. As of this writing, Abbas is serving the twentieth year of his four-year term, because—like Hamas in Gaza—he too was elected by the system of one man/one vote/one time. Unlike Hamas, which governs all of Gaza, Abbas's Palestinian Authority only governs roughly 40 percent of the West Bank, where practically all Palestinians live. But the reason he doesn't govern the equivalent of the entire West Bank is that he has turned down every peace plan ever proposed, refusing each time to even respond with counter terms. When the nations of the world gathered in Rome in 1973 to render apartheid illegal, this was not the situation they had in mind.

Here's the funny part: in Amnesty's eyes, Israel is an apartheid state *even when it adheres to international law*. You see, even if the West Bank and Gaza really were under Israeli occupation, Israel is *required* under international law to treat its residents differently from Israeli citizens. Amnesty was aware of this not-insignificant problem and said the following: "The law of occupation allows, and in some cases requires, differential treatment between nationals of the occupying power and the population of the occupied territory. However, it does not allow the occupying power to do this where the intention is to establish or maintain a regime of systemic racial oppression and domination."[33] In other words, adhering to international law doesn't matter. It's all about intent. It's all about racism.

This is where you begin to understand how the game is really played. Twisting the facts is only a starting point. The really earnest work is invested in twisting the law. The practice is sometimes referred to as "waging lawfare." Amnesty, for example, advocates for a "right of return" for the descendants of refugees, where they maintain a "close and enduring connection to the area" and "where this is feasible." Somehow, the only refugees that seem to match that criteria are—you guessed it—the descendants of Palestinian refugees.[34]

In the waging of lawfare, refugees are a sideshow. For those who wish to mobilize the law and march it off to war, there is another principle that is a far more effective tool. It is a lot like a Swiss Army knife. It can be used in any situation. It is a blunt instrument that doesn't do anything well. And lawyers waging lawfare carry it into battle whenever war commences (the one knife you can effectively bring to a gunfight).

It is the doctrine of proportionality.

* * *

In World War II, the commander of Germany's Army Group North, operating in Russia, was a mass-murdering sociopath named Field Marshal Wilhelm Ritter von Leeb.[35] Von Leeb encircled Leningrad and thereby set in motion a siege that would claim the lives of over 800,000 Russian civilians.[36] The siege was like the dropping of a slow-motion atomic bomb. The city and its inhabitants were largely eliminated. But it took two and a half years instead of two and a half seconds.

After the war, von Leeb was tried at Nuremberg as the most senior officer in one of the most famous legal proceedings in the history of international law, the High Command Trial. Situations of this kind are always judged on a spectrum. Everyone agrees that it is legal to lay siege to an army and starve it into submission. Indeed, a signature strategy of war is to cut off the enemy's supply line. On the other end of the spectrum, everyone agrees that it is illegal to deliberately kill civilians who put up no resistance. The problem is the situation in the middle. What happens if an army embeds itself inside a city populated with civilians and refuses to surrender?

At Nuremberg, the judges shocked the world and found von Leeb not guilty:

> A belligerent commander may lawfully lay siege to a place controlled by the enemy and endeavor by a process of isolation to cause its surrender. The propriety of attempting to reduce it by starvation is not questioned. Hence, the cutting off of every source of sustenance from without is deemed legitimate.... We might wish the law were otherwise but we must administer it as we find it.[37]

Von Leeb was found guilty of other things. But he was sentenced to time served and walked right out the courtroom door a free man. He lived out his days on the Bavarian estate that Hitler gave him, before dying fat, rich, and happy in his bed at the age of seventy-nine.

At least von Leeb stood trial. Those who ordered the bombing of civilian targets were never even prosecuted. General Telford Taylor, the Chief Allied Counsel for War Crimes at Nuremberg, wrote, "aerial bombardment of cities and factories has become a recognized part of modern warfare as carried out by all nations."[38] But what about collateral damage to civilians? The rule here was also established in Nuremberg in *United States v. Wilhelm List, et al.*, often referred to as the Hostages Trial. The court concluded that:

Military necessity permits a belligerent, subject to the laws of war, to apply any amount and kind of force to compel the complete submission of the enemy with the least possible expenditure of time, life, and money...it permits the destruction of life, of armed enemies and other persons whose destruction is incidentally unavoidable...but does not permit the killing of innocent inhabitants for purposes of revenge or the satisfaction of a lust to kill.[39]

This outcome left a bitter taste in many mouths. It took a few decades, but on June 8, 1977, 174 nations adopted Protocol I of the Geneva Convention.[i,40] It is a long document running to over a hundred articles. But the most oft-cited provision is Article 51, which bans "indiscriminate attacks" against civilians. This is defined as "an attack which may be expected to cause incidental loss of civilian life...which would be excessive in relation to the concrete and direct military advantage anticipated."[41] In shorthand, this is what people refer to as the doctrine of proportionality.

Since its adoption, the doctrine has never been reduced to a concrete set of rules for a simple reason: no one knows what it means. The international tribunal that investigated the 1999 NATO Air War against Yugoslavia said in its final report, "The main problem with the principle of proportionality is...what it means and how it is to be applied." Like most everyone else, the authors had little light to shed on the subject and concluded, "The answer to these questions is not simple. It may be necessary to resolve them on a case-by-case basis, and the answers may differ depending on the background and values of the decision maker."[42] A law that differs based on the

---

[i] The United States and Israel are among the few notable countries that have refused to sign Protocol I. This is because Article 1(4) says that the treaty covers those fighting "colonial domination and alien occupation and against racist regimes." This has been interpreted to mean that terrorists—who were traditionally treated as criminals under international law—were elevated to the status of soldiers, entitled to all the protections afforded soldiers. Paradoxically, though they've never officially adopted it, the United States and Israel have shown perhaps the greatest commitment to the principles enshrined in the Protocols. The international community has long demanded no less, even though neither country is an official signatory.

"background and values of the decision maker" is not a law, it is an ethical standard. And a murky one at that.

The Geneva Convention was a milestone in man's attempt to civilize himself. But it only works in situations where there is a clear, black-and-white rule. For example, it is illegal to shoot at a pilot parachuting to the ground after ejecting, or at a sailor flailing in the water after abandoning ship. These laws work well because they apply an *objective* standard that everyone understands. Once you adopt a *subjective* standard, such as proportionality, the legal application is a foregone conclusion. Everyone adopts the same rule: what *my* soldiers do is proportional; what *your* soldiers do is not.

The U.S. Army states in the *Department of Defense Law of War Manual* that "It is a legitimate method of war to starve enemy forces... Military action intended to starve enemy forces, however, must not be taken where it is expected to result in incidental harm to the civilian population that is excessive in relation to the military advantage anticipated to be gained."[43]

This is the law that American lawyers applied when President Obama ordered Operation Inherent Resolve, the war to drive the Islamic State out of Iraq and Syria. They considered all the precedents and concluded that it was proportional to use starvation as a tool of war. U.S. forces worked together with Iraqi troops to besiege the cities of Fallujah and Ramadi. No food, water, or fuel were allowed in.[44]

In truth, U.S. ground troops only played an advisory role. The larger U.S. contribution to the effort was in the air, which is where you really see the doctrine of proportionality in action. When confronting a military challenge, policymakers always face the same choice: use air power or use ground troops. Air power results in fewer of your own losses, but it greatly increases the dead and wounded among enemy civilians, as well as collateral damage to property. Using ground troops reverses that arithmetic: fewer enemy civilians die, but more troops return home in flag-draped coffins.

Obama never hesitated—he restricted U.S. combat troops to their bases.[45] Then he formed a coalition of allied air forces in which the U.S. supplied 70 percent of the air power, Britain 20 percent, and various other allies like Canada, France, and Australia the remainder. At a time in which fewer than a hundred Americans had been killed by ISIS terrorists on American soil, and most other countries sustained even fewer casualties, this coalition of enlightened nations took to the air. And then they flattened every city in their path.

The Iraqi security forces lost large swaths of the country to ISIS in 2014 because they had no will to fight.[46] They weren't much better in the effort to retake it. Whenever they took even small arms fire from a building, they demanded an air strike. At first, what is referred to as "Target Engagement Authority" was held exclusively by the overall commander of the operation, Lieutenant General Stephen J. Townsend. But requests for airstrikes became so numerous that authority was soon pushed down the chain. An American officer told me that the process continued until authority was exercised by "the dude on the ground."[47]

Western air forces have long adopted the use of very sophisticated (and very expensive) smart-bomb munitions. The hope was that "one shot, one kill" ordinance would minimize collateral damage. The problem in Iraq was that ISIS terrorists never got the memo, and didn't sit outside waiting to be bombed. Instead, they dug tunnels throughout the city for concealment and protection. This resulted in what one analyst called the "Precision Paradox." Driving the terrorists underground required more bombing to root them out. This generated "a creeping wave" of demolition that "further amplified destruction."[48]

The results were devastating. Mosul is the second largest city in Iraq—almost as large as Philadelphia. According to the Rand Corporation, the campaign resulted "in the city's effective destruction."[49] Two retired American army officers put the damage at $100 billion.[50] Ramadi, home to 400,000 people, was "reduced to rubble."[51] How many civilians were killed? No one really knows for sure. The Associated Press went to the central morgue in Mosul after the war and obtained the names of 9,606 people who were killed.[52] But many others were killed that were never brought to the morgue. Hoshyar

Zebari, who served as Iraq's foreign minister and deputy prime minister, and who is from Mosul, put the figure at 40,000.[53] *That was only in the city of Mosul*—a single battle in a war that stretched across numerous cities and towns in a landmass twice the size of Belgium.

In weighing the (supposed) requirements of "proportionality," Obama did what everyone else does: he chose the lives of American troops over the lives of enemy civilians. To this, I say, thank you, President Obama. Great Britain formally adopted the view that "the proportionality principle does not itself require the attacker to accept increased risk."[54] Do the good prosecutors working diligently in The Hague agree? It's hard to say. They handle proportionality on a case-by-case basis.

Obama has nothing to worry about. The United States has long made it clear that it has zero tolerance for any attempts to prosecute its soldiers or public officials. In 2017, the International Criminal Court attempted to investigate Americans for alleged torture of detainees during the Bush Administration. The Trump Administration slapped sanctions on the court's personnel. Those sanctions were only removed by the Biden Administration when the investigation was dropped.[55] That was for an *investigation*. Were anyone to *arrest* American personnel, the president has standing authority from Congress to use force to free them. The 2002 statute authorizing force has a section, number, and title befitting its place in the leatherbound books of federal law. [56] But everyone knows it by its unofficial name: the Hague Invasion Act.

* * *

On Passover night, March 27, 2002, a Palestinian laden with explosives walked into a hotel in the Israeli city of Netanya and blew himself up, murdering thirty people. The Park Hotel massacre, as it is known, pushed Israel's casualty toll for that month above a hundred killed. It was the worst urban carnage since the 1948 War, and for Prime Minister Ariel Sharon it was the last straw. He assembled his cabinet late that night, and they quickly voted to do what Israel had not done in twenty years: mobilize reservists and send them into battle.[57]

The first order of business was clearing the Palestinian terrorist group Islamic Jihad out of the West Bank city of Jenin. One Israeli soldier asked a reporter why they were being sent into Jenin's narrow alleys. The Americans would have just called out their air force and reduced the city to rubble.[58] But theirs was not to reason why, so in they went. The fighting went house to house, block to block. And when the guns fell silent, the Israelis sustained twenty-three killed. That is twenty-one more than the U.S. took in the destruction of Mosul.[59]

As for Palestinian casualties, Human Rights Watch did a study and concluded that a total of fifty-two Palestinians were killed. Of that, the authors found that "at least twenty-seven of those confirmed dead were suspected to have been armed Palestinians belonging to movements such as Islamic Jihad, Hamas, and the al-Aqsa Martyrs' Brigades." The cautious phrase "at least twenty-seven" means that the true figure was probably higher. But even if the lower figure is true, Israel would have achieved a kill ratio of terrorists to civilians that is better than one-to-one, something unheard of in modern urban warfare. We will never know what the kill ratio was in Mosul or Ramadi. One-to-one it certainly was not.

But here is how HRW judged the situation: "Human Rights Watch concludes that the Israeli military actions in the Jenin refugee camp included both indiscriminate and disproportionate attacks."[60] The Swiss Army knife got the job done again.

The nicest thing that one can say about the "human rights" community is that with the passage of time, they have become egalitarian: they now call practically everyone a war criminal. Amnesty International issued a statement on August 4, 2022, which said that "Ukrainian forces have put civilians in harm's way by establishing bases and operating weapons systems in populated residential areas.... Such tactics violate international humanitarian law."[61] The Russians pounced on the statement like a dog on a bone. Russia's ambassador to the United Nations said, "We don't use the tactics

Ukrainian armed forces are using—using the civilian objects as military cover...what Amnesty International recently proved in a report."[62]

Maybe it was the fact that America and Israel were not involved. Or maybe it was the fact that the soldiers and civilians on both sides of the war were white. Or maybe I'm just being unkind, and common sense can still occasionally make a cameo appearance in the tragicomedy called "human rights." But the Amnesty statement on Ukraine caused another outcry, not unlike the one surrounding Alexei Navalny. Among other things, Amnesty's Ukraine director resigned in protest.[63]

Amnesty quietly hired a panel of legal scholars to conduct an internal investigation. They concluded that Amnesty's charge against Ukraine was "not sufficiently substantiated." Amnesty spends a lot of time complaining about the lack of transparency by the governments it attacks. But it chose to bury the study, rather than release it to the press. It was eventually leaked to *The New York Times*.[64]

The episode was embarrassing. But it didn't leave any tarnish on the halo that shines its luminescent glow upon Amnesty. On the contrary, Amnesty and the other tillers and toilers in the human rights community share something in common with each other, and not just among themselves, but with other left-wing commentators, particularly those that comment on Israel.

They win a lot of awards.

VIII.

Lies on the Prize:
Mendacity and All Its Rewards

"History is the pack of lies that people have agreed upon."
—NAPOLEON BONAPARTE

On October 14, 1994, Shimon Peres and his aides sat nervously in his office in Jerusalem. A month before, Peres had travelled to Oslo, ostensibly to mark the one-year anniversary of the signing of the Oslo Accords. But the real reason for the trip, which he didn't even bother to conceal, was to lobby for something almost as close to his heart. He wanted a share of the Nobel Peace Prize.

The award is the most prestigious in the world. In his 1895 will, Alfred Nobel created it for the person or persons who in the preceding year, "shall have done the most or the best work for fraternity between nations."[1] Martin Luther King, Jr., Mother Theresa, Elie Wiesel—the laureates included some of the greatest names of the twentieth century. Nelson Mandela had won it the year before, in 1993. So when the Nobel committee in Norway issued its press release on the afternoon of October 14, there were hugs, cries of joy, and even a few tears. An elated Peres went before the press cameras and made the announcement. He had done it. He had won the Nobel Peace Prize.[2]

89

One of Peres' co-winners was Prime Minister Yitzhak Rabin. He was nowhere to be found. That was because five days before, an Israeli soldier named Nahshon Waxman had been kidnapped by Hamas near Ben-Gurion Airport. Unbeknown to Peres, Rabin was at that moment overseeing a rescue operation to free Waxman from his captors. The mission failed. Three of the Hamas kidnappers were killed, but so was one of the Israeli rescuers, along with Waxman, who was bound hand and foot and murdered in cold blood.[3] Rabin had broken off talks with Arafat earlier in the week when news of the kidnapping came to light. At the press conference announcing the tragic results of the operation, he signaled a willingness to go back to the negotiating table and did so shortly after that. But the Nobel Peace Prize was awarded during the hostage crisis, while the talks were frozen because of ongoing terrorism.

This caused more than a few people to wonder why the award was given to the third recipient—none other than Yasir Arafat. He remains part of Nobel's pantheon of luminaries, an exclusive club that includes the Dalai Lama and the Red Cross. Elena Bonner, the widow of the great Soviet dissident Andrei Sakharov, said that she couldn't believe that her late husband shared membership with Arafat in the "group of Nobel laureates."[4] One member of the Nobel Committee, Kare Kristiansen, resigned in protest, saying that Arafat was the "world's most prominent terrorist."[5]

Peres was livid at Rabin for not informing him of the rescue mission, leaving him to make a fool of himself celebrating before the cameras.[6] But he learned nothing from the experience. Neither apparently, did those who give out prizes. Just a month later, in November 1994, Peres went back to Europe to pick up a different prize, the Prince of Asturias Award from the King of Spain. This time a rabbi was murdered in the midst of the festivities. The picture of Peres smiling with Arafat was published in Israeli newspapers alongside the picture of the rabbi's distraught family, crying over his grave.[7]

When asked by reporters years later why the Nobel committee had given the world's most prestigious award to Arafat, Kristiansen said that the committee wanted to motivate the parties "to continue the hard work."[8] It's a nice theory. But there is a glaring flaw in the logic. In 2020, Netanyahu signed the Abraham Accords—four peace treaties with four Arab countries. There was no terrorism, there were no kidnappings, and no one had to hold out hopes for some future deal. The final treaties were signed right on the spot, tripling the number of Arab countries at peace with Israel.

As of this writing, none of the parties to the Abraham Accords have won a Nobel Peace Prize.

The inner workings of the Nobel Prize committee are a closely guarded secret, so the reason for the oversight is left to speculation. But this is where thought experiments can be a useful tool. Suppose the signatory for Israel on the Abraham Accords had been Rabin, or even his protégé Ehud Barak. Suppose the president of the United States had been Obama—who won the Nobel Peace Prize just a few months after taking office and before he accomplished much of anything. In this scenario, it is all but a foregone conclusion that *everyone* would have won a Nobel Peace Prize. The only question would have been how the committee divided it up amongst the parties, because the rules only allow the award to be given to a maximum of three people.

The obvious conclusion is that the Nobel Peace Prize committee is not just looking for the person who "shall have done the most or the best work for fraternity between nations." There is a branding issue as well. To win the coveted prize, you have to meet certain ideological criteria as well. The Nobel prizes in the sciences seem to be untainted by politics. Many conservatives, like Milton Friedman or even right-wing Israeli Robert Aumann, have won the prize in economics, just as I am sure conservatives have in fields like physics and medicine. But to award Arafat, but not Netanyahu, has to make you wonder if the judges could find "peace" in a dictionary.

I wish there were a Nobel Prize for Irony. In 1994, my candidates would have been the Norwegian judges who honored Arafat with the world's most prestigious peace award, at the very moment that he was leading a terror campaign. In other years, I would bestow the honor on American prize committee judges who hand out our most prestigious awards. They hand them out to honor the highest ideals of journalism and literature. And they give them to people who get things completely wrong.

* * *

On September 19, 1982, the world awoke to the news that Lebanese Christian militiamen known as Phalangists had perpetrated a massacre near Beirut in the Palestinian refugee camps of Sabra and Shatila, following the assassination of their leader Bashir Gemayel. Lebanon had seen far larger massacres in its recent past. But this time there were Israeli soldiers stationed down the road. So the world was mesmerized with the question of what the Israelis knew and when they knew it.

One of the people who wanted to know was a twenty-nine-year-old reporter for *The New York Times* named Tom Friedman. The massacre occurred while he was on vacation.[9] But after rushing to the scene from New York, he charged into the field seeking news fit to print. It did not take long before he found what he was seeking. This is what he reported:

> The Israeli Army began to learn on the evening of Thursday, Sept. 16, that civilians were being killed in Shatila, since the moment these armed men entered the camps, they began murdering people at random, and those who fled told the Israelis what was happening.... Yet, according to Defense Minister Ariel Sharon, the militiamen doing the killings were told by the Israelis they could stay inside the camps until Saturday morning, and the murders continued until they left.[10]

The callousness of the Israelis to the loss of civilian life was all the worse, Friedman reported, because they had a forward position atop a five-story building, and "from that position it is possible to see into at least part of the Shatila camp, including those parts where piles of dead bodies were found later."[11] An IDF colonel was quoted by him as saying that the goal of the operation was for the camps to be "purified."[i]

Friedman conceded that Israeli soldiers were not directly involved. Instead, he settled for the next best thing. "It seems clear," he wrote, "that there were militiamen from Major [Sa'ad] Haddad's group in the strike force that entered the camps on Thursday afternoon...the Israelis have sought to place blame solely on the [Lebanese Christian] Phalangists since Major Haddad's militia is virtually integrated into the Israeli Army and operates entirely under its command."[12]

The part about the Haddad militia being under Israeli command was true, so their participation in the massacre would have implicated the Israelis, if only indirectly. The Israelis therefore had a strong interest to steer blame away from Haddad and onto the Phalangists. But this Israeli ruse did not fool ace reporter Tom Friedman. "What is not clear is whether the Haddad militiamen could have reached the camps—far from their normal area of operations in the south along the Israeli border—without the knowledge or active cooperation of the Israelis." If newsprint could wink, there would be one after that last sentence. But just in case readers did not pick up on the nuance, he continued, "at the least, the circumstantial evidence indicates that some members of the Haddad militia passed through Israeli lines in an apparent effort to join up with the Phalangists going into the Palestinian camps."[13]

A star was born.

Friedman won the 1983 Pulitzer Prize for International Reporting. His dispatches were hailed as "a distinguished example of reporting of international affairs."[14] He also won the prestigious George Polk Award.[15] He had arrived on the Lebanon beat in April 1982, and less than six months later he was one of the most prominent figures in journalism.

---

[i] The Hebrew word for "purify"—"*letaher*"—is the same word used to describe a military "mopping up operation." To use that word as Friedman did would be the equivalent of an American soldier telling a reporter his unit was "mopping up" after a battle, and having it translated to mean they were engaged in a "purification" operation.

One group that heard of him was the Kahan Commission. It was formed by the Israelis in the wake of the massacre to find out what had really happened in Sabra and Shatila on September 16-18, 1982. In this task, it spared no effort. The Commission heard testimony from no less than fifty-eight witnesses and took written statements from almost two hundred others. The one person it never heard from was journalist Thomas L. Friedman. He refused to appear, claiming it would violate editorial policies of *The New York Times*. The Commission noted wryly that "we did not receive a satisfactory answer as to why the paper's publisher prevented its reporter from appearing before the commission and thus helping it uncover all the important facts."[16]

The Kahan Commission Report runs to ninety pages and gives an hour-by-hour description of what occurred. The key finding is a bit long, but it's worth reading the whole thing:

> It was alleged that the atrocities being perpetrated in the camps were visible from the roof of the forward command post, that the fact that they were being committed was also discernible from the sounds emanating from the camps, and that the senior IDF commanders who were on the roof of the forward command post for two days certainly saw or heard what was going on in the camps. We have already determined above that events in the camps, in the area where the Phalangists entered, were not visible from the roof of the forward command post. It has also been made clear that no sounds from which it could be inferred that a massacre was being perpetrated in the camps reached that place....
>
> Here we must add that when the group of [Palestinian] doctors and nurses met IDF officers on Saturday morning, at a time when it was already clear to them that they were out of danger, they made no complaint that a massacre had been perpetrated in the camps. When we asked the witnesses from the group why they had not informed the IDF officers about the massacre, they replied that they had not known about it. The fact that the doctors and nurses who were in the Gaza

Hospital—which is proximate to the site of the event and where persons wounded in combative action and frightened persons from the camps arrived—did not know about the massacre, but only about isolated instances of injury which they had seen for themselves, also shows that those who were nearby but not actually inside the camps did not form the impression, from what they saw and heard, that a massacre of hundreds of people was taking place.[17]

But why didn't the Israeli-controlled Haddad Militia inform their Israeli commanders of the carnage? The answer was simple: they weren't there.

The Commission found the following: "Rumors spread that personnel of Major Haddad were perpetrating a massacre or participating in a massacre. No basis was found for these rumors...no unit of that force had crossed [north of] the Awali River that week." The Commission noted that Haddad's men were practically at war with the Phalangists and that "it is inconceivable that a force from Major Haddad's army took part in military operations of the Phalangists in the camps, nor was there any hint of such cooperation."[18]

The Kahan Commission was no whitewash.[ii] Notwithstanding the findings above, it threw the book at all involved, finding they should have foreseen that a massacre might take place. Two senior generals were sacked. The Commission further made it clear that the chief of staff of the army would also have been sacked, but the term of his command was up. Most importantly, Ariel Sharon—the second most powerful man in the country—was compelled to resign and his political career was ended (or so everyone thought). There is literally no precedent for a nation punishing its own senior commanders for the acts of those beneath them. The My Lai massacre in Vietnam was carried out by American troops under American

---

ii The Commission was made up of the chief justice of the Israeli Supreme Court, a future chief justice, and a senior army general. The two lead investigators were women. One later became the first female chief justice of the Israeli Supreme Court (technically, the title in Israel is "president" of the Supreme Court). The other later became an associate justice of the Israeli Supreme Court.

command and not a single senior officer was cashiered. The commander in the field, Lieutenant William Calley, served all of three days in jail.[iii,19]

Imagine for a moment that you've won the Pulitzer Prize, the dream of every American author and journalist. Then, a commission inquiry report makes it clear that you got the whole thing wrong. What would you do? I would like to think that I would be honest enough to wipe the egg off my face and apologize.

So what did Friedman do?

Well, let's just say that winning a Pulitzer Prize means never having to say you're sorry. Friedman never did. To the contrary, like a fine yarn told round the campfire, the tale was only embellished with the passage of time. Years later, Friedman sat down to write about his experiences in Lebanon in his blockbuster memoir *From Beirut to Jerusalem*. The Sabra and Shatila massacre was recounted by him this way:

> Afterward, the Israeli soldiers would claim they did not know what was happening in the camps. They did not hear the screams and shouts of people being massacred. They did not see wanton murder of innocents through their telescopic binoculars.... This is true. Israeli soldiers did not see innocent civilians being massacred and they did not hear the screams of innocent children going to their graves. What they saw was a 'terrorist infestation' being 'mopped up' and 'terrorist nurses' scurrying about and 'terrorist teenagers' trying to defend them.... Many Israelis had so dehumanized the Palestinians in their own minds and had so intimately equated the words 'Palestinian,' 'PLO,' and 'terrorists' on their radio and television for so long...that they simply lost track of the distinction between Palestinian fighters and Palestinian civilians, combatants and noncombatants.[20]

---

iii Calley was initially convicted of killing at least twenty-two civilians. But his life sentence was reduced due to a public outcry, which included Governor Jimmy Carter of Georgia who called it "a blow to troop morale."

That's powerful stuff. But what proof does Friedman have? Here is the very next sentence: "The Kahan Commission...uncovered repeated instances within the first hours of the massacre in which Israeli officers overheard Phalangists referring to the killing of Palestinian civilians." In other words, he cites the Kahan Commission Report to back up his assertion that the Israelis knew a massacre was taking place—even though the Kahan Commission concluded the exact opposite.[iv,21]

Friedman does the same thing in his book when it comes to the even more explosive question of what the Israelis expected to happen when they were planning the operation in the first place. One can almost picture Friedman wagging his finger in anger as he says the following: "The Israelis knew just what they were doing when they let the Phalangists into those camps." This too he supports with a citation to the Kahan Commission Report.[22] Here's what the Kahan Commission really concluded:

> Contentions and accusations were advanced that...entry of the Phalangists into the camps had been carried out with the prior knowledge that a massacre would be perpetrated there and with the intention that this should indeed take place.... These accusations are unfounded. We have no doubt that no conspiracy or plot was entered into between anyone from the Israeli political echelon or from the military echelon in the IDF and the Phalangists, with the aim of perpetrating atrocities in the camps.... No intention existed on the part of any Israeli element to harm the non-combatant population in the camps.[23]

I would note, parenthetically, that the factfinding of the Kahan Commission has survived the test of time. In the ensuing forty years, no smoking gun memo has emerged, no deathbed confession has

---

iv A detailed description of what happened in Sabra and Shatila is beyond the scope of this account. Suffice it to say that each of the "repeated instances" cited by Friedman was reviewed by the Kahan Commission, and each was found to have been reasonably discounted.

come to light."[v,24] Friedman never uncovered any credible source that undermined anything in the Kahan Commission findings. To the contrary, he cited the Kahan Commission himself. So he read the words in the Report "no intention existed on the part of any Israeli element to harm the non-combatant population in the camps," and then wrote in his book "the Israelis knew just what they were doing when they let the Phalangists into those camps." He read all the passages cited above and wrote that the Israelis intentionally and maliciously ignored the cries of the innocents.

From Beirut to Jerusalem won the National Book Award. It was judged the very best nonfiction book of 1989.

I have focused on the Sabra and Shatila massacre because it is the story that brought Friedman fame. But it is only one episode in a book riddled with misstatements of fact, half-truths, and outright distortions. Like Jimmy Carter's *Palestine: Peace not Apartheid*, it is another of those books that says, wrongly, that Israel launched a "preemptive strike" against Jordan in 1967. And, of course, like every good critic of Israel, Friedman knows how to push the right buttons:

> It was enraging for Israelis to have these 'niggers' (sic.)—which was exactly how many Israelis viewed the Palestinians—these people whom they had given 'good jobs', medical care, and all the other benefits that Israelis claimed went into their 'enlightened occupation'—suddenly getting uppity and saying that they would not accept their second-class status any longer. More than a few Israelis wanted these 'thankless' Palestinian maids and waiters to be put back in their proper places.[25]

So how does a book like this win a National Book Award? One of the National Book Award judges in 2002 was the brilliant columnist, Michael Kinsley. He once wrote a hilarious piece describing the

---

[v] The closest thing to a bombshell revelation came in 1999 when a top Phalangist named Robert "the Cobra" Khatam published a memoir. He asserted that Elie Hobeika, the Phalange commander, was actually a Syrian agent, and that the Syrians engineered the massacre to embarrass Israel and damage the prospects for peace with Lebanon. It was said of Khatam that if a cobra bit him, the snake would die (hence the nickname). He was not a reliable figure, to put it mildly, so the veracity of this story is questionable.

experience of receiving over four hundred books in the mail and being asked to choose the best one. Among the four hundred books was a biography of Ben Franklin, and another that described the quest to find the giant antelope of Angola ("we gave the award to [Robert] Caro. But did I actually read every page? I'll never tell.")[26] His point was that the National Book Award is little more than a popularity contest, as the Pulitzer Prize no doubt is as well.

In this popularity contest, as well as others, the clique that controls the process looks to advance certain themes, all of which seem to cluster inside certain ideological zip codes. One has only to go down the list of movies nominated for an Oscar to see what I'm talking about. For years the bias was obvious, but at least it went unspoken. However, before the 2024 Oscars, the Academy of Motion Picture Arts and Sciences finally just came right out and said it. As described in a front-page story in *The New York Times*, the academy officially changed the rules. From now on, to qualify for the Best Picture award, "diversity in hiring…is considered. So is the movie's plot."[27] The academy publicly turned its back on half its audience, so that half of the audience returned the favor. The Academy Awards now receives less than half the ratings it did just ten years ago. The only thing surprising about this is that people are surprised.

Now, I have no idea what would motivate someone like Tom Friedman to cite a commission report for support, when it says the exact opposite of what he's trying to prove. But the tone of the book makes it clear that he set out to write an account to make liberal hearts go aflutter; namely, the story of a naïve Jewish boy from the Midwest who grows up loving Israel, only to learn the error of his ways.

Maybe Friedman deserved the accolades. In the end, everything is relative. And compared to his peers, he was a sober voice of restraint. *Time* magazine infamously reported that a secret section of the Kahan Commission Report found that Sharon "discussed… the need for the Phalangists to take revenge."[28] Essentially, *Time* claimed that although the Kahan Commission recommended sacking Sharon, it hushed up his most explosive crime. The story was absurd on its face. It would be like saying that Ken Starr found that the Clintons murdered Vince Foster but buried it in a secret portion of his report, and no one, including the Republicans, leaked it to the press. Sharon sued *Time* for libel. In 1983, as this was all playing out, *Time*'s Managing Editor Ray Cave was named editor of the year by *Adweek* magazine. A year later, in 1984, Sharon proved that the story was false and libelous.[29] In 1985 *Time* won the National Magazine Award for general excellence.[30]

Friedman would eventually finish his stint in Lebanon and assume the coveted post of Jerusalem Bureau Chief for *The New York Times*. The man he replaced, David K. Shipler, left the position to write his own memoir. Among other things, he claimed that Israel showed callous disregard for Palestinian life because in 1978, an Israeli lieutenant named Daniel Pinto was "convicted of strangling two [Palestinian] prisoners and throwing their bodies down a well," but he only served sixteen months in jail.[31] It was true that Pinto's punishment was reduced. But that was because the case against him was weak and because Pinto was the son-in-law of a legendary field commander, who may have intervened with the Army chief of staff to get the sentence reduced.[32] I'm obviously not defending the practice. But it's a far cry from the sort of "racism" that Shipler was trying to prove. In another portion of the book, Shipler described the reluctance of Jews to be treated in Palestinian hospitals in the West Bank and Gaza. Shipler attributed that to racism too.[33] Now, imagine you were Jewish and needed a procedure. Would you want the work done in Gaza? Neither would I.

Shipler's book won the Pulitzer Prize for General Nonfiction in 1987.[34]

Amnesty International won the Nobel Peace Prize.[35] Human Rights Watch won the United Nations Prize for Human Rights.[36] Left-wing Israeli author Amos Oz was a perennial favorite among London oddsmakers to win the Nobel Prize in Literature, though it eluded him. But his colleague, peace activist David Grossman, won the Man Booker International Prize.[37] I'll spare you commentary on the works they've written. Suffice it to say that neither wasted any ink defending the honor of the Jewish state.

Now, when I hear people like Michael Moore or Alexandria Ocasio-Cortez attack Israel, I understand it. My grandmother used to repeat an old saying (which sounds better in the original Yiddish), "You can't dance at every wedding," meaning no one can be an expert in everything. It is perfectly natural that those who identify with people of color, and whose knowledge of the Middle East is basic, will arrive at some upside-down conclusions about Israel.

Accolades aside, it is people like Friedman that have the most to answer for. These are the people who should know better. There is no shortage of them. There is, for example, Bernie Sanders, who volunteered to work on a kibbutz in the 1960s and is old enough to remember what happened in 1967. There is Jeremy Ben-Ami, the founder of J Street. But who I blame most is not a person, but an institution, one that is the very center of gravity for the Liberal Intellectual Complex. It is also, not coincidentally, still the most important journalistic institution in the world.

I blame *The New York Times*.

IX.

Groucho Marx Journalism

"Who are ya gonna believe, me or your own eyes?"

—MARX BROTHERS (1932)

On March 27, 1964, *The New York Times* shocked the world with a front-page story that would become famous:

> For more than half an hour 38 respectable, law-abiding citizens in Queens watched a killer stalk and stab a woman in three separate attacks in Kew Gardens. Twice the sound of their voices and the sudden glow of their bedroom lights interrupted him and frightened him off. Each time he returned, sought her out and stabbed her again. Not one person telephoned the police during the assault.[1]

The murder victim was Catherine "Kitty" Genovese, a twenty-eight-year-old bar manager whose name would become synonymous with urban indifference. The case spawned an entire field of psychology, which was dubbed the "bystander effect." It sparked studies, books, and movies. Genovese's brother Bill was greatly affected by what happened to his sister. Not wanting to be a bystander himself, he was inspired to join the Marines. Sadly, he lost both his legs in Vietnam.

As someone who grew up not far from where the murder took place—it happened just a few blocks from my elementary school—I often wondered later how anyone could have ever believed such a ridiculous story. Psychology studies show that under the right circumstances, there is indeed a "bystander effect." But New Yorkers are the most in-your-face, drop-everything-and-get-involved people on the face of the earth. The Kitty Genovese story seemed fishy to rival newspapers at the time, but no one would question it. It had to be true. It was reported in *The New York Times*.

It took decades, but the real story eventually came to light. From his wheelchair, Bill Genovese made a documentary film fifty years later that painted a completely different picture of what really happened. I won't bother you with the details. And my point is not to show that reporters sometimes get things wrong. Journalists are human and make mistakes just like the rest of us. The point is the outsized role that *The New York Times* plays in American journalism, particularly in our time of shrunken newsrooms and shuttered local newspapers. When *The New York Times* reports something, it becomes the truth for a large part of the population. Whether it actually happened is almost beside the point.

* * *

On December 18, 2003, Prime Minister Ariel Sharon gave perhaps the most famous speech in his long career and dropped one of the greatest political bombshells in Israeli history. During the election campaign earlier that year, Sharon had cried that Netzarim, the most isolated settlement in Gaza, was no different than Tel Aviv. Now he said that Netzarim and dozens of other settlements would all be dismantled. Israel was unilaterally withdrawing from Gaza. The plan was soon dubbed the "Disengagement."[2]

Israelis could hardly believe their ears. Could it be that the man who had spearheaded the effort to build the settlements in the 1970s and '80s was the very man who would now tear them down? It would have been as if Ronald Reagan had repudiated tax cuts, or Bernie Sanders universal healthcare. It is not every day that a politician disassociates himself from the very issue that defines him. Some thought Sharon did it to distract from an unrelated criminal investigation. Some thought he had dementia.

As we will see, he had some very good reasons to get Israel out of Gaza. For our purposes now, it is enough to say that Sharon went all-out in his effort to remove Israel and its army from every last granule of Gazan sand. Three of the Jewish settlements were built in the northern tip of the Strip in what was no man's land before 1967. There was a legitimate argument that this land was Israeli rather than Palestinian. But Sharon ordered those settlements dismantled as well.[3]

The political process that Sharon faced to achieve passage of the Disengagement was described by his righthand man, Dov Weissglas, in his 2012 memoir. The title of the chapter containing the description is "The Political Crisis: 'The Decisive Moment for Israel.'"[4] It was all that and more. When the crucial vote came up in the Knesset, television cameras memorably showed Sharon sitting in the center of the hall in the prime minister's chair, firm and unwavering, while his ministers were scurrying in the aisles trying to decide what to do.[5] Their political careers were all hanging in the balance. Massive protests boiled over across the country. In Israel, a land of hot weather and easy access to automatic weapons, there was a real fear of civil war, or at least large-scale refusal of soldiers to carry out orders. But Sharon handled the matter with the same determination that defined his entire career. He lost a referendum, so he ignored it. He was opposed by the chief of staff of the army, so he replaced him. One columnist said that Sharon was like a driver going ninety miles an hour the wrong way down a one-way street screaming, "Get out of the way! Get out of the way!"[6]

Everybody did. There was a lot of pushing and shoving. There was a lot of screaming and shouting. But in the end, no one was killed during Disengagement, no one was seriously injured, and the army cleared every last settler out of Gaza, including the dead. The army dug up Jewish cemeteries and brought the remains back to Israel for reburial. They didn't leave a bone in the ground; not a single Jewish molecule remained in Gaza. On September 21, 2005, the Israeli government declared Disengagement complete. From that moment forward, crossing between the Gaza Strip and Israel required an international passport.[7] The Israeli army no longer exercised any jurisdiction inside Gaza. It was a foreign country. For better or worse, the vaunted two-state solution had finally been realized.

Under international humanitarian law, an occupying power must assume responsibility for the health, safety, and well-being of the local population. A typical passage is Article 55 of the Geneva Convention (1949), which states that "To the fullest extent of the means available to it, the Occupying Power has the duty of ensuring the food and medical supplies of the population."[8] Israel performed this task and performed it admirably. After 1967, the material lives of West Bank and Gaza Palestinians improved dramatically by every material metric (per capita GDP, life expectancy, literacy, etc.).

But any responsibility to a local population disappears the moment the occupying army marches out of the territory. This rule, established in the 1907 Hague Convention, states, "Territory is considered occupied when it is actually placed under the authority of the hostile army. The occupation extends only to the territory where such authority has been established and can be exercised."[9] Secretary of State Colin Powell famously laid down the Pottery Barn Rule: you break it, you buy it. But the corollary to that is the Geneva Convention: you leave it, you lose it.

The trouble for Palestinians in Gaza was that they depended on Israel for everything. Food, water, fuel, electricity, jobs, medical care—it all originated from the Jewish state. What if the Israelis left? Who would support them? According to Weissglas, of all the critics of Disengagement, the most ferocious were Israeli Arab Members of Knesset. They understood all too well what it meant for Gazans.[10]

Israel's most strident critics were also thrown into turmoil. The whole thesis of their argument was that Israel was a racist-apartheid-colonizer because it was an occupier. The dog had finally caught the car. The Israelis were out of Gaza. What now?

I knew the U.N. would go right on condemning Israel, and the "human rights" community would as well. J Street would join the chorus several years later when it came into existence. But the media was another story. Reporters are supposed to be objective. How could they spin Israel's withdrawal as an evil act?

One approach was to play the motives game. Yes, the Israelis pulled out—but they did it for all the wrong reasons! Tom Friedman wrote that "[Sharon's] aides have made it clear that he is getting out of Gaza in order to entrench Israel even more deeply in the West Bank and the Jewish settlements there."[i,11] Another was to attack "the way" the Israelis withdrew, as if peace would have broken out if only Israel had withdrawn more politely.[ii,12] But these poison darts aside, I never expected what, in fact, happened next.

Because what happened was nothing. *The New York Times* and others went right on saying that Gaza was under Israeli military occupation, as if Disengagement had never occurred. Here is what the paper of record published on September 20, 2007: "Under international law, Israel is considered an occupying power in Gaza, even though it has removed its troops and settlers from the territory."[13]

International law? *Which international law is that?* The *Times* doesn't say. But it repeated this bizarre legal conclusion on a regular basis. On June 1, 2016, for example—over ten years after the pullout was completed—readers were told that Gaza is "a society long under the shadow of a military occupation."[14] An August 19, 2022 story accused Israel of "restricting and silencing criticism of its 55-year military occupation of the West Bank and Gaza Strip."[15] Note that I took these quotes from the *news* section. The op-eds and editorials in the *Times* are a whole other level of dysfunction and distortion.

---

i In the same speech Sharon announced he was also withdrawing from twenty-one additional settlements in the West Bank to show he was *not* doing it to entrench Israel in the West Bank. Paradoxically, it was the Bush Administration that convinced him to reduce that number to just four settlements in the West Bank. They did this for fear the whole plan would die in the Knesset if Sharon attempted too much at once. The four settlements were eventually dismantled.

ii The Israelis invited the Palestinian Authority to a flag lowering ceremony. They refused to attend.

But at least they are opinions. This is the news deemed fit to print. And these were not silly oversights that slipped through while the managing editor was on vacation—they reflect *all* the reporting of Gaza. Because even when the *Times* failed to say it outright, the unspoken assumption of every story was that Israel owed a duty of care to Palestinians because Gaza was still under occupation.

A 2015 article described the plight of a Palestinian woman in Gaza who could not reach her betrothed in the West Bank because the heartless Israelis would not permit her to travel across their country.[16] It is like criticizing the United States for not permitting people who lived in the Islamic State or the Taliban Afghanistan to travel across America. In the midst of the Covid crisis, the *Times* ran a story criticizing Israel for not sharing vaccines with Gaza and thus "not protecting Palestinians under its occupation."[17] Yet another article decried the "struggle" that Gazan athletes faced in reaching competitions because of "travel restrictions" placed by the Israelis.[18] Those words appeared right on the front page.

This is what I like to call Groucho Marx Journalism. Picture Groucho with the nose, the glasses, and the wiggling cigar saying, "who are ya gonna believe, me or your own eyes?"[iii] The editors of *The New York Times* ask a similar question with each story. Perhaps the Geneva Convention has its international law, but the editors have their own.

I have always looked at Disengagement as a kind of litmus test. I believe criticism of Israel for occupying Gaza was misplaced, given the circumstances, but it was still within the bounds of legitimate debate. I supported Disengagement myself. But to criticize Israel for occupation *after* Disengagement, well, that is the ultimate statement of bad faith. This is why I pay no attention to J Street when it offers the "solution" of Israel dismantling all settlements and withdrawing

---

[iii] Serious movie fans reading this are jumping up and down like Harpo Marx, honking a horn on their belt and stomping on their hat. It was not Groucho Marx that made that statement in the 1933 film *Duck Soup*; it was his brother Chico Marx dressed as Groucho. I like to think of myself as a stickler for accuracy. But I am going to lay down a rule that I hope will heretofore be known as Kaufman's Maxim: never ruin a good metaphor with the facts.

to the '67 boundary. Israel proved in Gaza that, should it do all that and more, J Street would still call it an occupier. *The New York Times* is no better.

And that only tells half the story. *The New York Times* doesn't just misstate the law. It also misstates the facts.

Ever since Disengagement, the *Times* has referred to Israel's "blockade" of Gaza. In at least two articles by different reporters, it referred to it as a "draconian blockade."[19] In recent years, someone in the *Times* finally looked at a map and realized that Gaza also borders Egypt, so its reporters began referring to it as "a blockade enforced by Israel and Egypt."[20] Even so, in the words of the *Times*, the blockade "has undermined the living conditions of more than two million Palestinians, and led to a nearly 50 percent unemployment rate that is among the highest in the world."[21] Note that the "blockade" is the source of the suffering, not the refusal of Gazans to sign a peace treaty. The blame rests on Israel.

But why quibble over minor details like that? The whole story was false. Because the truth is, there was no blockade at all.

Yes, Israel placed restrictions on military materials such as steel and concrete, and even that got through, as evidenced by the hundreds of miles of tunnels that Hamas dug throughout Gaza. But for everything else—food, clothing, diapers, etc.—obtaining supply was, in the words of Israeli general Yom-Tov Samia, "as difficult as making a telephone call."[22]

As of this writing, the most recent full year for which there is data was 2022. In that year, Israel supplied Gaza with 5.7 billion gallons of water.[23] Without it, Gaza would have died of thirst. Israel sent over 67,000 supply trucks filled with supplies. Without it, Gaza would have starved.[24] Gazans needed a means to pay for all this. So the IDF gave licenses to 17,000 of them to work inside Israel.[25] These steps are unprecedented in world history. How many North Koreans were earning a living in the U.S. during that conflict (or, for that matter, today)? How many trucks of supplies were sent into Islamic State?

In truth, Israel is a light unto nations. It is *the only country in the history of world that supplies its enemies in time of war, purely on humanitarian grounds.* But *The New York Times* flips the script. In its telling, Gaza is still under occupation, even though the Israelis withdrew. In its telling, Israel enforces a "draconian blockade," despite the unprecedented humanitarian supply. And who are ya gonna believe, me or your own eyes?

In this parallel universe of news fit to print—and print, and print, and print, ad nauseum—Israel "seized the West Bank from Jordan in the 1967 war."[26] I suppose that is technically true. It's just that the *Times* invariably leaves out the part about Jordan having seized it first in a war of aggression in 1948, and Israel winning it only after being *attacked by Jordan in 1967.* It is not unlike telling a history of World War II starting with the dropping of the atomic bomb, without bothering to mention what happened before. But again, it is technically true that Israel "seized" the West Bank in 1967, and given my level of expectation of the *Times* I probably shouldn't complain.

But here is something we should all complain about. The *Times* invariably explains Palestinian terrorism as a response to the "entrenchment of the Israeli occupation,"[27] an occupation "that critics increasingly describe as a kind of apartheid."[28] By their every action in word and deed, the Palestinians have demonstrated that violence has nothing to do with "occupation." Terrorism against Israelis was rife long before 1967; it continued in Gaza long after Israel withdrew. If you want to know what the Palestinians are really fighting for, all you have to do is listen to them. Hamas leader Ismail Haniyeh said in 2020, "We will not recognize Israel, Palestine must stretch from the river to the sea."[29] The Hamas Charter says that "there is no solution for the Palestinian problem except by Jihad."[30]

But why believe your own eyes? Everyone knows you can believe *The New York Times.*

* * *

After Donald Trump was elected president in 2016, the *Times* began a somber campaign, positioning itself as the very guardian of

America's freedom. "The Truth is Hard," the *Times* splashed across full page ads. "The Truth is Worth it." And my personal favorite, "The Truth Doesn't Report Itself."[31]

Lord knows they got that last part right. Nothing reports itself. So it pays to pause and try to understand how the *Times* arrives at "the truth."

You will recall that I noted earlier how the *Times* referred to the Palestinian terrorists who perpetrated the massacre at the Munich Olympics as "commandos." In truth, I could be accused of nitpicking on that one. The report might well have slipped out while the editor was out on vacation; the *Times* never refers to terrorists as commandos. It was a one-off.

But here is the more common practice. Timothy McVeigh, the Oklahoma City bomber, was referred to as a "Terrorist."[32] When an Irish journalist named Lyra McKee was gunned down on the streets of Northern Ireland in 2019, the *Times* quoted a police official who referred to it as a "terrorist incident." The piece went on to note that she was "the first journalist killed in the line of work in Britain since 2001, when...reporter Martin O'Hagan was murdered by Protestant terrorists."[33] A July 2023 piece spoke about "decades of murders by Basque terrorists."[34] The *Times* has no problem calling terrorists "terrorists" in these cases. They just have to pass the physical first. They have to be white.

But the Palestinians aren't white, they are people of color. In their case, the usual practice is to call them "militants." The *Times* standards department long argued that it could not call Hamas members "terrorists," since the group was the de facto administrator of territory, not a stateless terror group.[35] In other words, when it suits the *Times* to call Gaza occupied, it is occupied, but when it suits the Times to call it a state, it is a state. More importantly, the policy is not limited to Palestinians. The *Times* typically uses the term "militant" to describe the Nigerian terrorist group Boko Haram as well.[36] Sometimes the term "militant" doesn't fit because the killers are secular, not religious. When that happens, the practice is to fall back on the term "extremist" or even "fighter." The word "terrorist" is sometimes used in the worst cases. There is also a higher chance of it being used when the victims are Americans.[37] But there seems little doubt that on some visceral level, the *Times* feels a need to soften the blow when speaking of Arabs, who in America's culture wars are deemed "people of color." Liberal journalist Christiane Amanpour took the same approach. After an unarmed mother and her two daughters were gunned down in cold blood by Palestinian terrorists, she referred to the attack as a "shootout." "Shootouts" occur in places like the O.K. Corral where the bullets fly in both directions. This was a massacre (though to her credit, Amanpour apologized after the ensuing outcry).[38]

The bias confirmation extends not just to coverage of the Palestinians, but to coverage of the Israelis as well.

One of the most stubborn urban legends in Israeli history is the story of the "Yemenite Children." It has its source in a sensationalist Israeli weekly called *Ha-Olam Ha-Zeh* ("This World") which regularly published stories that turned out to be false (and thankfully went out of business in the 1990s). On January 11, 1967, it ran the headline "Yemenite Children Were Sold to America!"[39] The charge was that Ashkenazi (i.e. European) Jews had kidnapped immigrant Yemenite children in the early days of the state, and then sold them to wealthy, childless white families for adoption. The allegation is arguably the single most investigated story in all of Israeli history, having been looked at by no less than four commissions of inquiry, and an endless stream of journalists of every stripe. All arrived at the same conclusion: it never happened. The nastiest thing you could say is that there was insensitivity in the handling of dead bodies and that a few dozen of the dead babies could not be properly accounted for. A regrettable and even tragic story, yes, but hardly the stuff of "kidnapping."

Despite this voluminous record, the *Times* still ran a story on February 20, 2019, in which every old trope was repeated. The *Times* made mention of the commissions of inquiry in what journalists refer to as the "to be sure" paragraph. But most of the story pushed the old urban legend, quoting "advocates" who believed that the number of missing children was "as high as 4,500" while "their families believe the babies were abducted by the Israeli authorities in the 1950s and were illegally put up for adoption to childless Ashkenazi families."[40] The story also quoted someone who said that "during this period, similar incidents were happening in other parts of the world" such as aborigine children in Australia and indigenous children in Canada. This story might sound like another one-off, but it's right in the wheelhouse. It's white people behaving badly. That it happens to be a total fiction doesn't matter. That's the way white people behave, so it might as well be true.

In this environment, Israeli settlers don't have a prayer. The *Wall Street Journal* will sometimes refer to the West Bank as merely "the West Bank."[41] But the *Times* sets the tone for most of American journalism by always referring to the territories as "occupied," or sometimes "occupied Arab land." The starting point is that the land belongs to the Arabs. The Jews are occupiers. Wittingly or unwittingly, the *Times* is saying that when the Arabs invaded in 1948, the Jews were driven out legally. Never in history has ethnic cleansing been afforded such legitimacy.

Benjamin Netanyahu doesn't have much of a chance either, all the more so because he is opposed by the "moderate" Palestinian Authority president Mahmoud Abbas. I've seen that word appended to his name so many times that I often wonder if "moderate" is part of his official title. I typed the words "Abu Mazen"—Abbas' nickname—into the search bar of *The New York Times* in early 2024. After scrolling past the stories on the Gaza War, the first sentence of the first story that came up was this, from 2006: "The European Union is considering making direct payments to the moderate Palestinian Authority president, Mahmoud Abbas, as a way of supporting him."[42,iv]

Moderate? Dennis Ross, the Middle East envoy under President Clinton, described Abbas as even more uncompromising than Yasir

---

iv On January 25, 2025, following a prisoner exchange, Abbas called newly freed terrorist Yasin Abu Bakhar to praise and congratulate him. Bakhar had served over twenty years for murdering three Israelis, including a policeman and a nine-month-old baby.

Arafat. In the lead up to Camp David, he refused to make any concessions at all. When asked what the point of the Oslo peace process was if he wasn't willing to budge on anything, he replied, "Learning to live together." When Ross pointed out to Abbas that he had entered into an unofficial agreement in 1995 with the dovish Israeli politician Yossi Beilin—it is known as the "Unsigned Treaty"—he said, "It was never accepted."[43] Later, in 2008, Israel's prime minister, Ehud Olmert, made a shockingly generous offer to him that even included Israel absorbing thousands of the so-called refugees. It caused then-U.S. Secretary of State Condoleezza Rice to say that "Rabin had been killed for offering far less." Abbas refused to even reply with counter terms.[44] The *Times* does occasionally turn on its house "moderate," Abbas—every five years or so when he denies the Holocaust. I suppose it's nice to know that even the editors of *The New York Times* have their limits.

Here is another idea that doesn't have a prayer: territorial compromise. The slant of every news story, as well as practically every op-ed and editorial, is best summed up by this passage, written by the most famous of *Times* columnists, Tom Friedman:

> [Israelis] can have a democratic state in Israel and the West Bank, but…it may not be Jewish. They can have a state that is Jewish in Israel and the West Bank, but it won't be democratic. Or they can have a state that is Jewish and democratic, but it cannot permanently occupy the West Bank.[45]

Friedman has been spouting this "pick two out of three" business for decades. This is where he demonstrates his gifts as a writer, laying out something complicated in lively, easy-to-read language, almost short enough to fit into a haiku or a fortune cookie. The trouble is that it also demonstrates his other great gift, which is the ability to distort.

Here, Friedman employs the time-honored tactic of presenting false options. The two out of three choices is his way of saying that Israel must either withdraw from the West Bank or become an apartheid state. Those are the two options, and neither he nor the editors of *The New York Times* are interested in hearing about any others.

But there is another option. It's called territorial compromise.

Even now, despite all the "apartheid settlements" built on "occupied Arab land," the fact is that it wouldn't be all that hard to implement a two-state solution. It's just that it can't be premised on the '67 boundary. It has to be done the way the drafters of U.N. Security Council Resolution 242 envisioned it in the fall of 1967, and the way Rabin envisioned it in 1993. It has to be premised on territorial compromise. A 70-30 split of the West Bank in favor of the Palestinians would put pretty much all the settlers on one side of the boundary and pretty much all the Palestinians on the other. Why is this so unreasonable?

You can solve the problem of Jerusalem in a similar manner.

When the 1967 War ended, Moshe Dayan wanted Israel to keep the steep hills that ring Jerusalem. These are the "mountains" of the Bible. He figured he had a better chance of convincing the international community to let Israel keep a united "Jerusalem." So he took a pencil, drew a line on a map, and got the government to incorporate the hills surrounding Jerusalem into a new municipality he dubbed "Greater Jerusalem." This turned out to be an enormous blunder because the steep hills also contained twenty-eight Palestinian villages. Calling it "Greater Jerusalem" did nothing to convince the international community that it belonged to Israel. But it did everything to convince the Israeli public that giving up twenty-eight Palestinian villages that had never been part of Jerusalem would "divide the city."

By now, even right-wing Israelis recognize that the sensible solution is to roll the definition of "Jerusalem" back much closer to what it was on June 4, 1967. *That* Jerusalem would remain Israel's undivided capital. The hills and the twenty-eight Palestinian villages would go back to being hills and twenty-eight Palestinian villages. Or the Palestinians can call it "al-Quds"—their name for Jerusalem. Either way, most of what is referred to today as "East Jerusalem" would be under Palestinian rule. This approach puts practically all the Jews on one side of the border and practically all the Palestinians on the other.

It would also put all the holy sites under Israeli rule, which is the safest long-term solution, given the rising Islamist radicalism in Palestinian society. In 1967 Palestinians were divided between loyalty to Jordan and loyalty to the PLO. Thirty years later they were divided between the PLO and Hamas. Today their loyalty lies mostly with Hamas and Islamic Jihad. After that comes al-Qaeda and the Islamic State.

One has only to look at Iraq and Afghanistan to see that shrines of other religions don't do so well under the rule of Islamic extremists. What if the Palestinians decide one day to blow up the Church of the Holy Sepulcher because they don't want "infidels" defiling the holy capital of al-Quds? How about the Garden of Gethsemane, or the Via Dolorosa? To supporters of the Palestinians, this will sound like so much racism (as all criticism does), but the truth is that Palestinians have never respected a single Jewish holy site. Every one that has come under their control has been destroyed. Time and experience have shown that those who don't respect Jewish holy sites eventually get around to disrespecting the sites of other faiths as well. In the eyes of Islamist radicals, holy sites are a lot like potato chips: bomb one, you've got to bomb them all. Their hatred is hardly limited to Jews. As mentioned, the Taliban destroyed massive ancient Buddha statues in Afghanistan. Osama bin Laden and others spoke of defeating the "Crusader-Zionist alliance."[46]

You can agree with the idea of territorial compromise or disagree with it. Supporters of the Palestinians most definitely do not agree with it. I respect this as a position one can take on an issue in which reasonable minds can differ. But *The New York Times* rejects compromise as well, and I have no patience for the fantasyland logic trap this creates. The *Times* is supposed to be objective. An objective person would not be so dismissive of the efforts of Jews to reclaim a portion of what was taken from them in 1948. An objective person would not refer to the West Bank as "occupied." Why? Because an objective person does not change facts to fit a narrative.

Why do so many people take it as a given that the West Bank is "Arab land"? Why do so many accept the implicit presumption that when the Arabs invaded in 1948, the Jews were slaughtered fair and square? It is for the same reason that people once believed the story of Kitty Genovese: because *The New York Times* says it is true. If the Kitty Genovese story had been published in any other news outlet, it would have been forgotten by the next news cycle. And if *The New York Times* referred to the West Bank as "disputed," some would go right on calling it "occupied." But Jewish claims to their land would be viewed by many others as news fit to print. I wish other news outlets could offer their own account grounded in history and truth. But truth is hard. And sadly, it doesn't report itself.

* * *

Like many countries, Israel doesn't have a constitution. Constitutions are typically passed not by majorities but by super-majorities. An amendment to the U.S. Constitution requires a two-thirds vote of the House, two-thirds of the Senate, and three-quarters of the state legislatures. In Israel's tribal society, such majorities were never possible. The next best thing was to invent something in 1950 called a "Basic Law."

A Basic Law isn't much different from a regular law, save that the word "Basic" is added to the title. Like all Israeli laws, it can pass by a simple majority of the votes cast in the Knesset. For example, in the 120-member Knesset, a Basic Law could theoretically pass by a majority of 21 to 19, assuming eighty members fail to show up for the vote. But Basic Laws have been reserved for more important things, like the legal framework of the army and other national institutions. The intention was that adding the word "Basic" would cause members of Knesset to take them more seriously.

In the early days, Basic Laws probably did garner more attention. But by the 1990s, Israel was set in its ways, and Basic Laws, when they were proposed, were viewed as little more than political theatre.

Thus, on March 17, 1992, in a lame duck session—after the Knesset had disbanded and new elections were scheduled—a Basic Law on "Human Dignity and Liberty" came to the floor for a vote. It seemed innocent enough. Human Dignity and Liberty—who would oppose that? With practically no debate, this political cream puff passed by a vote of 32 to 20. In other words, a majority of the Knesset members didn't even show up for the vote. As later recounted by a member of Knesset named Michael Kleiner, "No one had any idea what they were voting for."[47]

On November 7, 1995, two days after Rabin's assassination, while the country was still in shock and completely distracted, the Supreme Court handed down a ruling in the case of *Bank Mizrahi v. Migdal*. The Bank Mizrahi case was over a minor commercial transaction. But using that minor case, while no one was paying attention, the court ruled that Basic Laws have greater legal power than regular laws. That meant that the Human Dignity and Liberty Basic Law overrode other supposedly lesser laws. And so, using that Basic Law and another even more obscure one as the basis of its authority, the justices arrived at a stunning conclusion: the Supreme Court had the power to strike down laws. All it had to do was find them "unreasonable."

This was nothing short of a revolution in Israel's governance. Indeed, it became known as the "Legal Revolution." It is true that judicial review is a hallmark of some democracies, most notably the United States. So by itself, this might not seem so revolutionary. Ah, but there is a huge difference.

In the United States, judges are selected by the people. At the state level, they run for election like all politicians. At the federal level, they are chosen by elected officials; the president appoints candidates and the Senate confirms them. One of the reasons you might vote for a Democrat versus a Republican is that you know that a Democrat will appoint a certain kind of judge, while a Republican will appoint another. These are the rights you enjoy if you are lucky enough to live in a democracy. Power comes from the people. Our leaders rule over us because we give them permission to. So far as I can tell, some variation of the two methods described above is the way judges are appointed in every democracy on the face of the earth.

Every democracy except one.

You see, in Israel, judges are selected through an insular committee that has nine members. Three of the members are supreme court justices, two are elected lawyers sent by the Israeli Bar Association. Three of the remaining four come from the ruling government coalition, while the final one comes from the opposition. By all accounts, the lawyers always vote in accordance with the wishes of the judges. Always. This is not surprising, since the lawyers have to appear before them in court. Who wants to anger a judge that will decide their next case? Former Justice Minister Daniel Friedman told a reporter that the lawyers themselves quietly admit that they do whatever the judges demand.[48] What this means is that the judges have a built-in majority of five. And it means something else: in Israel, the judges replace themselves. The public has practically no say whatsoever.

In America, voters that were unhappy with the overreach of the Warren Court could vote for Republicans and bring about a reversal of *Roe v. Wade*. As this account is written, Democrats are making their case to the American public to retake the court and shape it in their own image.

Israeli voters do not have this basic right—their judges get to replace themselves. These judges, not coincidentally, have two things in common: they don't care what the public thinks, and they are liberal. Radically liberal. One group of radical liberal judges replaces itself with another, and the Israeli public is powerless to change it. Aharon Barak, the architect of the Legal Revolution, stacked the fifteen-member court with eleven additional like-minded liberals.[v,49]

---

v An appointment to the Israeli Supreme Court requires a majority vote on the committee of 7-2. But even in recent years, when the Israeli right has always been in power, the 5 members in the judge's built-in majority could always join the one leftist representing the opposition, so they only needed one additional vote. They got it by occasionally letting in a token conservative. Also, lower court judges only need a 5-4 vote, so they all end up being liberal, leaving few candidates for elevation to the Supreme Court that are conservative.

A highly respected conservative legal scholar named Ruth Gavison was suggested for elevation to the Supreme Court. Barak blocked her, saying that she had an "agenda" (not like him). Sure she did—an agenda to return a bit of balance to the ideologically lopsided, out-of-control court.

Remaking the highest court in the land in his own image, and elevating it above the legislative branch while no one was looking, would have been enough for any normal megalomaniac. But that wasn't enough to satisfy Justice Aharon Barak. He also extended his enlightened judicial dictatorship to every aspect of Israeli life, reversing almost fifty years of precedent and ruling that every issue in Israel is subject to court review regardless of a litigant's interest in a particular case. Unlike in America, in Israel a litigant doesn't need standing, meaning they don't need to be somehow connected to the matter before the court. Any slob in a smelly t-shirt can walk into court and file action on anything under the sun. Don't like a law or treaty that was duly passed by the legislature? Take it to court where you can be certain the decision will always come down on the side of the radical left.

When Israel withdrew from the Sinai Peninsula in 1982 in accordance with the Camp David Peace Treaty with Egypt, it didn't even occur to anyone that the Israeli Supreme Court had a right to weigh in. But when Sharon passed Disengagement in 2005, the Supreme Court heard a case seeking to strike it down on the grounds that it wasn't "reasonable." Disengagement was allowed to stand. But the court's token conservative, Justice Edmond Levy, actually ruled in a dissenting opinion that it was unreasonable and had to be struck down. It would be as if President Biden needed to seek the approval of the U.S. Supreme Court to withdraw from Afghanistan and one justice said he couldn't.

Not everyone agreed with what Barak did. One of Israel's most famous Supreme Court Chief Justices, Moshe Landau—among other things, he presided over the Adolf Eichmann trial—said that Israeli judges seemed to have forgotten that they were qualified to judge, not to govern.[50] The distinguished American judge Richard

A. Posner said that "what Barak created out of whole cloth was a degree of judicial power undreamed of even by our most aggressive Supreme Court justices." The whole matter reminded him of Napoleon taking the crown out the pope's hands and putting it on his own head.[51]

This may seem to be hyperbole, but it is more than justified. In sum and substance, Barak's Legal Revolution was actually a classic, textbook case of white minority rule. It had the three hallmarks: You have a small minority ruling over the nation, with the majority of the public powerless to stop them. You have that minority exercising these superpowers, not because the public gave them this right, but because they arrogated these powers for themselves. And then you have the third hallmark of white minority rule: the judges are white.

As noted above, the Israeli Supreme Court has fifteen members. The court has long been diverse in terms of the number of women in its ranks. Indeed, as of this writing, three chief justices have been women. But of the fifteen members in early 2024, only two are Sephardic Jews, and only one is an Arab. Not a single justice is ultra-Orthodox, though two are observant to a lesser degree. By historical standards, this is one of the most diverse courts in Israeli history. But in the final count, twelve out of the fifteen are white and ten are WASPs. In Israel "WASP" stands for "White Ashkenazi Secular with Pull."

The real lack of diversity is in the rulings. To date, a quarter of the decisions striking down laws went against the interests of the ultra-Orthodox.[52] One ultra-Orthodox politician said that he would oppose enshrining the Ten Commandments as a Basic Law because the Supreme Court would interpret it to ban religion.[vi,53] Israel has an illegal alien problem like all wealthy Western countries. The

---

vi The court invariably finds that it is illegal for the ultra-Orthodox to be exempted from compulsory army service, but legal for the Arabs to be exempted. As any first-year law student will tell you, this is the exact opposite of a constitutional interpretation of "equality." This is because being a Jew instead of an Arab is an immutable characteristic, while being a yeshiva student isn't. To put it another way, anybody can choose to learn in a yeshiva and receive the draft deferment. But nobody can magically turn himself into an Arab.

Supreme Court has struck down all the solutions that have passed in the Knesset. And it ruled that even after Disengagement, Israel had to permit women from Gaza to be treated in Israeli hospitals. Try to imagine a court ruling that Germans had a right to seek treatment in American hospitals during World War II. In Israel, keeping out citizens of an enemy polity was deemed "unreasonable."[54]

At a time in which politicians with these views have not even been able to muster the 3.25 percent of the vote to get into the Knesset, this was the law of the land, and the Israeli public has been powerless to change it. The judges simply replace themselves with other like-minded judges—one group of WASPs replaces another. This is how white minority rule works. In Israel's case, it isn't apartheid because it isn't grounded in maintaining a system of racial superiority. But it's bad enough.

This is why every major Israeli politician has come out in favor of judicial reform at one time or another. But each backed down in the end. The political battle would have been too bruising. Instead, starting in 2014, a justice minister named Ayelet Shaked worked quietly to introduce more conservatives onto the court. The effort experienced limited success and kept the issue on a low boil.

But then, in 2023, an ultra-Orthodox politician named Aryeh Deri got elected and was appointed Interior Minister. Months before, Deri had pled guilty to a minor tax infraction, a technical violation for which he paid a small fine.[55] Even prosecutors said that he paid all taxes and intended to pay all taxes. But the Supreme Court ruled that such a man could not serve—it would not be reasonable.[vii] Deri was forced to resign, and with that, the inevitable had finally happened: the Supreme Court had reversed an election.

[vii] In 1989, my beloved hometown of New York City elected a courtly gent named David Dinkins to serve as mayor, despite the fact that he had been convicted earlier in his career of failing to pay his taxes. I did not vote for David Dinkins. But if a court had ruled that he could not serve, despite him winning the election, I would have been out in the streets protesting with everybody else, although I might not have put my whole heart into the ensuing riots.

That was the tipping point. An outcry went up. A new "Basic Law" was introduced in the Knesset to roll back the judges. Enough was enough.

Given the level of anger, the judicial reforms proposed in the Basic Law were surprisingly mild. I will spare you the details—suffice it to say that even had it passed, it would still have left Israeli judges with powers American judges can only dream of.

You would think that getting rid of white majority rule, promoting diversity, and giving power back to the people is something *The New York Times* would get behind. You would be wrong. Typical of how the paper described judicial reform is this, the first sentence from a 2023 article: "An Israeli government effort to weaken the country's judiciary, which critics call a threat to the nation's democratic foundations, is drawing unusually pointed protest from American Jewish leaders and organizations."[56] Another story said that Netanyahu was "pushing to upend the judiciary."[57] Few articles even described the plan, but the one that did came with this headline: "Netanyahu's Planned Judicial Overhaul Would Enfeeble Supreme Court."[58] Here's another headline: "Democracy May Hang On Israeli Court's Move: Parliamentary Challenge to Judiciary Creates Dilemmas Familiar to More Autocratic States."[59]

All the above came from the news section. The editorial page was even more strident. The Editorial Board of the paper issued this dire warning: "The Ideal of Democracy in Israel is in Jeopardy."[60] Tom Friedman called it a "judicial coup d'état masquerading as a 'judicial reform.'" Judge for yourself who carried out a coup: Netanyahu, who laid out his reform plan in an election and won, or the judges who seized power in an obscure decision while no one was paying attention. Friedman never had any doubt: "Israel cannot be allowed to turn into an autocracy like Viktor Orban's Hungary."[61]

The thing about bias and bias confirmation is that they park themselves so deeply in the human subconscious that they make people irony-proof without their even noticing it. The editors of the *Times* managed to display this unwittingly in the paper that appeared on February 21, 2023.

The front page of that edition carried the headline "In Mississippi, Racial Outrage At Court Plan." The story described a bill approved by legislators to "establish a separate court system for roughly one-fifth of Jackson [the state capital] run by state-appointed judges." The law sparked outrage because it replaced the existing system in which the judges were elected. Thus, the process of selecting judges was taken from the people and replaced with one in which "the proposed court system and the police force would be controlled almost exclusively by white officials in the state government." This, the reporter warned ominously, "evoked earlier eras in Mississippi's complicated racial history."[62]

But *in the same newspaper*, on page A8, the *Times* ran yet another story on judicial reform in Israel. That story described the attempt to take appointment of judges *away* from a committee, and give it *to* the people, as follows: "Israel's far-right government pushed forward with a divisive plan for a judicial overhaul that critics say will weaken and politicize the country's courts and undermine its democratic foundations."[63]

Note how it didn't even occur to the *Times* that there was a contradiction. It all seemed perfectly natural. In Mississippi taking selection of judges *from* the people was racist, so it was wrong. In Israel, giving that same process *to* the people was carried out by the evil Netanyahu, so it, too, was wrong. If nothing else, the editors proved themselves masters of juggling two conflicting thoughts in their heads without once noticing the contradiction.

This sort of thing is comical in the same way it is funny to watch someone slip on a banana peel. It is Groucho Marx Journalism at its finest. But *The New York Times* takes itself seriously, and Groucho was only joking. Of course, Groucho's entire point was that the truth matters.

But not so much at *The New York Times*.

* * *

Israel's liberal elites ran the country through the courts, even though they could no longer win elections. And they weren't going to give that up without a fight. Thousands of people took to the streets to protest judicial reform. These were the wealthiest segments of society, so they had plenty of money and talent behind them.[viii] They blocked highways. They burned tires. They attacked policemen. Chief Justice Barak said that "freedom of expression does not protect the 'freedom' to block firemen from reaching fires, or ambulances from reaching hospitals."[64] Great line, but he said it in 2005 when people who protested against Disengagement were severely punished. Protesters against judicial reform were treated differently; Israel's judges were not anxious to dismantle the powers they gave themselves. As late as July 7, 2023, after over six months of unrest, not a single protester was indicted.[65]

Opponents of judicial reform were emboldened. They said they would break every norm, and they broke them well and true. In March 2023, fighter pilots stopped showing up for flight training.[66] On July 21, 2023, 1,142 reservists in the Israeli Air Force, including 422 pilots, sent a letter stating that judicial reform would "leave us no choice, though with great pain, to cease volunteering for duty."[67] A colonel appeared on television and said that, "our goal is to cause the IAF to be unable to return to operations, not in peacetime and certainly not in an emergency."[68] Reserve officers in Israel's military intelligence threatened to stop showing up for duty, along with members of the elite cyber warfare unit.[69] Author Yuval Noah Hariri called on workers in the defense industry to "stop arming the government of Israel."[70]

Nothing like this had ever happened before. In an infamous incident in the 1948 War, men loyal to David Ben-Gurion opened fire on men loyal to Menachem Begin. Sixteen of Begin's men were killed. But Begin ordered his men to show up for duty the next day. At a closed-door meeting, someone secretly taped Netanyahu screaming at a group of pilots, "This is harming the security of the state! And it's not just disabling our capabilities, it's also what it does to our deterrent power!"[71]

---

viii A wealthy venture capitalist told one of the leaders of the judicial reform movement, "do you seriously think that my vote should count the same as a cab driver???"

Netanyahu was not the only one who thought that Israel looked weak. There were others outside the country that agreed with him. Some were in Iran. Some were in Lebanon. And some were in Gaza.

X.

October Surprise

"The world in general and Israel's enemies in particular should know that the circumstances which took the lives of the more than 2,500 Israelis who were killed in the Yom Kippur War will never ever recur."

—GOLDA MEIR[1]

For fifty years Golda was right.

I well remember that Yom Kippur day on October 6, 1973. I was a nine-year-old boy running around in the synagogue in New Haven, Connecticut where my father was the rabbi (and a young state senator named Joe Lieberman was a congregant). Out in the lobby, where my father couldn't see them, a group of men huddled in the corner around a transistor radio. This was something I have never seen before or since: a transistor radio brought into an Orthodox Jewish synagogue on Yom Kippur. They might just as well have brought in a ham and cheese sandwich. But there they were, listening nervously to the news. The State of Israel was at war. Egypt and Syria had launched a surprise attack.

Fifty years later, on October 7, 2023, I walked into a different Orthodox Jewish synagogue, this time in Long Island, on the holiday of Simchat Torah. A group of people were milling about nervously in the lobby. There was no transistor radio this time. But the news was the same: the State of Israel was at war. Hamas had launched a surprise attack.

* * *

On the night of October 12, 1953, Palestinian terrorists originating from the West Bank town of Qibya—then under Jordanian occupation—slipped into the Israeli town of Yehud and murdered a woman and her two small children. Maybe it was because there had been too many such attacks before—or maybe it was the fact that thirty-eight-year-old General Moshe Dayan was about to be named chief of staff of the army—but a tipping point had been reached. Up to then, Israel had let such attacks pass with a muted response, viewing them as a cost of living in a tough neighborhood. Dayan decided it was time to change the rules of the game.

Like all great leaders, Dayan was a man who understood men. He thus knew, instinctively, that for the mission he had in mind, he needed someone like twenty-five-year-old Ariel Sharon. Prime Minister Levi Eshkol once called Sharon a *vilde chaya*—Yiddish for "wild animal," the term used to describe an unruly child.[2] Dayan gave Sharon vague orders to send a message to Qibya and all the other Qibyas that terrorism would thereafter carry a heavy price for any village that harbored the attackers.

Sharon was the type of man that stepped into the twilight of vague orders the way one might step into a warm bath. He and his men entered Qibya with over half a ton of explosives and, by his own count, demolished forty-two of the village's "big stone buildings," killing sixty-nine villagers in the process.[i,3] The attack earned Israel a condemnation from the U.N. Security Council, but Dayan was satisfied with the results and sent Sharon on further missions.

Why would he place so much responsibility in such reckless hands? He had too much experience the other way. "I would rather

---

i Sharon and his men would forever insist they did not know that civilians were hiding in the basements.

contend with spirited horses that are hard to control," he famously said, "than lazy bulls that refuse to move."[4] The "spirited horse" that Dayan had discovered was indeed hard to control. But he got results. Terrorists based in Jordanian-controlled territory killed 111 Israelis in 1951 and 114 in 1952—but only thirty-seven in 1955.[5] It wasn't that the number of terrorists had suddenly decreased, or that Israel's defenses had suddenly improved. Rather, the policy of stiff retaliation forced the Jordanians to restrain the killers.

For a tiny army with meager resources, this was no small accomplishment. Henceforth operations were limited to military targets, something that prevented a repeat of the Qibya tragedy, but greatly increased the risk to Sharon and his men. Yet even after Arab countries came to expect retaliation and placed their soldiers on alert after each terrorist attack, Sharon somehow managed to achieve lopsided victories.

On the night of December 11, 1955, following a string of Syrian army attacks on Israeli fishing boats, a paratroop force led by Sharon assaulted enemy positions along the Sea of Galilee. Six of Sharon's paratroopers were killed. But his force killed fifty-four Syrians, wounded dozens more, and took thirty soldiers and officers as prisoners of war.[6] It earned the Israelis another stiff condemnation from the U.N. Security Council. But they did not take another casualty in that area for over six years.[7]

In time, people referred to the raids as Israel's "deterrent power." The goal was not revenge. It was striking back with enough force to induce neighboring countries to control violence, or at least reduce it to what became known, grimly, as a "tolerable level of terrorism." In effect, Israel was telling its neighbors—in the language that everyone understands in the Middle East—that terrorism was not just Israel's problem, but everyone's problem, because those who enabled terrorism would be made to pay as well.

The policy succeeded in reducing the number of attacks, but it never quite succeeded in eliminating them. The Palestinians were simply too determined. They convinced themselves that guerilla warfare would persuade the Jews to leave Israel, as it had persuaded the French to leave Algeria. Moreover, they wanted to ensure that the Jewish state would never achieve normalcy. With the right amount of luck, they might even spark a wider war with a coalition of Arab armies that would defeat and destroy it.[8] In the words of former Israeli Intelligence Chief Yehoshafat Harkabi, in the Palestinians' view, "the flame of the conflict should stay ablaze, as once it starts flickering it may go out."[9] For Israel, retaliation didn't extinguish the flame. But it reduced it to a low burn.

A quiet understanding emerged. Neighboring governments reduced terrorism to Israel's "tolerable level," and Israel kept its retaliation to a tolerable level in return. But what was "tolerable"? Figuring out these "rules" was a constant war of nerves. Following the Sea of Galilee incident, a nervous Prime Minister Ben-Gurion asked Sharon how the operation went. When Sharon replied, "B'seder" ["okay"], Ben-Gurion retorted, "It went a little too *b'seder!*"[10]

And what happened when one side broke the rules? This was when the game was at its most dangerous. More often than not, the rules were broken not by design but by accident. Low-level warfare and the Israeli response that was always sure to follow were inherently impossible to control. One side might have intended to inflict a "tolerable" number of casualties, only to have the situation get out of hand. An Israeli retaliatory strike on a Gaza police station in 1955 was supposed to be measured. But thirty-eight Egyptians were killed anyway, because the Israeli force unexpectedly came upon an Egyptian ambush and found itself compelled to fire on a truck carrying reinforcements.[11] Of course, the Egyptians weren't interested in explanations. They turned to the Soviets for arms, which in turn led Israel to turn to the British and French, which in turn led to the 1956 Suez War.

Something similar happened in 1967. Syria broke the rules by attacking too frequently, Israel broke the rules by retaliating too sharply, and before anyone knew it the region was plunged into war. Once the runaway train was sent hurtling down the track, it was anyone's guess where it might grind to a halt.

Had the 1967 war turned out differently, the military textbooks of the world would have added a chapter on the successful use of terrorism. The Palestinians—defeated, forgotten, and seemingly without hope—had kept their cause alive with easy, inexpensive attacks. They'd even managed to set off a chain reaction that plunged the region into all-out war. Admittedly, it had ended badly for them on this occasion. But that didn't mean they couldn't spark some future conflict that might end differently.

After 1967, the Arab populations of the West Bank and Gaza Strip could no longer take part in that effort. The Six-Day War left them neutralized under Israeli occupation. At least where these territories were concerned, the Israelis no longer had to retaliate in the hope that Jordan or Egypt would help reduce violence to the "tolerable level." With troops on the ground, they could control the situation from within.

In short, the Israelis no longer fought terrorism with deterrence only, but with occupation as well.

The years 1967-1980 might be considered the Golden Age of Occupation. The Israelis were able to control the populations of the West Bank and Gaza merely by moving training bases into the territories. Not only did the occupation cost nothing, it actually benefited both Israel's and the Palestinians' economies. The newly occupied territories supplied the Jewish state with a cheap source of labor, as well as a captive market for Israeli products. There was a brief spasm of violence in Gaza in the early 1970s that was quickly put down. But for the most part, the territories remained quiet.[12] Not a single settler was killed in the entire period. Paradoxically, the territories were a strange island of calm even during the worst waves of violence. The safest place for an Israeli soldier in the 1973 war was in the West Bank and Gaza.

* * *

On March 11, 1978, eleven Palestinian terrorists based in Lebanon eluded Israeli naval patrols, landed on the coast south of Haifa, and hijacked a bus. By the time they were stopped outside Tel Aviv, thirty-five Israeli civilians had been killed and dozens more wounded. The "bloody bus," as it became known, was the worst terrorist attack in Israeli history up to that point.[13] The government of Prime Minister Menachem Begin, less than a year old, determined that this unprecedented attack demanded an unprecedented response.

On March 15, 1978, Israeli ground forces launched a multi-pronged offensive into Lebanon. Resistance overall was light and ended after a few days.[14] "Operation Litani," so named because it ended at the Litani River, left the Israelis controlling a strip of land roughly six miles wide in southern Lebanon.

But what next? For the first time, the Israelis handed off authority to local allies who likewise viewed the PLO as a threat. No Israeli soldiers or advisors stayed behind. Instead, a new miniature regime was set up to police the area and keep it free of hostile forces. This miniature regime ignored Beirut and took its orders from Jerusalem.

In short, the Israelis carved out a strip of land in which they carried out regime change.

A local 1,200-man militia called the "Army of Free Lebanon" was formed under the command of a Lebanese Major named Sa'ad Haddad. The Israelis gave work permits and health care to the families of their newfound allies. In return, local residents manned Haddad's militia and provided Israel with security along its border.

By any yardstick, this first experiment with regime change was a complete success. Haddad proved himself an able, durable, and loyal ally. The Lebanese Civil War that had raged since 1975 was shocking in its brutality even by the standards of the Middle East. Yet somehow Haddad held together a multi-ethnic force that gave stability to local residents and kept the area free of the PLO. He even managed to get American Televangelist Pat Robertson to fund a Christian radio and television station called the "Voice of Hope."

The success of the endeavor was limited only by its small size. "Haddad-land" covered less than 5 percent of Lebanon. It didn't take long before people made the obvious leap and began to wonder what might be accomplished in the other ninety-five. The right regime in Beirut could do far more than a mere Haddad. Haddad could only fight terrorism. A government could sign a peace treaty.

Thus did Defense Minister Sharon launch Israel's First Lebanon War in 1982. The plan was ambitious, but it was well thought-out. Israel invaded Lebanon in June. Lebanese elections were scheduled for August. Arafat and the PLO were driven out. Sharon saw to it that his Christian ally Bashir Gemayel was elected president by Lebanon's parliament.

For the briefest period in early September 1982, it looked like the Israelis had pulled it off. Peace between Israel and Lebanon was on the table. Although Israeli opposition leader Shimon Peres was a sharp critic of the war, in early September 1982 he quietly gathered the senior leadership of his Labor Party and told them the following:

> Many of our dire predictions turned out to be wrong. Against our earlier fears, the war has been an enormous success. It's very close to achieving most of its main goals. In just a few days— it's impossible to escape from the facts—a peace treaty will be signed between Israel and Lebanon. This will be [Likud's] second peace treaty [after having concluded a treaty with Egypt in 1979]. They will also succeed in scattering Arafat and all his terrorists to the four winds and in breaking the PLO. Whoever wants to continue opposing the war and make a fool out of himself, that's his business. But whoever does that is also our representative. And with his opposition he is making fools of *us*—and this is our business.[15]

It all looked so promising. But then the Syrians assassinated Gemayel on September 14, 1982, in a massive bombing that killed twenty-six other Christian politicians.[16] With that, the whole plan unraveled, peace treaty and all. When the Israelis used deterrence to fight terrorism, they lost about twenty lives per year. The first year of the Lebanon War claimed five hundred lives, all of them young soldiers.[17] The Israelis abandoned the effort in 1985 and never attempted regime change again.[ii,18]

But they didn't abandon the idea of occupation. Haddad, in the meantime, had died of cancer. And a new, radical Shiite terrorist group called Hezbollah, or "Party of God," emerged that was too powerful for the militia that Haddad had founded to control. So the Israelis formed a narrow "security zone" in southern Lebanon, which they occupied. The strategy worked well in the 1980s. But in the 1990s, Hezbollah adapted and began a guerilla warfare campaign that claimed the lives of hundreds of soldiers. This was more than the Israeli public would tolerate.

Finally, on the night of May 22, 2000, the skies above Lebanon ignited with the phosphorus flashes of Israeli outposts being detonated by retreating soldiers. The last soldier returned to Israel and closed the gate behind him two days later. The Lebanon War was finally over.

The PLO had been driven out in the initial phase of the war in August 1982, though at a cost that was far higher than Israel had ever paid while controlling terrorism with deterrence. The eighteen years after that were a futile exercise in regime change and occupation that left Israel with hundreds killed, thousands more wounded, billions spent, and nothing to show for it. The painful but obvious lesson was that occupation and regime change were poor strategies to control terrorism. Deterrence was a poor strategy also—the only thing it was better than was everything else.

---

ii The United States would have done well to learn from the Israeli experience before launching the catastrophic Iraq War in 2003. One of the most prominent boosters of that war was *New York Times* columnist Tom Friedman, who wrote that a "right reason" to go to war was "the need to partner with Iraqis, post-Saddam, to build a progressive Arab regime." I will never understand how the man who wrote *From Beirut to Jerusalem*—mocking the Israelis in a tone dripping with sarcasm—could have seen regime change resulting in democracy as a realistic outcome in a country like Iraq. The blundering analysis did nothing to hinder the conspiracy of praise surrounding Friedman's work. In 2002, he won the Pulitzer Prize once again, this time for commentary "for his clarity of vision, based on extensive reporting, in commenting on the worldwide impact of the terrorist threat."

So after coming full circle, the Israelis made an announcement: from now on, every attack would be met with a devastating response.

* * *

On May 15, 1974, Palestinian terrorists belonging to Nayef Hawat-meh's Democratic Front for the Liberation of Palestine took 115 high school students and teachers hostage in the northern Israeli town of Ma'alot, demanding the release of twenty convicted terror-ists.[19] The parents of the children pleaded with the chief of staff of the army, General Mordechai "Motta" Gur, to give in to the terror-ists' demands. But Gur replied that the country could never allow itself to enter into such a bargain, or the price it would pay in the future would be exponentially higher.[20] A commando force stormed the building and killed the three hostage-takers. But twenty-two children and three teachers were killed as well.[21]

There was a time when the Israelis were viewed as the very role model for how Western nations should deal with the scourge of hos-tage-taking. The norm was not to negotiate with terrorists. In the few cases that deals were struck, they were always premised on trad-ing roughly one for one, as in a July 23, 1968, plane hijacking of an El Al passenger jet, which ended with twenty-four jailed Palestinians traded for a similar number of Israelis and crewmen.[22] The more common practice was to launch rescue missions. Some, such as the commando raid on Entebbe Airport in Uganda, are among the most storied military operations in Israeli history.

It all changed in 1978.

A group of six Israeli soldiers went on a joy ride in Lebanon at the conclusion of Operation Litani and somehow got waved through a checkpoint into Palestinian-controlled territory. One remarkably escaped to tell the tale. But of the remaining five, four were shot dead and the fifth was captured by Ahmed Jibril's Popular Front for the Liberation of Palestine—General Command.

Negotiations ensued over the release of the soldier. A terrorism expert named Ariel Merari advised taking it slow. This is how you negotiated in the Arab souk. Most importantly, he counseled politicians against meeting the family of the captured young man.

Both pieces of advice were ignored. The boy's mother met with Defense Minister Ezer Weizmann first. Merari later remembered that "Weizmann had a hard time standing up to the pressure. He caved in to the family and declared that they had an open line to him whenever they wanted." The same thing happened when the family met with Prime Minister Begin.

It resulted in what became known as the "First Jibril Deal." The soldier was freed in return for nineteen Palestinians captured during Operation Litani, as well as seventy-six convicted terrorists. Many of the terrorists were convicted murderers. Merari did a calculation and concluded that they had combined sentences remaining of over 2,800 years.[23]

It only got worse from there. There was a "Second Jibril Deal" seven years later. This time, for the freedom of just three soldiers, Jibril received 1,150 convicted terrorists, including 400 murderers, some of whom were the most notorious in Israeli history.[24] Merari asked one of the negotiators how he could have agreed to such an irresponsible deal. The negotiator, Shmuel Tamir, one of the toughest and most famous lawyers in Israeli history, responded angrily, "Let's see what you would have done with Miriam Grof [the mother of a soldier] fainting on the table in front of you." Merari responded that this was why he had always insisted that parents not be permitted to meet with negotiators or politicians.[25] Yitzchak Rabin later admitted in characteristic candor that he knew it was wrong to do the deal, but he couldn't withstand the pressure of the mothers.[26]

This was a terrible outcome, particularly for a country that premised its strategy on deterrence. How do you deter terrorists when they know that one day they will be set free?

The actions of the terrorists, once they were let out of jail, showed just how laughable the idea of deterrence had become. The prisoner deals did not send freed killers to some faraway place where they could do no harm. Most were permitted to walk out the prison gate and go right back home to the Palestinian territories. What happened next was inevitable. A 2009 study found that fully two-thirds of those freed went right back into terrorism.[27]

A total of 6,912 terrorists were freed between the signing of the Oslo Accords in September 1993 and the outbreak of the al-Aqsa Intifada in September 2000. Most were released as goodwill gestures to the newly created Palestinian Authority, though some because they had served out their term. A victims group called Almagor issued a study that found that in the first five years of the Intifada, those freed from jail killed at least 177 Israelis.[28]

In 2004, Israel broke yet new ground in undermining its own security by agreeing to the "Tenenbaum Deal." This time, Jerusalem freed 435 terrorists in return for one live Israeli and the bodies of three soldiers.[29] The living Israeli wasn't even a soldier captured while on active duty, but a retired colonel named Elhanan Tenenbaum who was kidnapped in Dubai, then transported to Lebanon, while attempting to engineer an illegal drug deal. A study done by a team of Israeli journalists in 2011 showed that at least twenty-seven Israelis were subsequently murdered by those freed in the Tenenbaum swap.[30]

The Israelis still learned nothing from any of this. So "hostage inflation" continued to rise.

On June 25, 2006, a group of Palestinians attacked an Israeli tank on patrol near the Gaza border. Two of the tank crewmen fought back and were killed. The Palestinians threw a grenade into the tank and wounded a third. But then, as the Palestinians retreated back to Gaza, the fourth Israeli soldier in the tank popped out and surrendered. That soldier's name was Gilad Shalit.[31] By now the floodgates had all burst open. Hamas, which held Shalit, demanded nothing less than Israel freeing every terrorist that it held behind bars, a cohort numbering almost five thousand men.[32]

Palestinians held inside Israeli prisons were represented by two "emirs." One led prisoners from the West Bank. His name was Saleh Arouri. The other led Palestinians from Gaza. His name was Yahya Sinwar.

Sinwar was jailed in 1989 for murdering five Palestinians who were suspected of collaborating with Israel. Three were tortured first. Israeli security officials said that at least one of the five had nothing to do with Israel, and was killed for making pornographic movies and for alleged sex crimes with young girls. They described Sinwar as "a tough, merciless, and stone-cold killer."

The negotiations over Shalit dragged on for years. Finally, Arouri asked for a private meeting with a prison official and told him that Sinwar was vetoing any proposal that did not include the freeing of every Palestinian prisoner. The only way to get a deal done, Arouri said, was if Sinwar was placed in solitary confinement so that he couldn't communicate with the Hamas leadership abroad. Prison officials heeded the advice and in 2011, five years after Shalit was captured, the two sides finally concluded a deal. [33]

The Shalit deal dwarfed every arrangement that came before it. In return for a single soldier, Jerusalem agreed to free 1,027 convicted terrorists.[iii,34]

The prime minister that approved the deal was none other than Benjamin Netanyahu. In 1986, Netanyahu edited a book entitled *Terrorism: How the West Can Win*, in which he argued forcefully against just such a dangerous capitulation.[35] Why then did "Mr. Security," as he is known, agree to the scandalous humiliation?

In his memoir, Netanyahu writes he did it because he needed to win the support of the Israeli public for a potential military operation against Iran's nuclear program.[36] Only Netanyahu knows his own motives. But if that lame excuse is the best he could come up with, then it seems clear that this time, his critics were finally on to something. They argued that he did the Shalit deal because Israel was then riven with protests over the high cost of living, Netanyahu feared for his political standing, and he needed to change the public conversation.[37] In short, they said Netanyahu did it because he would do anything to stay in power.

---

iii Of that number, the Israelis were permitted to select 550 of the prisoners, so they chose minor figures that would have been freed within a few months anyway. But at least 280 of the remaining 477 were convicted murderers serving life sentences.

The strategy worked for Netanyahu politically. The public became distracted with the drama of the Shalit deal and the protests died down. But it was a complete disaster for Israeli security. Arouri was set free and eventually made his way to Lebanon to assume a senior Hamas role. Sinwar was freed as well. He chose to return home to Gaza.

The night before his release, Sinwar got down on his knees in his cell and kissed the shoes of those who were left behind. With tears in his eyes he made a solemn vow. One day he would free them all.[38]

* * *

Sometime in 1969, a tall, handsome, impeccably dressed man walked into the Israeli embassy in London and asked to speak to a Mossad agent. "I want to work for you," he said. "I will give you information that you could only hope to obtain in your wildest dreams. I want money, a lot of money. And believe me, you will be happy to pay."[39] The Israeli intelligence community was indeed happy to pay. When word got back to Tel Aviv, the heads of Mossad and IDF Military Intelligence practically fell out of their chairs. Because the individual who offered his services was no less than the son-in-law of Egyptian president Gamal Abdel Nasser. Later he was appointed chief of staff to Nasser's successor, Anwar Sadat. His name was Ashraf Marwan.

Marwan sold the Israelis a mountain of information that was described as "once-in-history material." But there was one piece of intelligence that was so important that it seized control of Israel's strategy, and a new Hebrew term was coined to describe it. Israeli military planners called it the *Conceptzia*—"the Concept." The *Conceptzia* said that Egypt would not go to war unless and until it received the most advanced Soviet fighter jets, which in those days were the MIG-23 and the MIG-25. Since those fighter jets were not scheduled for delivery until late 1974, and since it took about a year to train pilots to fly them, Israeli intelligence concluded that war was impossible in 1973.

On October 6, 1973, the Yom Kippur holiday, the Israelis found out that Anwar Sadat had *Conceptzias* of his own. The Egyptians and

Syrians launched a surprise attack that caught Israel completely off guard. The Israelis regrouped and ultimately won a stunning victory. But it almost ended in disaster.

After the war, Israeli intelligence decided that it would never again rely on *Conceptzias*. Every piece of information would be looked at with fresh eyes. But analysts soon realized that this was simply impossible. You can't run any large organization without having core assumptions. You can't even live your life without them. For example, when you cross the street, you do it based on the core assumption that motorists will stop at a red light. If the core assumption turns out to be wrong—if someone drives through the red light—you may be run over and killed.

The failure of core assumptions is often the cause of disaster, and not just in military affairs. The 2008 U.S. financial crisis—the worst crisis since the Great Depression—happened because certain core assumptions about the American housing market, which had always held true, were no longer accurate. Commercial real estate owners are today going bankrupt because, in the post-Covid era, core assumptions about people working in office buildings are no longer true.

Military history is the field in which the failure of *Conceptzias* stands out most prominently. French military planners were certain that German tanks could not penetrate the thick Ardennes Forest in World War II. German panzers overran them in just a few weeks in 1940, doing exactly that. In 1967, the Egyptians likewise believed that certain areas of the Sinai Peninsula could be left unprotected because the sand dunes were impassable. Israeli tanks drove right over them.[iv,40]

---

iv The thing about *Conceptzias* is that they usually are correct, and in at least one instance, saved Israel from mistakenly mobilizing for war (and possibly even preempting). In the 1990s, a Mossad agent named Yehudah Gil said that a Syrian general had warned him of an impending attack. The report made no sense; according to a longstanding *Conceptzia*, Syria would never go to war without Egypt. Israeli leaders followed the *Conceptzia* rather than mobilize. Then, Gil was secretly taped and found to have fabricated the whole thing. He was tried, convicted and sent to jail.

The best analogy to what went wrong for Israel on October 7, 2023, is the Munich Olympics in 1972. Why were the games left completely unprotected? Because it never occurred to anyone that terrorists would attack them. Even if someone had warned German security officials, they would have scoffed. Why would anyone attack the Olympics? Wouldn't that spark global outrage? Wouldn't it hurt the cause of the attackers rather than help it? It turned out that the *Conceptzia* was all wrong. For terrorists, there is no bad publicity—all publicity is good because it puts the cause back on the global agenda. This is doubly so for the Palestinians because they enjoy broad support in the international community, as well as in academia and media, no matter what atrocities they commit.

General Aharon Haliva, the head of Military Intelligence on October 7, 2023, later told friends that had he been awakened in the night and told that a massive attack had taken place with over a thousand people killed or kidnapped, he would have assumed it had come from Hezbollah. Had he then been told that the attack had not come from Lebanon, he would have assumed it had come from the West Bank. The idea of an invasion from Gaza had barely crossed his mind.[41]

Why was an attack by Hamas so unthinkable? To answer that question, we must return to Ariel Sharon and his plan of Disengagement from the Gaza Strip.

* * *

The architects of Disengagement never had any illusions about peace breaking out once the Israeli army withdrew. Rather, the thinking was that Gaza could be controlled more effectively from the outside than from within. To put it another way, Israeli military planners concluded that they would take fewer casualties and spend less money fighting the Palestinians with deterrence rather than occupation.

For a long time, it looked like they were right. In the twelve years between 1993 and 2005, 376 Israelis were killed by terrorists based in Gaza, or 2.6 per month. But in the eighteen years between 2005 and 2023, only 164 were killed, or 0.76 per month—a drop of more than 70 percent.[42]

Another big savings was in money. Prior to the Disengagement, it had taken over 20,000 soldiers to defend just 8,600 settlers in Gaza.[43] Withdrawing the settlers from Gaza relieved the army of that burden. It allowed Israel to drastically reduce its defense budget, so that by 2023, it was only spending 3.5 percent of GDP on defense, the lowest in its history and less than the United States.[44] Perhaps the greater financial burden was supporting the local Palestinian population, paying salaries of teachers, picking up the trash and performing all the services of local government, as required by international law. The Israeli army never released figures for these items. But in 2008, when Jerusalem contemplated reoccupying Gaza, someone leaked an internal memo to the press that showed the cost at $1.5 billion a year, or fully 1 percent of Israel's entire GDP.[45] One of the reasons that Israel's economy took off in the twenty-first century was that it was relieved of this grinding budgetary burden.

But if the plan had worked out so well, then why did Israel contemplate reoccupying Gaza? The answer was rockets. Hamas took control of Gaza in 2007, after a short civil war with the rival Fatah movement that dominates the Palestinian Authority. Prior to its seizing power, Gazans had fired a total of about 3,300 rockets and mortar shells into Israel in the four years between 2001 and 2005. But then, after Disengagement, they fired over 2,800 in 2007 alone, and over 3,100 in 2008.[46]

The shelling led to a series of short wars between Hamas and Israel, beginning with Operation Cast Lead on December 27, 2008.[47] The next war in 2012, Operation Pillar of Defense, was the first in which Israel introduced Iron Dome, a rocket-interception system that proved remarkably effective.[48]

That was followed in 2014 by Operation Protective Edge, a fifty-five-day war that resulted in the deaths of 72 Israelis and 2,125 Palestinians,[49] and was by far the longest and most destructive of the wars. It was so destructive that it caused Hamas leaders to embrace what Israeli defense officials called "the arrangement."

The arrangement was a deal whose terms were simple enough: cash for quiet. Israel allowed money supplied by Qatar—after Iran, the biggest state supporter of Hamas—to be handed over to Hamas officials.[50] Moreover, in addition to the food, water, electricity and fuel the Israelis already allowed into the Strip, the number of Gazans permitted to work in Israel was gradually increased, reaching 17,000 in September 2022.[51]

In return, Hamas was expected to keep terrorism down to Israel's "tolerable" level. A further aspect of the deal related to targeted killings. The assassination of senior Hamas leader Ahmed Jabari, for example, had touched off Operation Pillar of Defense in 2012.[52] Israel quietly agreed to stop the practice—once again, so long as rocket fire and terrorism were kept down to the tolerable level. Deterrence was thus enforced both with carrots and sticks. Hamas could take the jobs in Israel, plus the Qatari cash, and live. Or it could fight the Israelis and die.

Admittedly, the unholy bargain had the air of paying protection money. But it was hard to argue with success. The next war with Hamas did not break out for another seven years, and it only lasted eleven days. The Israeli Air Force had by then developed technology to find and destroy tunnels; Hamas and Islamic Jihad lost many men as a result. Israeli officers celebrated the air strikes as a huge success that reinforced deterrence. Haliva—then army chief of operations—told a reporter that there would be five years of quiet on the Gaza border.[53]

He got that wrong. Another war broke out the next year, in 2022. But it was the shortest of them all, at only three days, and Israel fought it against Islamic Jihad only. Hamas refused to join the fight. Senior Israeli columnist Ben Caspit wrote "Hamas continues to invest in rebuilding Gaza, raising the standard of living, and keeping things quiet with Israel...if this isn't deterrence then there is no deterrence."[54] The head of the Knesset's powerful Foreign Affairs and Defense Committee said that every army officer from the chief of staff on down had agreed with the *Conceptzia* of deterrence, so it was never questioned.[55]

Haliva's predecessor as head of Military Intelligence was Gen. Tamir Hayman. In August 2023, just two months before the October 7 attack, he said "we are not about to find ourselves in a multi-front war as on Yom Kippur in 1973.... You don't need to see the intelligence signs. It's enough to see the interests of the other side."[56] On September 29, 2023, less than two weeks before the October 7 attack, the respected military commentator Tal Lev-Ram wrote, "Hamas isn't interested in any military escalation.... Hamas [wants] pressure on the Qataris and the international community for more money and greater economic easing."[57]

As noted, Israel supplied Gaza with its food, water, electricity and fuel. The number of Gazans given permits to work in Israel was set to rise to 20,000 in late 2023.[58] In June 2023, Netanyahu announced plans to advance development of a natural gas field in the Mediterranean off the coast of Gaza, to foster "Palestinian economic development and maintain security stability in the region."[59] Just days before the October 7 attack, the Netanyahu government announced a willingness to expand Gazan fishing waters and allow in more Qatari cash.[60]

In short, there was broad consensus that the policy of deterrence had succeeded. All of Israel's intelligence analysts agreed that Hamas would never cut off its only economic lifeline. All agreed that its leaders would never choose to commit national suicide.

This is a classic example of what psychologists call projection. The officers who commanded Israeli intelligence wanted to raise their families and live well and figured that, at least to some degree, the Palestinians wanted to do the same. It was only after the October 7 attack that Hamas leaders gave interviews showing how they really thought. Former Hamas leader Khaled Mashal said that 30 million Russians had died expelling Hitler, 6 million Algerians had died expelling France, and if millions of Palestinians had to die to destroy Israel, well, he was perfectly willing to follow suit.[61] Hamas leader Ali Baraka told Russian television that "we made them think that Hamas was busy with governing Gaza and that it wanted to focus on the 2.5 million Palestinians [in Gaza] and has abandoned the resistance altogether."[62]

In truth, there were Israelis who questioned the conventional wisdom. There was a young intelligence officer—whose name has not yet been released—who warned that Hamas might be planning a large-scale attack.[63] The story garnered media attention because the officer is a woman, so it was a wonderful media opportunity to confirm people's biases about the patriarchy. But those in the know insisted that her being a woman had nothing to do with her warning going unheeded, and anyway, there are numerous women in senior positions of Israel's defense establishment. The problem was that she was a junior officer and her work never even reached senior officers, because it was stopped by middle management, which came from other branches of the service and didn't understand intelligence work.[64]

The real problem was a lack of diversity.

The leaders of Military Intelligence looked like they had been plucked by human resources from the country's high-tech sector. One senior officer described himself as "an Ashkenazi from Ra'anana [a wealthy suburb] who speaks a little Arabic." He could have been describing pretty much all of them. They grew up in relatively wealthy Western-oriented homes and were primarily secular, so not only did they fail to understand Arab culture, they didn't understand the pull religion can have on the human psyche.[65]

Dr. Aryeh Eldad formerly commanded the IDF Medical Corps., retiring with the rank of general. After taking off his uniform, he entered politics as a candidate of a radical right-wing party. One of his former superiors ran into him and said angrily that had he known how right-wing Eldad was, he never would have allowed the promotion to go forward. Eldad said that this was why he made sure to keep his political views to himself.[66] The fact that right-wing people seem to suffer from discrimination of this kind is probably why the senior leadership of the Israeli defense establishment is so much more left-wing than the rest of the country. And this is why, when intelligence analysts were struggling to understand Hamas' intentions, a critical point of view was missing. The head of the IDF Manpower Department, General Yaniv Asor, said as much when he left the army in late 2024.[67]

The one person that saw what was coming was Michael Ben-Ari, a deeply religious member of Knesset . Ben-Ari belongs to the far-right "Jewish Power" party headed by Itamar Ben-Gvir. But Ben-Ari stands out even in that crowd. He is to the right of Ben-Gvir. He is so far off the deep end that in 2019, Israel's Central Elections Committee took the extraordinary step of disqualifying him from running for Knesset.[68] Supporters of al-Qaeda have been allowed to run, but Ben-Ari was not. In 2018, he wrote that "Gaza is a roadside bomb that will blow up in our faces... What do they want?... They want to enter kibbutzim along the border... They dream of murdering everyone that lives there."[69] This was dismissed as racism.

I am no supporter of Ben-Gvir, Ben-Ari, or anything that they stand for, but I too believed in the *Conceptzia* of carrots and sticks. Before October 7, I too would have dismissed Ben-Ari as a radical. But striving to be intellectually honest, I have to admit that he got it right and I got it wrong. Israeli intelligence needed fewer people like me and more like Michael Ben-Ari.

But there was one final blunder that was perhaps the biggest of them all.

Intelligence officers were hardly alone in slavishly following a *Conceptzia* off a cliff—many have made this mistake before, and no doubt many will in the future. But in one respect, the October 7 catastrophe stands out from the others. Israeli military leaders were so sure of themselves that they never performed a simple cost-benefit analysis.

Golda Meir and her generals could be forgiven for failing to mobilize the army in 1973. Calling up the reserves brought the economy to a standstill, and risked sparking a crisis that could touch off a war. The security officials at the Munich games in 1972 could likewise be forgiven. Protecting the thousands of athletes and hundreds of thousands of spectators that attend an Olympics is a monumental undertaking. It is not the sort of thing one does to be safe rather than sorry.

But on the night of October 6, the IDF didn't need to do any of these things. When reports came in that Hamas terrorists were massing near the fence, all it had to do was ruin a holiday weekend and order the men in surrounding bases to the border. When reports came in that Hamas terrorists were ordered to insert Israeli SIM cards into their phones, all IDF chief of staff Herzi Halevi had to do was contact the commander of the air force and tell him to prepare a few squadrons of fighter jets, attack helicopters, and armed drones.[70]

Instead, the senior generals got on a conference call at 3 a.m. in the early hours of October 7. They agreed that Hamas was planning nothing more than a raid, and only brought in a small force.[71] They agreed that more forces might be needed. But they would wait to see what happened the following morning.[72]

XI.

The Gaza War

"We may not be unbeatable, but we are unbreakable."

—YOSSI SARIEL,
commander of Israel's Intelligence Unit 8200[1]

It is best not to write history about an event until at least forty years have passed, after passions cool, memoirs are published and classified information is released. Journalism is history's first draft, but even that must often be submitted on deadline while the story is still unfolding.

Legendary British journalist Alistair Cooke faced just such a dilemma on August 6, 1974. The Watergate scandal had by then reached what appeared to be a climax, and there were rumors that Nixon might resign any day. Unfortunately, Cooke could not wait to find out what would happen. He had to record his popular BBC radio program "Letter from America" that day in Washington, so that the tape could be put on a plane to Britain and broadcast from London several days later. How do you report on an event before it happens?

Cooke gave a history of what had occurred up to that point. Then he laid out three options for what might happen in the next few days. He brought it all to a climax and concluded confidently: "the rest you know."[i,2]

* * *

On the morning of October 7, 2023, at approximately 6:30 a.m., Hamas fired an estimated 2,200 rockets into Israel, the largest single barrage in the history of the Arab-Israeli conflict, and probably the entire Middle East.[3] Thousands of Hamas terrorists simultaneously blew holes in the border fence and came pouring through on pickup trucks and motorcycles. They were inside Kibbutz Nahal Oz just fifteen minutes later.[4] One of the first targets they hit was the Kerem Shalom crossing, where thousands of trucks passed into Gaza each month. The bewildered Israeli officer who commanded the crossing said that Palestinians had attacked the very hand that fed them.[5]

Everything the Palestinians did was calculated to demonstrate that they would never accept a Jewish presence in the Middle East. The people who lived in the kibbutzim surrounding Gaza included some of the best-known peace activists in the country. They were people like Vivian Silver, a Canadian-Israeli, who had co-founded the group Women Wage Peace and served on the board of the leftist NGO B'Tselem, and who long volunteered to drive sick Gazans to medical treatment in Israel. Hamas knew her address from her humanitarian work, and had terrorists drive straight to her home and kill her. Then they burned her house to the ground.[6]

There is an old saying in Vaudeville: you don't know your act until everything goes wrong. It's the same with a military plan.

Israel spent over $1 billion building a high-tech fence around Gaza.[7] Upon its completion in December 2021, Defense Minister Benny Gantz hailed it at a ceremony, saying, "Our mission is to always stay one step ahead of the enemy."[8] The fence would come in for a great deal of criticism after the October 7 attack. It was proof, critics said, that Israel relied too much on technology. In truth,

---

i Cooke's report aired just hours after Nixon resigned. Listeners, who had no idea that it had been taped days before, hailed the "masterly" ending as "dramatic" and "tasteful, not rubbing his nose in it."

the fence performed the two tasks it was designed to carry out: it gave warning of a breach, and it prevented tunnelling from Gaza into Israel.[9] But as early as 2018 the contractor said that it was not designed to prevent thousands of people from crashing through.[10]

The failure of the fence was not an overreliance on technology, but an overreliance on a flawed *Conceptzia*. In gaming out a Hamas attack, military planners expected a commando raid to kidnap a soldier, similar to the one that captured Gilad Shalit in 2006. For such a mission, they foresaw Hamas breaching the fence in at most four places and attacking with no more than seventy men.[11] As it turned out, Hamas breached it in forty-eight places and attacked with over three thousand.[12]

The Israelis had sensors and robot machine guns in place. But the robots were not designed to stop three thousand men and, in any case, Hamas used thirty-five suicide drones to take them all out in the opening blow. In the weeks leading up to the war, Hamas had eliminated three Israeli lookout balloons, but in a way that convinced operators that the balloons had fallen out of the sky for technical reasons. None were repaired prior to October 7. The Israeli Air Force was not informed that anything unusual was afoot, so it only had two attack helicopters on standby for the entire country.[13] By the time fighter jets took to the skies, sensors and communications had been knocked out, making it impossible for pilots to discern between friend and foe.[14]

Meanwhile, on the ground, Israeli forces were at half-strength for the holiday weekend. Even at full strength, the line was lightly manned because, with the fence in place, the Israelis figured they could move forces elsewhere. More importantly, they wanted fewer men on the line since it meant fewer targets for Hamas to kill or kidnap.[15] The goal of Israel's war plan, in other words, was to stop a kidnapping, not an invasion.

Had Israeli military bases been fortified in even the most basic way, the Hamas invaders would have been wiped out. Soldiers firing machine guns from pillboxes would have mowed down the attackers, who only had small arms and no armor. But no one thought

there would ever be an invasion, so no one thought to build fortifi-
cations. In some cases, the Israelis didn't even bother to man their
guard posts. An IDF veteran told his wife before the war that the
army base where their daughter served—and was later killed—was
unguarded and reminded him of the comically incompetent army
unit from a famous Israeli satire.[16] When Hamas fired its opening
salvo of rockets, men and women on bases piled into protective
bunkers, exactly as they had been trained. When they came out, the
Hamas fighters were already there waiting for them.[17]

Once inside, Hamas knew where everything was located. Palestinians with permits to work in Israel had scouted the area and given
Hamas the location of high-value targets.[18] At least one dead terrorist was found with his work permit still in his pocket.[19] But it was
obvious that a far more serious intelligence breach had occurred.
Hamas fighters knew that the back gate of the most important signal
intelligence base was left unguarded. Once they blew it open, they
knew where to find the commander's office as well as his living
quarters. Three Israeli colonels were killed on October 7, something
that hadn't even happened in the surprise attack on Yom Kippur in
1973.[20] Hamas' men also knew where to find something still more
valuable: the computer servers. A major intelligence catastrophe was
averted when Israeli special forces arrived just as the Hamas fighters
emerged, and killed them before they could bring the information
back to Gaza.[21] But overall, senior Israeli intelligence officers in Tel
Aviv watched the massacre in real-time, viewing it on Palestinian
social media sites as the terrorists posted selfies and videos online.
There was little they could do. In Kibbutz Nir Oz, where a quarter of
the members were killed or taken hostage, reinforcements did not
arrive until seven hours after the initial attack.[22]

If there was any consolation for Israel, it was the fact that it all
could have been much worse. The Hamas terrorists would have
killed far more people had they not wasted valuable time raping and
torturing the early victims. Moreover, instead of focusing on wanton
acts of butchery, they could have attacked far more important targets, such as the Sdot Micha Airbase located just twenty-five miles

from Gaza, where the Jewish state reputedly stores its nuclear weapons.[23] Had they driven a little further they could have attacked the nuclear reactor in Dimona.

If anything limited the unfolding catastrophe it was the courage of ordinary Israelis, who grabbed their guns and drove straight into battle. Although many of them died, the army later identified the bodies of over a thousand terrorists killed in the attack, which meant, remarkably, that when the sun set on October 7, there were about as many dead terrorists as dead Israelis.[24]

According to published reports, as of March 15, 2024, the Israelis have captured approximately two thousand terrorists, some on October 7 and some later.[25] During questioning, they have often asked their interrogators, "When are we going to be freed? When is there going to be a prisoner swap?"[26]

* * *

While Israel buried its dead, *and before its ground operation in Gaza even began,* eighteen progressive members of the U.S. Congress signed a resolution calling for "an immediate de-escalation and cease-fire in Israel and occupied Palestine." One was quoted as saying "when we say Black Lives Matter, what's really being said inside of that statement is a history of oppression."[27] More than a thousand black pastors representing hundreds of thousands of congregants later pushed the Biden Administration for a ceasefire as well. "We see them as a part of us," one reverend told *The New York Times.* "They are oppressed people. We are oppressed people."[28]

Another bastion of Hamas support was American college campuses. On December 7, 2023, in a congressional hearing, the presidents of Penn and Harvard were asked if calling for the genocide of Jews constituted bullying and harassment on their campuses. Both answered that it depended on the context.[ii,29]

---

ii Claudine Gay, the president of Harvard, was soon forced to resign, in part due to allegations of plagiarism. In a *New York Times* op-ed, she argued that the question "does calling for the genocide of Jews violate Harvard's rules of bullying and harassment?" was an unfair curveball in the dirt, and that she fell victim to a "well-laid trap." She was targeted, she insisted, because she was "a Black woman selected to lead a storied institution."

The October 7 attack stunned the Israeli left, but soon it regained its footing as well. Author David Grossman, who as mentioned before won the Man Booker International Prize, said that his concern in the wake of the attack was that Israel would emerge "more right-wing, militant and racist."[30]

And then there was Tom Friedman. Under the title "Israel Has Never Needed to be Smarter" he penned a column that was never dumber. The reason Israel was caught off guard, he explained, was not because of the *Conceptzia* (as every Israeli military leader and commentator said) but because the evil Netanyahu divided Israeli society by seeking to "get control of the courts." The army's officers "took their eyes off the ball" because of "extremist settlers." In explaining the reason why Hamas launched the attack, he made no mention of Sinwar wanting to extract Palestinian prisoners from Israel's jails. The reason Hamas did it, he said, was to "trigger an Israeli overreaction, like an invasion of the Gaza Strip, that would lead to massive Palestinian civilian casualties and in that way force Saudi Arabia to back away from the U.S.-brokered deal now in discussion." Moreover, "Hamas and Iran absolutely do not want Israel to refrain from going into Gaza." I take the double-negative to mean that Friedman believed that Sinwar wanted Israel to go into Gaza and tear the place apart. Yeah, right.[31]

For Israel, perhaps the biggest disappointment of all came from the "human rights" community.

Amnesty International condemned Hamas, but only while pointing out what it described as "Israel's well-documented record of war crimes" and the fact that "the latest attacks in Israel must be seen in the wider context of the situation in Israel and the Occupied Palestinian Territories."[32] In its press release on October 26, before Israel's ground campaign began, it called for "an immediate ceasefire by all parties in the occupied Gaza Strip." Gaza was "occupied," in Amnesty's view, even though the only Israelis in it were the hostages. Amnesty urged the pause, in part, so that "the root causes of the conflict [could] be addressed, including dismantling Israel's system of apartheid against Palestinians."[33]

Human Rights Watch picked up on these themes with its first press release after the attack, which began: "Palestinian armed groups carried out a deadly assault on October 7, 2023, that killed several hundred Israeli civilians and led to Israeli counterstrikes that killed hundreds of Palestinians."[iii,34]

But these statements were expected. What was not expected, and what sparked genuine outrage, was what the so-called human rights community ignored.

Reports of mass rape of Israeli women began streaming in as early as the morning of October 7.[35] In our time it is enough for women to level an allegation of sexual misconduct and, even if the incident occurred years or decades before, women's groups and human rights organizations spring into action. The righteous rage never leaves any room for the rights of those accused, a troubling phenomenon that Professor Alan Dershowitz dubbed "guilt by accusation." But in the case of Israel, credible allegations by multiple witnesses and victims were met with a wall of silence. The shameful disregard sparked a new moniker: "Me Too, Unless You're a Jew."[36]

On November 27, almost two months after the attack, the U.N. Human Rights Council finally announced that it would commence an investigation.[iv,37] By the time the report was issued in March, the IDF had already released a taped rape confession by one of the terrorists, and a courageous Israeli woman had stepped forward to confirm that she had been raped.[38] The U.N. Report concluded that there was an attack on October 7 by "Hamas commandos." It also found instances of rape. But it was careful not to put two and two together, stopping short of accusing Hamas "commandos" of rape.

---

iii On March 28, 2024, two workers from a left-wing NGO called Looking the Occupation in the Eyes were shot and wounded in the West Bank by an Arab terrorist who was also a policeman in the Palestinian Authority. The two—who were driving in a new car, because their old one had been stolen by Arabs—were in the territories on a stated mission to protect Palestinian shepherds from alleged settler violence. Though it was nearby settlers who came out and treated the workers, the NGO issued a statement saying, "this incident will not prevent us from continuing to work to protect the Palestinians and demanding freedom and equality for all those that settle the land."

iv Human Rights Watch responded cautiously, saying that "when more than a thousand people are killed in a single day, untangling what happened takes time."

The authors wrote that "the mission was not investigative, it did not gather information and/or draw conclusions on attribution of alleged violations to specific armed groups."[39,v]

I typed the word "rape" into the search bar on Amnesty International's website in early May 2024. 2,632 different matches came up. There was rape in Darfur, rape in Rwanda—rape in every corner of the planet. Not a single entry mentioned the October 7 attack.[40] When I entered "Hamas Rape," one entry came up that touched on the Gaza War. But it was an allegation that Amnesty leveled *against Israel,* claiming that an arrested Palestinian was threatened with rape.[41]

Here one has to put in a good word for *The New York Times,* which ran a December 4, 2023 story about Hamas' sexual crimes.[42] But even that rape story caused a minor revolt inside the paper, as staffers questioned the veracity of the sourcing. It spilled out into the open initially as the *Times* spokesperson split hairs as to whether the Hamas rapes were "weaponized sexual violence" or merely "systemic use of sexual assault."[vi,43]

Rape story or not, the massacre did not shake the *Times* from the practice of referring to Hamas terrorists as "militants"; in at least one place, it described the October 7 terrorist attack as "a sweeping raid."[44] Another recurring theme of *Times* reporting was not so much *schadenfreude* about the attack, but *Bibifreude.*[vii] From the beginning, Netanyahu was cast as a villain, or worse. For years the paper of record had complained mightily that Israel maintained a "draconian blockade" of Gaza. Now it shifted gears, did a complete

---

v A detailed forensic study released in Israel over a year after the October 7 attack found that sex crimes were even more widespread than originally feared. The terrorists managed to cover up much of what they had done, in part, by shooting and mutilating the vaginal areas of their victims.

vi A leak by disgruntled employees of the staffroom controversy caused the *Times* to commission a leak investigation to get at the source. This is a hell of a thing for any news organization to do, given their reliance on leaks and the constant preaching of their need to protect sources. The Times Guild, the newsroom union that represents almost 1,500 journalists at the paper, filed a formal grievance.

vii Netanyahu was not even informed by his generals that anything unusual was afoot until after the attack began.

about-face, and fired off a new complaint: the evil Netanyahu had let money *into* Gaza.

Here's what happened. In 2018, Palestinian Authority President Mahmoud Abbas froze salaries of workers in Gaza after a dispute with Hamas. Hamas responded by rioting on the fence with Israel. To stave off a "humanitarian collapse," and with the blessing of Washington, the European Union and Israel's entire defense establishment, Netanyahu arranged for cash to be supplied to the Strip by Qatar.[45] The money was supposed to go directly to Palestinians, but like the salaries paid by the PA, much of it ended up in the hands of Hamas through a system of "taxation" (or blackmail; it depends who you ask).[46] Try to imagine the outcry if he had *not* allowed the cash in and Hamas had gone to war. No doubt, the *Times* and others would have then complained about the "draconian blockade."

After the October 7 attack, the *Times* did a complete about-face. It ran two front-page stories attacking Netanyahu for letting the money in, quoting critics who said that "his approach to Hamas had, at its core, a cynical political agenda: to keep Gaza quiet as a means of staying in office without addressing the threat of Hamas or simmering Palestinian discontent."[47] What those critics ignored was the fact that the "cynical" program was deemed so successful at keeping the border quiet, that Netanyahu's political rival and successor, Prime Minister Naftali Bennet, had doubled down and allowed in even more cash.[48] Most importantly, the *Times* never explained how it could be wrong, or even possible, for Israel to be carrying out a "draconian blockade" even as it was letting in hundreds of millions of dollars of Qatari cash. But in reporting two conflicting ideas as fact, the *Times* confirmed what it had long said: The Truth is Hard (at least for them).

The willingness of Netanyahu to allow the Qatari payments to continue, together with an agreement to increase the number of Palestinian workers in Israel and develop offshore natural gas for Gazans, demonstrates the absurdity of another "fact" that appeared in all the *Times* reporting: the idea that the Netanyahu government was the "most right-wing in Israeli history." It was more accurate to say that of the three coalition partners in Netanyahu's ruling coalition, the smallest was made up of some very radical people.[viii] Those radicals were marginalized by Netanyahu from the very beginning. Although he carried the title Minister for National Security, radical right-winger Itamar Ben-Gvir was not invited to join Netanyahu's war cabinet. Instead, Netanyahu brought in two retired chiefs of staff from the opposition, Benny Gantz and Gadi Eisenkot.

It was obvious to all that, like the Fedayeen terrorists of the 1960s, Hamas hoped to touch off a regional war. Moreover, an Arab diplomat with good connections to Hamas told an Israeli reporter that Sinwar only expected to capture perhaps several dozen hostages, and never dreamt the border would be as unguarded as it was. He also gambled that, like the other wars of the previous fifteen years, the Israelis would not want to take the casualties of a large ground operation in tunnel-infested Gaza.[49]

These core assumptions demonstrated that flawed *Conceptzias* were hardly limited to the Jewish state. Israeli intelligence had failed badly because it did not understand Hamas. Hamas and the people of Gaza were about to find out that they did not understand the Israelis either.

* * *

On October 23, 2023, President Biden sent a delegation of American officers to Israel headed by Marine Lieutenant General James F. Glynn. The Americans met with their Israeli counterparts to offer advice, based on their experiences in Iraq and Afghanistan.[50] General Glynn told minister Gantz that any ground campaign would accomplish little and cost the lives of at least twenty Israeli soldiers per day. Better, he advised, to manage expectations as to the war's goals and focus on pinpoint raids. Gantz listened politely and then responded that Glynn's plan made a great deal of sense for fighting

---

[viii] At a time in which the radical right won elections in the United States, Italy, Poland, Hungary, Brazil, Argentina, won a plurality in the Netherlands, and garnered more than 40 percent of the vote in France, the most surprising thing about the radical right in Israel is that it only got 11 percent of the vote.

terrorists on the other side of the world. But Israel's enemies were several hundred yards from its towns and cities.[51]

Netanyahu, Gantz, and other Israeli leaders defined their war goals as bringing back the 251 hostages and "dismantling" Hamas, which they defined as depriving the terror group of the ability to govern the Gaza Strip. The most obvious way to accomplish that would have been to invade the city of Rafah in south Gaza, and cut Hamas off from its Egyptian sources of supply. The Israelis did not do that, and one day when records are declassified we will find out why. I was told off the record that Egyptian officials—who did not want to lose the revenue they earned from cross border smuggling—complained to Biden Administration officials, who vetoed the operation.

Instead, the Israelis did the next best thing. On October 27, 2023, the IDF's 36th Armored Brigade plowed a path through the middle of the Gaza Strip, splitting it in two and creating what became known as the "Netzarim Corridor."[52] This would serve throughout the war both as a logistical hub and as a barrier, preventing enemy movement between the north and south of the territory.

Looking back several months after Israel entered the Gaza Strip, Israeli combat officers gave high marks to the skills of Hamas frogmen who, on October 7, eluded Israeli naval defenses and murdered nineteen civilians sunbathing on a beach.[53] But all other Hamas terrorists were described by the Israelis with unvarnished contempt. Their descriptions included words like "no fighting spirit"; "they don't know what landed on them"; and "we are not an army against an army or even an army against a terrorist group…all they do is pop out of tunnels and try to 'tail' us."[54]

In truth, once the IDF mobilized, the Hamas terrorists never really had a chance. Failures on October 7 notwithstanding, the modern miracle known as Israeli technology quickly made itself apparent on the battlefield. Each Israeli tank and armored vehicle was equipped with a miniature "Iron Dome" anti-missile defense system that could intercept incoming projectiles. Hundreds of anti-tank rockets and RPGs were fired at Israeli vehicles. The defense system, called "Windbreaker," stopped practically all of them.

Meanwhile, the Israeli Air Force provided ground support as never before.[55] By March 15, 2024, it had flown no less than 24,000 fighter-jet sorties, 4,000 attack helicopter sorties and 3,600 more with combat drones.[56] Practically all the ordnance the IAF fired were precision munitions. The Israelis took conventional bombs and attached American-made JDAM guidance systems that turned them into smart bombs.[57] On the ground, buildings were cleared and tunnels uncovered using specially trained combat dogs as well as robots, one of which was built to resemble a snake so that it could slither around obstacles.[58] The American casualty predictions proved grossly pessimistic. Israeli losses in the ground campaign were fewer than two a day.

Of course, Hamas carried out the October 7 attack knowing that all this technology would be brought to bear. But its leaders had a strategy for dealing with it and every other thing the Israelis might throw at them. A Hamas lawmaker named Fathi Hammad said as early as 2008 that Palestinian women, children and elderly "excel" at the "industry of death" and at forming "human shields."[59] In an interview with Al Jazeera television on October 23, Hamas leader Ismail Haniyeh said, "the blood [spilled] in the Gaza Strip, alongside the resistance…will defeat this occupier.… As I said and I repeat every time, the blood of the children, women and the elderly…we need this blood so that it will ignite within us the spirit of revolution."[60]

Haniyeh and the Hamas leadership indeed needed the blood of women and children. And they would go on to use it. They used it when they deliberately placed military assets under hospitals and schools. They used it in at least one notorious incident when they sent a large group of women and children to act as human shields against IDF troops attacking a key Hamas compound.[ix,61] But they were not just looking to ignite "the spirit of revolution." They were

---

[ix] This is another of those things that even the Nazis didn't do. When the allies began bombing German cities, they evacuated their women and children to the countryside.

looking to ignite something very different. Something that held out the hope of saving their skins.

* * *

In 1996, Hezbollah started one of its periodic wars against Israel. When an Israeli artillery shell accidentally killed 106 civilians, the Clinton Administration demanded that Israel enter into a ceasefire, and thus prevented Israel from achieving victory.[x,62] Not surprisingly, after the ceasefire was declared, Hezbollah went right back to firing rockets into northern Israel.

This history repeated itself in 2006 when Hezbollah started a war yet again. Another errant Israeli artillery shell accidentally killed dozens of civilians in the exact same village in southern Lebanon. But this time the story had a different president, so it had a different ending. President George W. Bush was caught on a hot mic telling British prime minister Tony Blair that they had to "get Hezbollah to stop doing this shit."[63] Washington made no demands for a ceasefire, Israel pounded Hezbollah into dust, and the Lebanese-Israeli border was quiet for seventeen years.

The difference between the two approaches was obvious. The Republicans allowed Israel to win, even in the face of collateral civilian casualties. The Democrats didn't want the Israelis to lose, but didn't want them to win either. They wanted a mixed outcome to match their mixed feelings about the conflict.

Everyone in the region took notice. Hamas started a war with Israel on December 27, 2008 when it knew that Obama was three weeks away from being sworn in. But apart from that, Hamas and Hezbollah knew not to start any wars while Bush was in office, or during the four years of the Trump Administration. They and Iran didn't even start a war after Trump ordered the killing of the head

---

[x] That Hezbollah used the 106 civilians as a vast human shield was never disputed. A U.N. spokesman stated that the "terrorists drew Israeli fire deliberately towards the U.N. position where the Lebanese civilians were seeking protection.... Hezbollah forced the IDF to respond and fire in the area of the U.N. position." One of three U.N. peacekeepers wounded by the Israeli strike was quoted as saying, "The IDF is not to blame and we are not angry at them."

of the Iranian Revolutionary Guard, Qasem Soleimani. By contrast, Hamas started two wars while Obama was in office, plus a third in 2021 during the Biden years. Gaza-based Islamic Jihad started yet another in 2022. And, of course, there was the attack on October 7, 2023.

For Hamas, the strategy was as obvious as it was cynical: place enough civilians in harm's way, and the Biden Administration would put a stop to the war. The civilian casualties caused by the explosion near the al-Ahli Hospital on October 17 almost gave Hamas the lifeline it was looking for. When it emerged that the rocket that caused the explosion was a malfunctioning rocket fired by Islamic Jihad, one commentator said only half-jokingly that the group did more for the Palestinian cause by killing its own people than it ever did killing Israelis.

The number of civilian casualties became an international obsession. In general, terror groups are not given much credibility by the media. No one quoted the "Islamic State health ministry" for casualty figures when Obama was busy flattening cities in Iraq and Syria. Nevertheless, Hamas' health ministry became a modern-day Walter Cronkite, the Most Trusted Name in News. Everyone quoted it. The media continued the practice even after it became self-evident that the health ministry figures were statistically impossible. For one thing, the number of dead rose in a linear fashion, in an almost straight diagonal line across a graph, unrelated to the ebb and flow of combat.[64] More importantly, on February 19, 2024, a Qatari-based Hamas leader told Reuters that the group had lost 6,000 fighters in the war up to that point. That was only half the Israeli estimate of 12,000,[xi,65] but even if one sticks with the Hamas number, the health ministry said on that same day that 29,000 Palestinians had died since the beginning of the war and that two-thirds of the dead were women and children.[66] Quick arithmetic shows that for all these numbers to be true, 19,500 of the dead civilians would have

---

[xi] During Operation Cast Lead, Hamas claimed that only forty-nine of its fighters were killed. But two years later, it acknowledged that the true number of lost men was seven hundred, the figure that the IDF had said all along.

to be women and children, while only 3,500 could be men (since the remaining 6,000 dead were acknowledged to be fighters). A ratio like that would mean the Israelis had invented a magical weapon, a precision bomb that almost exclusively killed women and children.

The Gaza health ministry left much of the propaganda to others. The ministry only issued the total number of Palestinians it said were killed, without saying how many were civilians and how many were combatants, leaving it to the media to pick up the narrative from there. Progressives were so anxious to cast Israel in the worst light possible that they seized upon the health ministry number and said that *all* the dead Palestinians were civilians. A BBC reporter named Wyre Davies got into hot water for doing this, reporting that 24,000 Palestinians had been killed according to the Gaza Health Ministry, and that all were civilians.[67] Lucy Hockings, a well-known BBC anchor, did the same thing on November 24, when the health ministry number was 14,000.[68] Senator Bernie Sanders did it when the health ministry number was 15,000 ("The killing of nearly 15,000 Palestinian civilians since the war began is unacceptable").[69] So did Spain's Foreign Minister in an interview with Christiane Amanpour.[70]

But at least their bias was grounded in a number. Rep. Alexandria Ocasio-Cortez called the war an "unfolding genocide." South Africa filed a complaint against Israel with the International Court of Justice, claiming it was committing genocide (never mind that it is Hamas that howls its wish to commit genocide). South Africa's ruling African National Congress, which harbored Sudanese warlords wanted for genocide in Darfur, was then in financial turmoil, its assets seized by creditors. But shortly after it filed the complaint, it announced that its finances had "stabilized," leading many to speculate that Iran had bought off its leaders.[71]

Eventually the lies caught up with the Most Trusted Name in News. On April 6, 2024, the Gaza health ministry acknowledged that it had "incomplete data" on fully a third of the deaths it claimed had occurred.[72] And on May 13, a U.N. spokesman said that only 24,686 Palestinian deaths could be documented out of a claimed

34,622.[73] Hamas continued to claim that the missing 10,000 dead were "buried in the rubble," but offered no evidence to back that up.[74] In June, Congress voted by a lopsided, bipartisan majority to an amendment "limiting the use of unverified statistics from the Gaza Ministry of Health."[75] When you consider that the dead also included those who died by errant Palestinian rockets, as well as those who died of natural causes, it meant that it was a near certainty that far fewer than one civilian died per terrorist, a ratio unheard-of in modern urban warfare.

Still, *The New York Times* clung to its biases, reporting on April 22 that the Gazan death toll was "34,000, according to health officials there." To hammer home how high that death toll was, the reporter added that in the siege of Mosul "by Iraqi forces and the U.S. Air Force 3,000 civilians were killed as a result of Iraqi and U.S. military action, by some estimates."[76] Those "estimates" could only have come from people who don't know how to count. As noted earlier, the Associated Press plucked 9,606 names out of the morgue and Kurdish authorities said the death toll was 40,000.[xii,77]

After the al-Ahli story failed to stick, Hamas tried a different tack. It agreed to a ceasefire on November 24, 2023, that included a hostage deal on terms that were—comparatively speaking—extremely favorable to Israel. The Jewish state only had to exchange three terrorists for each hostage, and all but a few of the Palestinian prisoners were minor figures who would have been freed within a few months anyway.[xiii,78] Hamas' decision-making is completely opaque, but many speculated that Sinwar had agreed to the deal hoping that the pause would permit reporters to enter Gaza, film the destruction, and cause Washington and the international community

---

xii The coverage of the October 7 attack raised serious ethics questions because many of the Gazan "journalists" who sent pictures in real time plainly had ties to Hamas and knew of the planned massacre in advance. One was freelance photojournalist Yousef Masoud, whose work appeared in *The New York Times*. He won a Polk Award for what one judge called "magnificent reporting."

xiii As they were led out, the Israeli hostages were jeered by angry mobs. Not one came back with a story of a Palestinian that showed them kindness or a single act of humanity. A little girl came home from the seven-week ordeal thinking she'd been in captivity for a year.

to put an end to the fighting.[79] The weeklong ceasefire resulted in eighty hostages being swapped for two hundred and forty Palestinian prisoners. But Hamas suspended further swaps when it became apparent that the war wouldn't be brought to an end.[xiv,80]

The Biden Administration didn't end the war. But from Hamas' standpoint, it did the next best thing: it launched what I'll call Operation Hypocrisy. It ignored America's recent history of engaging in siege warfare against Islamic State and demanded that Israel be the only country in history to supply its enemies in the middle of a war.[xv] Biden took this extraordinary step without even demanding that Hamas free eight American citizens among those held hostage. The administration even went so far as to parachute supplies into Gaza. When Biden was vice president, the only thing American planes dropped on Mosul, Fallujah, and Ramadi were bombs. And if some country had parachuted supplies down to America's enemies, Obama would have ordered the planes shot out of the sky.[xvi,81]

The Israelis continued their campaign through the areas of Jabalia, Shuja'iyya, and Khan Yunis. They killed four senior Hamas leaders, including Sinwar's old cellmate Saleh Arouri, who was assassinated in Lebanon. They scored a major victory when they lured the terrorists into returning to the Shifa Hospital in Gaza City before surrounding it and closing in, killing or capturing hundreds.[xvii,82] This was accomplished without a single civilian casualty.[83] Early in

---

xiv On February 12, 2024, Israeli commandos rescued two of the hostages in a daring raid. *The New York Times* ran a column saying that the raid "came with enormous cost" because "Gazan health officials said at least 67 Palestinians died in the effort."

xv On May 5, 2024, *The New York Times* ran a full-page analysis on "Gaza and the Law on Starvation." It was highly critical of Israel, and all but accused it of a war crime, even though trucks with supplies were rolling into Gaza every day. Among others, it quoted British foreign minister David Cameron who conveniently forgot that as prime minister he had helped enforce a siege of food and water against cities under the control of Islamic State. The *Times* reporter, Amanda Taub, apparently forgot this as well, because the words "Fallujah," "Ramadi" and "Obama" don't appear anywhere in her analysis.

xvi Despite all the cries of "food insecurity" and "starvation," a study in May 2024 showed that flour was cheaper in Gaza than in Israel.

xvii The terrorists apparently believed they would be safe in Shifa because it was a hospital. This also explains why there were thirty-six "hospitals" in Gaza, while Queens, New York, which has a slightly larger population, has only fourteen. In Shifa, the Israelis waged gun battles in the pediatric ward and found weapons hidden in MRI machines.

the war, on November 13, Biden said that Shifa Hospital "must be protected," and called for "less intrusive action" by Israeli forces.[84] But while he was vice president, on December 7, 2016, American planes deliberately bombed the al-Salem Hospital in Mosul, Iraq and destroyed it.[xviii,85]

By the end of March 2024, Israel had dismantled twenty of twenty-four Hamas battalions. Sinwar and the other Hamas leaders still alive were thought to be holed up with the remaining hostages in the southern Gaza Strip city of Rafah. As noted above, Rafah was also the location of the tunnels into the Sinai Peninsula through which Hamas smuggled all its military supplies. So one would have expected the IDF to go in and finish the job. But everything came to a screeching halt in January 2024. For months, Israeli media reported on what it called a "*dishdush*," a negative connotation that loosely translates to mean running in place or treading water. Why had the IDF suddenly stopped attacking just when it seemed to be on the verge of victory? The reason for the delay first appeared on the news site *Axios* and then on Israeli television: the IDF could not continue its operation because the Biden Administration would not supply it with badly needed ammunition.[86]

Like Clinton and Obama, Biden didn't want the Israelis to lose, but he didn't want them to win either. Kamala Harris gave an interview to ABC News on March 24, 2024, in which she suggested that there would be "consequences" for Israel if it entered Rafah. Expressing concern for the 1.4 million Palestinians who were then encamped in Rafah, she said "Let me tell you something: I have studied the maps. There's nowhere for those folks to go."[87] It was a curious observation. The Palestinians in Rafah had traveled there from elsewhere in Gaza. There was no reason why they couldn't just go back.

The following day, in a move widely seen as a slap at Israel, Biden allowed the U.N. Security Council to pass a resolution calling for

---

xviii Article 19 of the Geneva Convention permits the bombing of hospitals when they are used for any acts "outside their humanitarian duties" that are "harmful to the enemy."

a ceasefire. The resolution made no mention of Hamas or of who started the war, and though it called for the freeing of the hostages, it did not condition the ceasefire on their release.[88] In a truly unprecedented step, Democrat Chuck Schumer took to the Senate floor and called on Netanyahu to resign. The *Wall Street Journal* described it as "the latest in a series of high-level warnings and White House moves aimed at pressuring Israel...to rethink its war plans."[89] The Biden Administration was so anxious to keep Israel out of Rafah that the *Washington Post* reported that it offered Jerusalem "sensitive intelligence" to help it locate Hamas leaders.[90] Predictably, the *Post* story raised even more eyebrows. Why hadn't Washington been sharing this intelligence with Israel already?

The Biden people turned to a favorite conduit for making their position known: Tom Friedman. In an April 28 column, he reported that "privately, they [Biden Administration officials] are being more blunt and telling Israel: No massive invasion of Rafah, period." Were the Israelis to proceed with the operation, it would "force a real breach with the Administration" and "President Biden would consider restricting certain arms sales to Israel."[91]

Hamas almost caught a lucky break on April 2, 2024, when the IDF accidentally killed seven aid workers operating in Gaza. White House spokesman John Kirby said the United States was "outraged," raising the specter that Israel would be forced into a ceasefire, and Hamas handed victory.[92] Nancy Pelosi joined thirty-six other Democrats in demanding that Washington cut off all arms shipments to Israel.[xix,93] The threat only dissipated after Biden forced Israel to open yet more crossings and step up the already unprecedented level of aid it sent to its enemies.[94]

With this, Operation Hypocrisy reached a high-water mark. On October 3, 2015, when Obama was president and You-Know-Who was vice president, American warplanes accidentally bombed a Doctors Without Borders hospital in Afghanistan, killing forty-two

---

xix On April 8, Senator Elizabeth Warren added her voice to the Progressive chorus, accusing Israel of committing genocide.

aid workers and patients.[95] The idea that, as a result of this tragedy, the United States had to agree to a ceasefire and hand the Taliban a victory was never entertained in the media or anywhere else, just as it was never entertained when NATO planes accidentally bombed the Chinese embassy in Belgrade during the air war in Yugoslavia, or when U.S. troops massacred hundreds in My Lai during the Vietnam War. Indeed, Israel is the only country in history fighting under Progressive Rules of Engagement: civilians are accidentally killed, so therefore there must be a ceasefire.

Equally striking was *The New York Times*. In the 2015 bombing by the U.S. Air Force, the *Times* headline the next day was "Airstrike Hits Doctors Without Borders Hospital in Afghanistan." The headline left out who may have perpetrated the attack, suggesting that some other air force operating anonymously in Afghanistan might have been the culprit. The first paragraph of the article was equally cautious, saying that "the American military acknowledged that it may have killed 19 patients, staff members and others."[96] In Israel's case the accidental killing was the lead story in the *Times* for four straight days and the tone was set by the very first headline: "Strikes by Israel Kill Aid Workers and Draw Outcry." The sub-headline read "Logo was on Vehicles: 7 Deaths in Food Convoy in Gaza—'Everybody Feels Endangered.'"[97]

In accordance with the laws of physics, in May 2024 *The New York Times* won the Pulitzer Prize for International Reporting. In the words of the judges, the Paper of Record was honored for its "wide-ranging and revelatory coverage of Hamas' lethal attack…and the Israeli military's sweeping, deadly response in Gaza."[xx,98]

---

xx The winner in the history category was a work about the struggles of black workers in Boston during the civil rights era. Two shared the prize in biography, one for a work about Martin Luther King, Jr. and the other for telling the story of an enslaved African-American couple that escaped from Georgia in 1848. The winner in nonfiction was a work about "life under Israeli occupation" in the West Bank. Two others won for reporting on racism, another for a "sobering examination of the AR-15 semiautomatic rifle," and there was a Special Citation for journalists that died "in the effort to tell the stories of Palestinians and others in Gaza." For those seeking an award given to a conservative, I say to you what was once said to fans of the Brooklyn Dodgers: wait till next year.

* * *

The *dishdush* finally ended on May 6 when Netanyahu ordered the army to launch the long-awaited attack on Rafah. It was obvious that he did not coordinate with American officials, because they were quoted saying that they did not believe the air and ground assault represented the start of a major operation.[99] The Palestinians never got the memo from Kamala that there was "nowhere for those folks to go." As early as May 17, over 800,000 had relocated peacefully, just as the Israelis had predicted.[100]

Along the border with Egypt, the Israelis found a tunnel every ten meters. In the words of Alon Ben-David, one of Israel's most distinguished military commentators, "the entire border was criss-crossed with tunnels for smuggling that led to tunnels for firing rockets that led to tunnels for command and control." Though he initially questioned the wisdom of the operation, he wrote that "now that it is clear what a lifeline the tunnels in Rafah were to Hamas, it is hard to see how Israel could withdraw."[101]

The operation proceeded with remarkable speed. In a speech before Congress, Netanyahu said that the IDF killed "1,203 terrorists," further asserting that—apart from a single tragedy in which forty-six were killed because Hamas positioned an ammunition dump in a tent camp—the number of civilian dead was "practically none." Fact-checkers questioned the "practically none" assertion, but were only able to point to perhaps several dozen more civilian fatalities.[102] This was still a tiny fraction of the number of Hamas fighters killed, and an even smaller fraction of what the Biden Administration predicted. Then, on July 13, the IDF scored one of the biggest victories of the war, killing Muhammad Deif, a legendary Hamas leader who had survived seven previous assassination attempts.[103]

All of this success was tempered by an unavoidable problem: the mighty Israeli Army was running out of ammunition. There were four thousand desperately needed bombs that were being held up by the Biden Administration because of the Rafah operation.[104] On June 18, 2024, Netanyahu made what had to have been one of the most difficult decisions of the war. He went public about his dispute with Biden, releasing a film in which he said that it was "inconceivable that in the last few months, the administration has been withholding weapons and ammunition to Israel."[105] You would have expected the defense minister, army chief of staff, and others to stand behind him in solidarity, but Netanyahu stood alone.

Netanyahu's detractors often accused him of delusions of grandeur, thinking himself an "Israeli Churchill," but this was indeed his finest hour. The speech led to an outcry, and denials from the Biden Administration. Back home, Netanyahu came under withering criticism. How could he anger the White House? Didn't he know that Washington was Israel's only lifeline?

Netanyahu doubled down and repeated the charge a week later. Israel needed ammunition and the Biden Administration was holding it up.[106]

The second verbal assault partially broke the ice. On June 27, the Biden Administration announced that it was sending some of the arms shipment. As reported by *Axios*, "the White House wants to decrease some of the tension between President Biden and Israel's supporters over his decision to withhold this specific shipment."[107] But many critical munitions and badly needed armored bulldozers were not released to Israel until January 25, 2025, after President Trump assumed office.[108] Jeremy Ben-Ami of J Street posted on November 17, 2024 in support of a Senate resolution disapproving arms sales to Israel. The "pro-Israel" Ben-Ami declared that "the moment demands a clear and powerful statement of disapproval of how this war has been conducted."[109]

The resolution failed, but Democrats still seemed as determined as ever to see an inconclusive outcome to the war. After the Israelis assassinated Deif and cut off smuggling into Gaza from Egypt, Hamas reportedly softened its demands for a hostage deal. But then on July 25, Kamala Harris, by then the Democratic nominee for president, gave a speech in which she said, "What has happened in Gaza over the past nine months is devastating. The images of dead children and desperate hungry people fleeing for safety sometimes displaced for the second third or fourth time. We cannot look away in the face of these tragedies, we cannot allow ourselves to become numb to the suffering, and I will not be silent."[110]

The following day, Hamas rejected any hostage deal and refused to even attend the talks.[111]

Who could blame them? Sinwar's primary demand in all the talks had been that Israel commit to end the war and leave Hamas in power. The vice president all but said that if elected, she would see to it that those demands were met. Hamas not surprisingly chose to wait it out and see who won the election.

The Gaza War did not figure prominently in the American presidential campaign. The American people were more concerned with kitchen table issues like inflation. But it did figure prominently in Michigan, a large battleground state with a sizeable Muslim population. Bill Clinton gave a speech to a packed West Michigan church in which he said that "Hamas did not care about a homeland for the Palestinians, they wanted to kill Israelis and make Israel uninhabitable."[112]

The next day, the *Huffington Post* ran the following headline: "Bill Clinton Justifies the Mass Killing of Palestinians in Racist Michigan Speech."[113]

* * *

Starting the day after the October 7, 2023 attack, Hezbollah fired thousands of rockets into northern Israel in solidarity with Hamas. Israelis living in border communities all fled for their lives and remained refugees for close to a year. Finally, on September 17, 2024, the IDF set off bombs inside Hezbollah pager devices that Israeli intelligence had secretly boobytrapped. The attack decimated Hezbollah's ranks, killing dozens and severely wounding over three thousand. It was hailed as one of the greatest intelligence victories of the twenty-first century. But Leon Panetta, who served as CIA director under President Obama, called it an act of "terrorism."[114]

That Friday, September 20, 2024, Hezbollah leader Hassan Nasrallah gave a sermon by video link. The fire in his eyes had dimmed;

rumors spread through Lebanon that the security breach had occurred because his son Jawad had taken a fat commission on the acquisition of the pagers.[115] Nasrallah vowed revenge. But then, on September 27, 2024, he convened a meeting of the senior leadership of Hezbollah in a bunker buried deep beneath a residential block in south Beirut. The Israelis leveled the entire complex with a massive air strike that killed Nasrallah and practically the entire senior leadership of the organization.

Hezbollah agreed to a ceasefire with the Israelis on November 27, 2024. With the group neutralized, Syria's leader Bashar al-Assad no longer had his most important ally to prop up his regime. Syrian rebels drove him out of the country less than two weeks later. An Iranian Revolutionary Guard leader said that for Tehran, Bashar's fall was like the collapse of the Berlin Wall.[116]

Meanwhile, the Israelis killed Yahya Sinwar on October 17, 2024. *The New York Times* reported that death of this "militant" would pave the way for a hostage deal.[117] Actually, what paved the way for a hostage deal was the election on November 5, 2024, of Donald Trump. He announced on December 4, 2024, that there would be "all hell to pay" if Israeli hostages were not released by the time he took office on January 20, 2025.[118] Hamas dropped its requirement that Israel agree to end the war. And on January 15, 2025, Israel and Hamas announced a ceasefire. The first Israeli hostages were exchanged for jailed Palestinian terrorists on January 19, 2025.

The rest you know.

XII.

Coda

"The revolution wasn't about the price of watermelons."
—AYATOLLAH RUHOLLAH KHOMEINI[1]

I n the play *The Visit* by the Swiss dramatist Friedrich Durrenmatt, a wealthy old woman returns to the town of her youth and presents its impoverished citizens with a devilish proposal. She will make an enormous donation to the people that will solve all their economic troubles, but on one condition: the town must murder her former lover, who, years before, impregnated and abandoned her.

The townspeople react in horror. How could she think that they would do such a thing? They are civilized, law-abiding people. They throw her out, even as she declares that the offer remains on the table.

But then, a strange thing happens. The target of the old woman's wrath, until then a respected shopkeeper, changes in the eyes of the citizenry: He is dishonest. He is a profiteer. The town's troubles are all his fault. The old woman's offer is the furthest thing from anyone's mind, of course, but no one is above the law. The end of the story is by now obvious: the townspeople find the shopkeeper guilty of a litany of crimes and kill him after dimming the lights.

171

When a reporter arrives, the doctor tells him that the man died of a heart attack.

As I researched this book, I was reminded of that story, plus a wonderful quote that is said to date back to the 1780 Gordon Riots, the most destructive urban violence in British history: "I would rather be governed by an ill-dressed mob than a well-dressed mob." In the Eurovision music competition in 2024, Israel and Ukraine got the highest and second highest number of online votes from the voting public. That's too much of a coincidence to be a coincidence. One observer said that Israel's performance "earned the most amount of public love out of the entrants."[2] But then the appointed judges hammered Israel, placing it thirteenth in their scoring. In other words, Israel did great among the ill-dressed masses, and poorly only among the well-dressed elites.

It brings everything back to the question with which this book began: why? Why is Israel, like Durrenmatt's shopkeeper, surrounded by a well-dressed mob of politicians, journalists and human rights workers, and accused of a laundry list of imagined crimes? The reason the shopkeeper in the play was persecuted is obvious. But what is behind Israel's predicament?

Whenever I confront weighty questions like this, the first thing I do is consult with the Lord—Rabbi Lord Jonathan Sacks.

Until his death in 2020, Rabbi Sacks was the chief rabbi of Britain, a member of the House of Lords, and one of the most influential theologians of our time. He argued that antisemitism is a mutating virus that adapts in each period and place, always casting the Jews as the "other." When society was deeply Christian, the Jews were Christ-killers. When society was Communist, the Jews were money-grubbing capitalists. When society was capitalist, Jews were godless Communists. In our time, people in the West are more sensitive to the legacy of racism and apartheid. So the Jews are colonial oppressors.

This current mutation of antisemitism leads to strange outcomes. In World War II, trains carrying German prisoners of war often travelled across the American south on their way to detention camps. More than a few people noticed that if a train stopped in Alabama or Mississippi, the Nazi POWs could eat in the restaurants because they were white, while the American soldiers guarding them couldn't because they were black. This is the same phenomenon we witness when we see progressives, left-wing feminists and "Queers for Palestine" marching in solidarity with Hamas. These are the crazy outcomes you get when you judge people by the color of their skin and not the content of their character.

The brilliant British author Douglas Murray has pointed out that generals aren't the only ones who fight the last war.[3] Cultural warriors do the same thing. The young people treating the quad at Columbia University as if it were the Edmund Pettus Bridge in Selma all aspire to be a modern-day John Lewis, manning the ramparts as he did in the fight against racism. I saw the same thing when I was in college in the 1980s. Back then we called it "Sixties Envy." It often seemed, even then, that the civil rights movement had morphed into something akin to a societal autoimmune disease. It ran out of bacteria to destroy. So it started to attack healthy tissue.

It is a problem for Israel. But it is a far bigger problem for the United States.

* * *

In 1979, as angry crowds gathered in the streets of Iran to topple the Shah, *The New York Times* ran an editorial describing Ayatollah Ruhollah Khomeini as an "enigma." Bernard Lewis was then perhaps America's leading scholar on the Islamic world. He had read Khomeini's works, many of which had been translated into English and were easily accessible. Far from an "enigma," Lewis concluded that Khomeini possessed the virtue of candor (to put it mildly), and that in every other respect he was a perfect lunatic. But Lewis had been largely discredited as a "racist," so his offer to write a piece for the *Times* fell on deaf ears. The head of the Iran desk at the paper was even heard to say that Lewis was merely a Zionist agent spreading disinformation.[4]

Among other things, Khomeini had written that girls should be married off before puberty ("Do your best to ensure that your daughters do not see their first blood in your house").[5] His own father—who was stabbed to death when Khomeini was a baby—married his mother when she was just nine years old. Khomeini himself took his wife when she was ten years old and had her pregnant by the age of eleven. Khomeini blamed poverty in Iran on foreigners and Jews,[6] and argued that the idea of nationalism and nation-states were nothing but a western plot to weaken Islam.[7]

At the heart of Khomeini's program was conquest. In the words of Vali Nasr, one of the world's leading authorities on Shia Islam:

> Khomeini's ambitions extended beyond Shiism. He wanted to be accepted as the leader of the Muslim world, period. At its core, his drive for power was yet another Shia challenge for leadership of the Islamic world. He saw the Islamic Republic of Iran as the base for a global Islamic movement, in much the same way that Lenin and Trotsky had seen Russia as the springboard country of what was meant to be a global communist revolution.[8]

No price was too high to pay in the jihadist drive to create a Shiite Caliphate. During the blood-soaked Iran-Iraq War of the 1980s, an ayatollah named Mehdi Haeri Yazdi approached Khomeini, his mentor, while he was sitting alone on a rug in his garden facing a pool. The hopeless war was consuming hundreds of thousands of young lives, Yazdi said. Was there no way to stop the slaughter? Khomeini replied reproachfully, "Do you also criticize God when he sends an earthquake?"[9] The economic costs of creating a caliphate were a secondary concern for Khomeini as well. He famously cried that "economics is for donkeys," and "the revolution was not about the price of watermelons."[10]

This ideology continued long after 1989, the year Khomeini died. In 2021, a former senior Syrian official named Firas Tlass told an interviewer that, "The Iranians have an authoritative plan to take control over the entire region." Their strategy was as brilliant as it was simple. They went to any country that had Muslims and a political vacuum. There they set up a school system in which they indoctrinated children with their vision of violent, expansionist, radical Shiite Islam. Twelve short years later they had legions of young fighters eager to do their bidding. The strategy was implemented in an arc of ruin that extended from Lebanon through the Levant and down to Yemen. Tlass said that there were whole swaths of Syria that were controlled by Iran and its Lebanese proxy Hezbollah, where the Bashar al-Assad regime had no control and no idea of what was going on. The Iranians even attempted to gain a toehold on the European continent in the 1990s, in Kosovo.[11] Tlass added that in the mid 2000s, former Iranian president Muhammad Khatami predicted, in a private conversation between the two, that in twenty years Iran would be the counterweight to the United States.[12]

This prophesy would be realized almost exactly twenty years later during the Gaza War, when the world got its first taste of the radical Shiite coalition. Tehran mobilized its multi-tenacle proxy army. Though Israel ultimately triumphed, as we have seen, the world got its first taste of the dangers of the would-be Shiite Caliphate. There was unprecedented shelling by Hezbollah, which rendered an entire region of northern Israel uninhabitable. There was disruption of international shipping by Iranian-backed Houthi rebels in Yemen. And at the very moment that Iraq's prime minister was in Washington hoping to negotiate a much-needed economic package, a Shiite militia in his country joined Iran's April 13, 2024 assault that launched hundreds of rockets into Israel. A senior member of Iraq's security forces named Abdul Aziz al-Mohammedawi made no secret of his allegiance to Iran and its supreme leader Ayatollah Ali Khamenai.[13]

In the face of this challenge, American allies in the region, and particularly the Saudis, were dumbfounded by Washington's foolishness.

Under the banner of "human rights," the Biden Administration undermined Saudi Arabia's war against the Iranian backed Houthis of Yemen. As a senior Saudi journalist put it, "You wouldn't let us fight the Houthis, so now you have to."[14] Biden Administration envoy Amos Hochstein reportedly offered Hezbollah an aid package to rebuild southern Lebanon after the war, if the terror group agreed to stop firing into Israel.[15] A problem like Hezbollah is solved not with carrots, but with sticks. The Administration should have slapped punishing sanctions on Lebanon's battered economy the minute Hezbollah launched its first rocket. Even over 130 attacks on U.S. troops by Iranian proxies drew little or no response.[16] On January 28, 2024, Iranian-backed militias killed three American troops stationed in Jordan. [17] The Biden Administration carried out a measured response in Iraq and Syria but left Iran out of the fray, even lifting sanctions to permit Tehran to raise oil exports from 300,000 barrels a day to 2 million.[18]

And then there was the Iran Deal. Experts still debate how long it would have delayed Iran obtaining a bomb—the deal, by its very terms, only placed restrictions on Iran for fifteen years—but all agree that it gave Tehran access to over $100 billion of its previously frozen assets in foreign banks. To this President Obama said, "Our best analysts expect the bulk of this revenue to go into spending that improves the economy and benefits the lives of the Iranian people."[19] This statement showed a fundamental misunderstanding of Iranian priorities.

Israel was caught off guard on October 7 because it never thought that Hamas would commit an act of national suicide. There is a great deal of confusion hanging over the region as the new "rules" are being sorted out. But the one thing that can be said with certainty is this: Hamas signed its own death warrant on October 7, 2023. The 17,000 Gazans who used to work in Israel had better get their resumes together. They won't be coming back to Israel anytime soon. The 5.7 billion gallons of water they used to receive from Israel, as well as the 67,000 supply trucks, the electricity, the fuel, the offshore natural gas—it's all finished. Gaza is going to become a ward of the international community living on humanitarian assistance, not unlike the rebels living in Idlib in northwestern Syria. And yet, in the face of all this, opinion polls show that Hamas remains popular both in the West Bank and even in Gaza. As pollster Khalil Shikaki put it, "The support for Hamas comes from various sources, but the most important one is because Palestinians share Hamas' values."[20]

This is why the story of the Gaza war is so much bigger than Israel and Hamas. If a radical Islamic proxy like Hamas is willing to commit national suicide for the greater cause of Jihad, then what does it say about its patron, Iran? *What does it say about a nuclear Iran?* Can the ayatollahs be deterred like the leaders of other nuclear powers, or do they view mutually assured destruction ("MAD") as an incentive?[i,21]

Setbacks notwithstanding, there can be no doubt that the Iranians will attempt to rebuild and ultimately create their Shiite Caliphate. It is, after all, their highest national priority. It is also why the Saudis are almost certain to sign a peace treaty with Israel after the Gaza war ends, Palestinian state or not. Numerous Gulf Arab leaders told author Dan Senor that the event that convinced them to normalize relations with Israel and sign the Abraham Accords was Benjamin Netanyahu's March 3, 2015, speech before Congress, arguing against the Iran Deal. Here at last was a Western leader who both understood the Iranian peril and had Washington's ear.

But will Washington listen?[ii,22]

That the ayatollahs present a clear and present danger to the United States is as obvious as one of the Supreme Leader Ayatollah Ali Khamenei's speeches. Speaking on November 2, 2017, over cries of "Death to America!," he declared that "America is the number one enemy of our nation."[23] But rather than rally to meet the challenge, left-wing Americans are working against allies and themselves. When Ukrainian President Volodymyr Zelensky spoke before Congress on December 21, 2022, all members of Congress attended. But

---

i On April 10, 2024, a camera caught Hamas leader Ismail Haniyeh at the very moment he learned that three of his children and three of his grandchildren had been killed in combat, fighting the Israelis. He didn't flinch and was seen uttering what appeared to be a prayer. After Haniyeh himself was killed by the Israelis on July 31, 2024, his widow was captured on camera wishing him 72 virgins in Paradise.

ii On July 31, 2024, Tom Friedman said, "we were never, ever, ever, ever, ever, ever going to bomb Iran and take out its nuclear reactors from a standing start. It was not that big a strategic threat to us."

when Netanyahu spoke before Congress on July 24, 2024, about half the Democrats and their eventual candidate for president, Kamala Harris, chose to boycott the event.[24] Of course, half of Democrats only represent the views of about a quarter of the American people. But that quarter includes about 60 percent of the journalists, 90 percent of the filmmakers, and 100 percent of the people who hand out awards to journalists and filmmakers.

On paper, Iran constitutes a far smaller threat to the United States in the twenty-first century than Fascism or Communism did in the twentieth, but the American people were much more united in the twentieth century in rising to meet the challenge. Yes, there were isolationists ("Who wants to die for Danzig?"), but very few people identified with fascists or communists. By contrast, many Americans in our time identify with Iranians or Palestinians, not because of what they stand for, but because they see them as "people of color" fighting oppression. Perhaps the most prominent African American official in the Carter Administration, U.N. Ambassador Andrew Young predicted, "[Ayatollah] Khomeini will be somewhat of a saint when we get over the panic."[25] In May 2024, Iranian Supreme Leader Ayatollah Ali Khamenei sent a letter to pro-Palestinian college protesters, praising them for "standing on the right side of history" by forming "a branch of the Resistance Front."[26] When a man accustomed to leading cries of "Death to America" finds common cause with Americans, you know that something is awry.

But all is not lost. Yes, Nancy Pelosi described Netanyahu's 2024 speech as "by far the worst presentation of any foreign dignitary invited and honored with the privilege of addressing the Congress of the United States."[27] But the majority of Congress disagreed, giving him one standing ovation after the other. Israel might be losing the battle on progressive college campuses and in Pelosi's San Francisco. But it is winning the battle practically everywhere else. Even after six months of the withering and dubious criticism in the media described above, a May 2024 Harvard-Harris Poll showed 80 percent of Americans supporting Israel.[28] When Keir Starmer recently ran for prime minister of Britain, he described himself as a former prosecutor, but never how he really began his career, which was as a human rights lawyer. There was a time when that profession was seen as a noble calling. Now it is a topic to avoid.[29] The elites may shower the NGOs with prizes and accolades. The rest of the public knows exactly what role they play.

And that's why I haven't given up on progressives either. The biases, the cognitive dissonance—these things will only last so long. Politics makes for strange bedfellows, as the old saying goes. But eventually people wake up and find themselves lying next to their enemy. That is, unless that enemy kills them first in their sleep.

But like most Americans, I'm an optimist. So I'm going to end with a prediction. One day those who share Israel's liberal values will look back upon our time. They will look back upon progressives, who hate everything about Palestinians and Iranians except their struggle with Israel. They will look back at the tortured truths progressives employed to support this strange bias. And like racism itself, they will realize just how crazy the whole thing was.

Uri Kaufman
Lawrence, NY
January 27, 2025

Endnotes

I. Strange Bedfellows

1 Leon Festinger, Henry Rieken, and Stanley Schachter, *When Prophecy Fails* (Blacksburg: Wilder Publications, 2011), p. 7.

2 *Maariv Hamosaf*, October 27, 2023, p. 6.

3 "New Tally Puts October 7 Attack Dead In Israel At 1,163," *Agence France Presse*, February 1, 2024, https://www.barrons.com/news/new-tally-puts-october-7-attack-dead-in-israel-at-1-163-78182279.

4 "October 7: How Hamas Attacked Israel, Minute by Minute," *Haaretz*, April 18, 2024, https://www.haaretz.com/israel-news/2024-04-18/ty-article-static-ext/.premium/what-happened-on-oct-7/0000018e-c1b7-dc93-adce-eff753020000.

5 Israel Channel 14 TV, January 17, 2024.

6 *Yediot Achronot, 7 Yamim*, March 29, 2024, p. 34.

7 *Maariv, Sofshavua*, January 12, 2024, p. 19.

8 "IDF publishes audio of Hamas terrorist calling family to brag about killing Jews," *The Times of Israel*, October 25, 2023, https://www.timesofisrael.com/idf-publishes-audio-of-hamas-terrorist-calling-family-to-brag-of-killing-jews/.

9 Karin Laub, "Palestinian poll shows a rise in Hamas support and close to 90% wanting US-backed Abbas to resign," Associated Press, December 13, 2023, https://apnews.com/article/israel-hamas-palestinians-opinion-poll-wartime-views-a0baade915619cd070b5393844bc4514; Zach Kessel, "Over 70 Percent of Palestinians Support Hamas's October 7 Terror Attack: Poll," *National Review*, March 21, 2024, https://www.nationalreview.com/news/over-70-percent-of-palestinians-support-hamass-october-7-terror-attack-poll/.

10 Gianluca Pacchiani and Michael Bachner, "Hamas official says group aims to repeat Oct. 7 onslaught many times to destroy Israel," *The Times of Israel*, November 1, 2023, https://www.timesofisrael.com/hamas-official-says-group-aims-to-repeat-oct-7-onslaught-many-times-to-destroy-israel/.

Endnotes

11 J. Sellers Hill and Nia L. Orakwue, "Harvard Student Groups Face Intense Backlash for Statement Calling Israel 'Entirely Responsible' for Hamas Attack," *Harvard Crimson,* October 10, 2023, https://www.thecrimson.com/article/2023/10/10/psc-statement-backlash/.

12 *The Wall Street Journal,* November 7, 2023, p. A17.

13 *Ma'ariv Sofshavua,* May 17, 2024, p. 30. There were 1,398 articles in the study period.

14 "A Sudden Blast, Then Carnage in a Hospital Courtyard," *New York Times,* October 20, 2023, https://www.nytimes.com/2023/10/18/world/middleeast/gaza-hospital-deaths-aftermath.html.

15 Margherita Stancati et al., "U.S., Experts Say Evidence Suggests Palestinian Militants' Rocket Hit Gaza Hospital," *The Wall Street Journal,* October 18, 2023, https://www.wsj.com/world/middle-east/israel-tries-to-back-up-claims-it-didnt-attack-gaza-hospital-a8cc3405.

16 "Editors' Note: Gaza Hospital Coverage," *New York Times,* October 23, 2023, https://www.nytimes.com/2023/10/23/pageoneplus/editors-note-gaza-hospital-coverage.html.

17 David Alexander, "Israel tried to limit civilian casualties in Gaza—U.S. military chief," Reuters, November 6, 2014, https://www.reuters.com/article/uk-israel-usa-gaza-idUKKBN0IQ2LB20141107.

18 *Colonel Richard Kemp,* "UK Commander Challenges Goldstone Report—UN Watch Oral Statement," UN Human Rights Council: 12th Special Session, UN Watch, October 16, 2009, https://unwatch.org/dramatic-u-n-testimony-uk-commander-challenges-goldstone-report/.

19 Tom Segev, *One Palestine, Complete: Jews and Arabs Under the British Mandate* (New York: Macmillan Publishers, 2001), p. 212.

20 Ehud Olmert, *B'Goof Rishon* ("In Person") (Rishon LeZion: Miskal—Yedioth Ahronoth Books and Chemed Books, 2018), p. 336.

21 See, e.g., Stefan Arestis, "Top 20 gay vacation spots in the world," *Nomadic Boys,* July 9, 2024, https://nomadicboys.com/best-gay-vacation-spots/.

22 "Gay Palestinian Ahmad Abu Marhia beheaded in West Bank," BBC, October 7, 2022, https://www.bbc.com/news/world-middle-east-63174835.

23 Rothna Begum, "The Deadly Toll for Palestinian Women," *The New Arab,* September 19, 2019, https://www.hrw.org/news/2019/09/19/deadly-toll-palestinian-women.

24 Office of Rep. Jim Jordan (R-OH), "Jordan statement on Security Council resolution on Israel," December 23, 2016, https://www.legistorm.com/stormfeed/view_rss/957567/member/846/title/jordan-statement-on-security-council-resolution-on-israel.html.

25 "Bernie Sanders on NATO," *Feel The Bern,* https://feelthebern.org/bernie-sanders-on-nato/.

26 Hanna Trudo, "Progressive Caucus withdraws letter on Ukraine strategy amid blowback," *The Hill,* October 25, 2022, https://thehill.com/homenews/house/3703331-progressive-caucus-withdraws-letter-on-ukraine-strategy-amid-blowback/.

27 Vice President Kamala Harris, "Remarks by Vice President Harris on the Conflict Between Israel and Hamas," White House website, December 02, 2023, https://www.whitehouse.gov/briefing-room/speeches-remarks/2023/12/02/remarks-by-vice-president-harris-on-the-conflict-between-israel-and-hamas/.

28 *Yediot Achronot Hamosaf Leshabbat,* May 31, 2024, p. 15; Jessica Kiang, "'Sabaya' Review: Devastating Doc on the Frontline Fight to Rescue Women and Girls From ISIS Slavery," *Variety,* February 2, 2021, https://variety.com/2021/film/reviews/sabaya-review-1234893481/.

29 Michael Moore, "Tax Day in America....Time to Fund the Killing of More Palestinians!," *Michael Moore* (podcast), May 18, 2021, https://michaelmoorepodcast.com/episode/tax-day-in-america-time-to-fund-the-killing-of-more-palestinians/.

30 "Monstrous dose of reality | Susan Sontag on 9/11," *Biblioklept* (blog), September 11, 2021, https://biblioklept.org/2021/09/11/monstrous-dose-of-reality-susan-sontag-on-9-11/.

31 Alan Dershowitz, *The Case Against Israel's Enemies* (Hoboken: John Wiley & Sons, Inc., 2008), p. 105, quoting *La Jornada* (Mexico), September 15, 2001.

32 David L. Graizbord, "Israel's mosaic of Jewish ethnic groups is key to understanding the country," *The Conversation,* November 30, 2023, https://theconversation.com/israels-mosaic-of-jewish-ethnic-groups-is-key-to-understanding-the-country-217893.

II. Jimmy Carter—The Phenomenon in the Flesh

1 Napoléon Bonaparte Quotes, *GoodReads,* https://www.goodreads.com/quotes/753029-to-understand-the-man-you-have-to-know-what-was.

2 *The New York Times Book Review,* January 7, 2007, p. 25.

3 *The New York Times,* December 7, 2006, p. A35.

4 Jimmy Carter, *Palestine: Peace not Apartheid* (New York: Simon & Schuster, 2006), p. 59.

5 *Milkhemet Sheshet Hayamim, Sikum Seminar "Sugyot B'Bitakhon Yisrael" 1996* ("The Six Day War, Summary of the Seminar 'Topics on Defense', 1996") (Israel: Efi Meltzer, Ltd., 1996), p. 53; Abba Eban, *Personal Witness: Israel Through My Eyes* (New York: G.P. Putnam's Sons, 1992), p. 409.

6 Carter, *Palestine Peace not Apartheid,* pp. 148 and 152.

7 Dennis Ross, *The Missing Peace: The Inside Story of the fight for Middle East Peace* (New York: Farrar, Straus & Giroux, 2005), pp. 754-755.

Endnotes

8   *The New York Times*, January 12, 2007, p. A16; Ross, *The Missing Peace*, map in the first section of the book, on an unnumbered page.

9   UN Secretary-General, *Report of the Secretary-General on the Implementation of Security Council Resolutions 425 (1978) and 426 (1978)*, S/2000/460, New York, NY: UN Headquarters, May 22, 2000, p. 3, https://digitallibrary.un.org/record/416349?ln=en&v=pdf.

10 James Kanter and Jodi Rudoren, "European Union Adds Military Wing of Hezbollah to List of Terrorist Organizations," *New York Times*, July 22, 2013, https://www.nytimes.com/2013/07/23/world/middleeast/european-union-adds-hezbollah-wing-to-terror-list.html.

11 Carter, *Peace, Not Apartheid*, pp. 71 and 98.

12 Carter, *Peace, Not Apartheid*, pp. 254 and 256.

13 Dershowitz, *The Case Against*, p. 29.

14 Jimmy Carter, *A Full Life: Reflections at Ninety* (New York: Simon & Schuster, 2015), p. 3.

15 *Id.* p. 4.

16 *Id.* pp. 4-5.

17 *Id.* p. 4.

18 *Id.* p. 24.

19 Jonathan Alter, *His Very Best: Jimmy Carter, A Life* (New York: Simon & Schuster, 2020), p. 36.

20 *Id.* pp. 34-35.

21 *Id.* p. 46.

22 *Id.* p. 108.

23 *Id.* p. 128.

24 *Id.* p. 131.

25 *Id.* p. 163.

26 *Id.* p. 166.

27 *The Wall Street Journal*, September 19-20, 2020, p. C4.

28 Dennis Ross, *Doomed to Succeed: The U.S.-Israel Relationship from Truman to Obama* (New York: Farrar, Straus & Giroux, 2015), pps. 176-177.

29 Riad, pp. 90-91; U.S. Department of State Archive, https://2001-2009.state.gov/r/pa/ho/frus/johnsonlb/xx/2673.htm.

30 *The New York Times*, November 21, 1977, p. 17.

31 Mohamed Ibrahim Kamel, *The Camp David Accords* (London: KPI Ltd., 1986), p. 126.

32 Ezer Weizman, *The Battle for Peace* (New York: Bantam Books, 1981), p. 299.

33 William Quandt, *Camp David: Peacemaking and Politics* (The Brookings Institution, Washington, D.C., 1986), p. 177.

34 Kamel, *The Camp David Accords*, p. 296.

35 Moshe Dayan, *Breakthrough: A Personal Account of the Egypt-Israel Peace Negotiations* (New York: Alfred A. Knopf, 1981), pp. 161 and 163.

36 Kamel, *The Camp David Accords*, p. 270.

37 Kamel, *The Camp David Accords*, p. 149.

38 Kamel, *The Camp David Accords*, pp. 216-217.

39 Kamel, *The Camp David Accords*, pp. 368.

40 Dayan, *Breakthrough*, pp. 187-188.

41 Quandt, *Camp David*, p. 204.

42 William Safire, *Safire's Washington* (New York: Times Books, 1980), p. 319.

43 Jimmy Carter, *White House Diary* (New York: Farrar Straus & Giroux, 2010), p. 218.

44 Carter, *White House Diary*, p. 231.

45 *Yediot Achronot, 7 Yamim*, November 11, 2023, pp. 20 and 22.

46 Shlomi Eldar, *Lehakir et Hamas* ("Getting to Know Hamas") (Jerusalem: Keter Books, 2012), P. 281.

47 *Yediot Achronot, 7 Yamim*, March 1, 2024, p. 26.

48 Jim Michaels, "Jimmy Carter calls for recognizing terror group Hamas," *USA Today*, August 5, 2014, https://www.usatoday.com/story/news/world/2014/08/05/carter-israel-hamas/13640905/.

49 Dayan, *Breakthrough*, p. 177.

50 Quandt, *Camp David*, p. 31.

51 Carter, *Palestine: Peace not Apartheid*, pp. 27-28.

52 Segev, *One Palestine, Complete*, p. 142; David Fromkin, *A Peace to End all Peace: Creating the Modern Middle 1914-1922* (New York: Henry Holt & Company, 1989), p. 529.

53 Arthur James Balfour to Lord Rothschild, "Text of the Balfour Declaration," November 2, 1917, https://www.jewishvirtuallibrary.org/text-of-the-balfour-declaration.

54 "The Ogre of Land Speculation: The 1920 Ordinance," *The Palestine Post*, January 27, 1935, https://www.nli.org.il/en/newspapers/pls/1935/01/27/01/article/25/.

55 Moshe Aumann, "Land ownership in Palestine, 1880–1948," The Rohr Jewish Learning Institute, https://lessons.myjli.com/survival/index.php/2017/03/26/land-ownership-in-palestine-1880-1948/; *Palestine Royal Commission (i.e. Peel Commission) Report*, Chapter 9, July 7, 1937, https://www.jewishvirtuallibrary.org/text-of-the-peel-commission-report.

56 Edward Said, *The Question of Palestine* (New York: Vintage Books, 1979), pp. 65, 66, 74, 75 and 76-77.

57 Said, *The Question*, pp. 83 and 123.

58 Carter, *Palestine: Peace not Apartheid*, p. 62.

59 Carter, *Palestine: Peace not Apartheid*, p. 203.

60 Carter, *Palestine: Peace not Apartheid*, p. 15.

III. Bill Clinton, George Mitchell, and a Tale of Two Peace Processes

1 George Mitchell, *Making Peace* (New York: Alfred A. Knopf, 1999), p. 186.

2 Ross, *The Missing Peace*, pp. 100-101; Uri Savir, *The Process* (New York: Random House, 1998), p. 59; Yuval Bloomberg, *Malkodet Oslo* ("The Oslo Trap") (Israel: Sella-Meir Publishers, 2023), pp. 37-38.

3 *Ma'ariv Sofshavua*, May 9, 2003, p. 82.

4 Ross, *The Missing Peace*, pp. 120-121; Ronen Bergman, *V'Hareshut Nitna: Ayfo Ta'eenu? Kakh Hafkha Ha'Reshut Hafalestinit l'pas Yitzur shel Shekhitut V'Terror* ("And Permission was Given: Where Did we Go Wrong? How the Palestinian Authority became a production line for Corruption and Terrorism") (Tel Aviv: Miskal—Yediot Achronot and Chemed Books, 2002). p. 88.

5 Mitchell, *Making Peace*, pp. 17-18; The Joint Declaration of 15 December 1993 (Downing Street Declaration), paragraph 9.

6 Mitchell, *Making Peace*, p. 27.

7 Mitchell, *Making Peace*, pp. 35-36.

8 Ross, *The Missing Peace*, p. 118.

9 *Ma'ariv, Mosaf Chag,* September 27, 2002, p. 9; Bloomberg, *Malkodet Oslo,* p. 75.

10 *Ma'ariv, Sofshavua,* January 30, 2004, p. 40.

11 *Ma'ariv, Sofshavua,* January 30, 2004, p. 40.

12 Ross, *The Missing Peace*, p. 127.

13 Ami Ayalon, *Esh Kochotaynu* (Tel Aviv: Miskal-Yediot Achronot & Chemed Books, 2022), p. 113.

14 *Ha'aretz,* September 13, 2002, p. B4.

15 Ayalon, *Esh Kochotaynu,* pp. 111-112.

16 Ross, *The Missing Peace*, pp. 117-119; Amit Segal, *Sipuro Shel Hapolitika Hayisraelit* ("The Story of Israeli Politics") (Israel Amit Segal, Ltd., 2021), p. 150.

17 Ayalon, *Esh Kochotaynu,* p. 114.

18 Ross, *The Missing Peace*, p. 189.

19 Moshe Ya'alon, *Derekh Arukha K'tzara* ("The Longer Shorter Way") (Tel Aviv: Miskal-Yediot Achronot & Chemed Books, 2008), p. 82.

20 Mitchell, pp. 19-20.

21 Mitchell, pp. 41-42.

22 Mitchell, p. 48.

23 Mitchell, p. 134.

24 Mitchell, pp. 135-136.

25 Mitchell, p. 132.

26 Mitchell, p. 187.

27 Benjamin Netanyahu, *Bibi: My Story* (New York: Simon & Schuster, 2022), p. 258.

28 Shaul Mofaz, *Shaul Mofaz: Hamasa Hayisraeli Sheli* ("Shaul Mofaz: My Israeli Journey") (Tel Aviv: Miskal-Yediot Achronot & Chemed Books, 2022), p. 166.
29 Ayalon, *Esh Kochotaynu*, p. 149.
30 Ross, *The Missing Peace*, p. 267.
31 Ross, *The Missing Peace*, p. 449.
32 Ross, *The Missing Peace*, p. 350.
33 Netanyahu, *Bibi*, p. 291.
34 Netanyahu, *Bibi*, p. 307; Haggai Huberman, *Hanan Porat, Sipur Khayuv* ("Hanan Porat—Biography) (Tel Aviv: Miskal-Yediot Ahronot & Chemed Books, 2013), pp. 284-285.
35 Segal, *Sipuro Shel Hapolitika Hayisraelit*, p. 217.
36 Uri Avnery, *Optimi II*, ("Optimistic II") (Tel Aviv: Miskal-Yediot Achronot & Chemed Books, 2016), p. 495.
37 "Comprehensive Listing of Terrorism Victims in Israel (September 1993–Present)," Jewish Virtual Library, https://www.jewishvirtuallibrary.org/comprehensive-listing-of-terrorism-victims-in-israel.
38 Ross, *Missing Peace*, pp. 503 and 628-629.
39 Ya'alon, *Derekh Arukha K'tzara*, p. 89.
40 Ya'alon, *Derekh Arukha K'tzara*, p. 74.
41 Bloomberg, *Malkodet Oslo*, p. 80.
42 *Ha'aretz Magazine*, September 6, 2002, p. 21.
43 Ya'alon, *Derekh Arukha K'tzara*, p. 75.
44 Ya'alon, *Derekh Arukha K'tzara*, p. 80.
45 Ross, *Missing Peace*, p. 190.
46 Ross, *Missing Peace*, p. 620.
47 Ya'alon, *Derekh Arukha K'tzara*, p. 100.
48 Ross, *Missing Peace*, p. 688.
49 Ross, *Missing Peace*, p. 699.
50 Ross, *Missing Peace*, p. 705.
51 Rashid Khalidi, *The Hundred Years' War on Palestine* (New York: Metropolitan Books, 2020), p. 211.
52 Ross, *Missing Peace*, pp. 710-711.
53 "Case Dismissed," *Deutsche Welle*, October 10, 2008, https://www.dw.com/en/court-throws-out-restitution-claim-by-ethnic-germans/a-3703582; *The Wall Street Journal*, August 11, 2004.
54 Adi Schwartz and Einat Wilf, *Milkhemet Z'khut Hashiva* ("The War of the Right of Return") (Hevel Modi'in: Kinneret, Zmora-Bitan, Dvir, 2018), p. 183.
55 Schwartz and Wilf, *Milkhemet Z'khut Hashiva*, pp. 56, 77, and 176.
56 *Ma'ariv, Mosaf Shabbat*, November 30, 2007, p. 3.
57 *Yediot Achronot, Hamosaf L'Shabbat*, October 23, 2020, p. 11.

Endnotes

58 *Yediot Achronot, Hamosaf L'Shabbat,* March 3, 2006, p. 11.

59 Ross, *Missing Peace,* p. 730.

60 Ross, *Missing Peace,* p. 729.

61 Ya'alon, *Derekh Arukha K'tzara,* p. 102.

62 "The Sharm el-Sheikh agreement," BBC News, October 17, 2000, http://news.bbc.co.uk/2/hi/middle_east/976760.stm.

63 *Sharm El-Sheikh Fact-Finding Committee Report ("The Mitchell Report"),* United Nations website, April 30, 2001, p. 3, https://www.un.org/unispal/document/auto-insert-200482/.

64 *Mitchell Report,* p. 2.

65 *See, e.g.,* Khalidi, *The Hundred Years' War,* pp. 207-209.

IV. Thus Spake Obama

1 Bloomberg, *Malkodet Oslo,* p. 79.

2 Joshua 10:12-13, New King James Version.

3 Steve Law, "Is This Solar Eclipse Really Joshua's Miracle?," *Patterns of Evidence,* November 10, 2017, https://www.patternsofevidence.com/2017/11/10/is-this-solar-eclipse-really-joshuas-miracle/.

4 *Akhbar al-Yom,* October 11, 1947; David Barnett and Efraim Karsh, "Azzam's Genocidal Threat," *Middle East Forum,* Volume 18: Number 4, meforum.org/3082/Azzam-genocide-threat; David G. Dalin and John F. Rothmann, *Icon of Evil: Hitler's Mufti and the Rise of Radical Islam* (Random House: New York, 2008), p. 5.

5 Huberman, *Hanan Porat,* pp. 11-12.

6 Huberman, *Hanan Porat,* p. 28

7 Segal, *Sipuro Shel Hapolitika Hayisraelit,* p. 75.

8 Neumark, *Mishtar H'Neo-Baath B'Suriya, 1966–1970, Politika U'Mediniut* ("The Neo-Baath Regime in Syria, 1966–1970: Politics and Policy") (Bar-Ilan University Press: Ramat Gan, 2002) pp. 146-147.

9 Huberman, *Hanan Porat,* pp. 33-34.

10 *Convention (IV) relative to the Protection of Civilian Persons in Time of War. Geneva, Part 1, Article 2,* August 12, 1949, https://ihl-databases.icrc.org/en/ihl-treaties/gciv-1949/article-2?activeTab=.

11 David A. Korn, *Stalemate: The War of Attrition and Great Power Diplomacy in the Middle East, 1967-1970* (Westview Press: Boulder, 1992), pp. 33-34.

12 Aaron David Miller, "Why the Oslo Peace Process Failed," *Foreign Policy,* September 13, 2023, https://foreignpolicy.com/2023/09/13/oslo-accords-1993-anniversary-israel-palestine-peace-process-lessons/.

13 Akiva Eldar and Idith Zertal, *Adonay Ha'aretz* ("Masters of the Land") (Kinneret, Zmora-Bitan: Dvir Publishing House, Ltd., Or Yehuda, 2004), pp. 218-219, 238.

14 Eldar and Zertal, *Adonay Ha'aretz,* p. 239.

15 Eldar and Zertal, *Adonay Ha'aretz*, p. 183.
16 Ross, *Missing Peace,* p. 717; George Mitchell and Alon Sachar, *A Path to Peace* (Simon & Schuster: New York, 2016), p. 134.
17 Segal, *Sipuro Shel Hapolitika Hayisraelit*, p. 177.
18 Ross, *Missing Peace,* p. 679.
19 Author's notes; Olmert, *B'Goof Rishon,* p. 814.
20 *Ma'ariv Erev Rosh Hashana*, September 6, 2002, p. 11; *Ma'ariv Mosaf Shabbat,* June 20, 2003, p. 2.
21 Dov Weissglas, *Arik Sharon Rosh Memshala: Mabat Ishi* ("Arik Sharon Prime Minister: A Personal Look") (Israel: Miskal-Yediot Achronot & Chemed Books, 2012), p. 176, 182, and 208.
22 Weissglas, *Arik Sharon,* p. 232.
23 "President George Bush to Prime Minister Ariel Sharon," White House website, April 14, 2004, https://georgewbush-whitehouse.archives.gov/news/releases/2004/04/20040414-3.html.
24 Barack Obama, *A Promised Land,* (New York: Crown, 2020), p. 632.
25 Netanyahu, *Bibi,* pp. 420-423.
26 Bill Clinton, *Hard Choices* (New York: Simon & Schuster, 2014), p. 316.
27 "Netanyahu: Obama threatened me, made 'slitting throat' gestures," *Al Mayadeen English* (Source: Israeli media), October 17, 2022, https://english.almayadeen.net/news/politics/netanyahu:-obama-threatened-me-made-slitting-throat-gestures.
28 David Axelrod, *Believer: My Forty Years in Politics* (New York: Penguin Press, 2015), p. 446.
29 Obama, *A Promised Land*, pp. 631-632.
30 Obama, *A Promised Land,* p. 633.
31 *Yediot Achronot, Hamosaf LeShabbat,* August 31, 2012, p. 9.
32 Netanyahu, *Bibi,* p. 456.
33 Netanyahu, *Bibi,* p. 459.
34 Netanyahu, *Bibi,* pp. 461 and 477.
35 Netanyahu, *Bibi,* p. 504.
36 *The Good Friday Agreement—Policing and Justice, BBC,* https://www.bbc.co.uk/northernireland/schools/agreement/policing/prisoners2.shtml.
37 Netanyahu, *Bibi,* p. 518.
38 Netanyahu, *Bibi,* pp. 507-508; *The New York Times,* December 24, 2014, p. A19.
39 Allison Kaplan Sommer, "Obama: Peres Understood the Jewish People 'Were Not Born to Rule Another,'" *Haaretz,* September 30, 2016, https://www.haaretz.com/israel-news/2016-09-30/ty-article/obama-peres-understood-the-jewish-people-were-not-born-to-rule-another/0000017f-dc8c-df9c-a17f-fe9ccfca0000.
40 Rhodes, *The World,* p. 202.
41 Rhodes, *The World,* p. xvi.

Endnotes

V. Cognitive Dissonance: The Tragedy of the Israeli Left

1 *The New York Times*, January 14, 2023, p. A20.
2 Festinger, Rieken and Schachter, *When Prophecy Fails*, pp. 29-30.
3 Festinger, Rieken and Schachter, *When Prophecy Fails*, pp. 150-151.
4 Festinger, Rieken and Schachter, *When Prophecy Fails*, p. 25.
5 Festinger, Rieken and Schachter, *When Prophecy Fails*, pp. 7-8.
6 Barbara Tuchman, *The March of Folly: From Troy to Vietnam* (New York: Alfred A. Knopf, 1984), p. 4.
7 Tuchman, *The March of Folly*, p. 33.
8 Bloomberg, *Malkodet Oslo*, pp. 159-160.
9 Bloomberg, *Malkodet Oslo*, p. 102.
10 *Yediot Achronot*, April 25, 2003, p. 2.
11 *Ma'ariv Sofshavua*, April 25, 2003, p. 38.
12 Bloomberg, *Malkodet Oslo*, pp. 98-99 and 514.
13 *Ma'ariv Sofshavua*, June 21, 2002, p. 18.
14 *Ha'aretz Magazine*, November 12, 2004, p. 6.
15 *Ha'aretz Magazine*, November 12, 2004, pp. 7-8.
16 "Clinton says if Rabin had lived, Israelis and Palestinians would have peace," i24 News, March 11, 2017, https://www.i24news.tv/en/news/international/americas/139810-170311-clinton-says-if-rabin-had-lived-israelis-and-palestinians-would-have-peace; author's notes.
17 Segal, *Sipuro Shel Hapolitika Hayisraelit*, p. 123.
18 Bloomberg, *Malkodet Oslo*, p. 176.
19 *Yediot Achronot, Hamosaf Leshabbat*, November 14, 2005, p. 19.
20 Netanyahu, *Bibi*, p. 244.
21 *Ha'aretz Magazine*, November 4, 2005, p. B2.
22 *Ma'ariv Sofshavua*, March 27, 2002, p. 5.
23 *Ma'ariv Mosaf Shabbat*, December 5, 2003, p. 3.
24 *Ha'aretz Magazine*, November 8, 2002, p. 13.
25 "GDP (current US$)—Israel," World Bank Group, https://data.worldbank.org/indicator/NY.GDP.MKTP.CD?locations=IL.
26 Dayan, *Breakthrough*, p. 193.
27 Weissglas, *Arik Sharon*, p. 189.
28 Netanyahu, *Bibi*, p. 429.
29 Mitchell and Sachar, *A Path to Peace*, p. 172.
30 Stuart Winer, "Haaretz in government crosshairs after publisher calls terrorists 'freedom fighters,'" *The Times of Israel*, October 31, 2024, https://www.timesofisrael.com/haaretz-in-government-crosshairs-after-publisher-calls-terrorists-freedom-fighters/.
31 Yemini, *Ta'asyat Hashkarim*, ("Industry of Lies") (Tel Aviv: Miskal—Yedioth Ahronoth Books and Chemed Books, 2014), pp. 292, 294-297.
32 Ayalon, *Esh Kochotaynu*, p. 185.

33 Segal, *Sipuro Shel Hapolitika Hayisraelit*, p. 115.
34 Netanyahu, *Bibi*, p. 336.

VI. The Anti-Israel Advocacy Group J Street

1 "75 best advertising quotes from industry rulers," August Communications, December 5, 2018, https://itsaugust.com/75-best-advertising-quotes-from-industry-rulers/.
2 Jeremy Ben-Ami, *A New Voice for Israel: Fighting for the Survival of the Jewish Nation* (New York: Palgrave Macmillan, 2011), p. 66.
3 *Id.* at 59 and 61.
4 *The New York Times*, March 25, 2019, p. D8.
5 *Id.* at 109.
6 *Id.* at 110.
7 *Id.* at 126.
8 *Id.* at 88.
9 *Id.* at 89.
10 *Israeli-Palestinian Interim Agreement on the West Bank and Gaza Strip, Article XI,* UN website, September 28, 1995, https://www.un.org/unispal/document/auto-insert-185434/.
11 *Israeli-Palestinian Interim Agreement on the West Bank and Gaza Strip, Article XXXI,* UN website, September 28, 1995, https://www.un.org/unispal/document/auto-insert-185434/.
12 Jeremy Ben-Ami, "On The Movement For Black Lives," J Street website, August 23, 2016, https://jstreet.org/movement-black-lives/.
13 "Trump's Golan Tweet is About Helping Netanyahu—Not Advancing US or Israeli Interests," J Street website, March 21, 2019, https://jstreet.org/press-releases/trumps-golan-tweet-is-about-helping-netanyahu-not-advancing-us-or-israeli-interests/#.Y5ansuzMKBs.
14 Sam Dagher, *Assad or We Burn the Country: How one Family's Lust for Power Destroyed Syria* (New York: Little, Brown & Company, 2019), p. 406.
15 "Don't Call J Street 'Anti-Israel,'" J Street website, May 1, 2009, https://jstreet.org/dont-call-j-street-antiisrael_1/.
16 Ben Smith, "Ackerman blasts J Street," *Politico*, January 25/2011, https://www.politico.com/blogs/ben-smith/2011/01/ackerman-blasts-j-street-032783.
17 Congress.gov, "S.1322 – 104th Congress (1995-1996): Jerusalem Embassy Act of 1995," October 13, 1995, https://www.congress.gov/bill/104th-congress/senate-bill/1322.
18 "US Closure Of Jerusalem Consulate is Another Blow to Diplomacy, Gift for Settlement Movement," J Street website, October 18, 2018, https://jstreet.org/policy/jerusalem/.
19 Netanyahu, *Bibi*, p. 633.
20 Netanyahu, *Bibi*, p. 632.

Endnotes

21 Josephine Franks, "10 predictions about the future that turned out to be very wrong," *Sky News*, January 2, 2023, https://news.sky.com/story/10-predictions-about-the-future-that-turned-out-to-be-very-wrong-12763530.

22 List25 Team, "25 Famous Predictions That Were Proven To Be Horribly Wrong," List25, July 20, 2024, https://list25.com/25-famous-predictions-that-were-proven-to-be-horribly-wrong/.

23 Izzat Tannous, *The Palestinians: Eyewitness History of Palestine Under British Mandate*, (I.G.T. Company, 1988), pp. 310-314; Bergman, *V'Hareshut*, pp. 59-60.

24 "News Roundup," J Street website, September 16, 2020, https://jstreet.org/news-roundups/news-roundup-for-september-16-2020/.

25 *UAE-Israel Comprehensive Economic Partnership Agreement*, United Arab Emirates Ministry of Economy, April 1st, 2023, https://www.moec.gov.ae/en/cepa_israel.

26 "Israeli-Arab Normalization and Advancing Israeli-Palestinian Conflict Resolution: Symposium Report and Compendium," December 19, 2022, https://jstreet.org/wp-content/uploads/2022/12/J-Street-Policy-Center-Symposium-Summary.pdf.

27 "A Saudi-Israeli Peace Deal? Who Wants What and Why," *The Washington Post*, October 9, 2023, https://www.washingtonpost.com/business/energy/2023/09/22/a-saudi-israeli-peace-deal-who-wants-what-and-why/9284a33c-595b-11ee-bf64-cd88fe7adc71_story.html.

28 "Issue Brief: Israel-Saudi Arabia Normalization Must Advance US & Regional Interests," August 15, 2023, https://jstreet.org/wp-content/uploads/2023/08/Issue-Brief-UPDATED_-Israel-Saudi-Arabia-Normalization-Must-Advance-US-Interests-081523-1.pdf.

29 See e.g., "J Street Welcomes State Department Condemnation Of Settlement Expansion, Urges Further Action," J Street website, October 26, 2021, https://jstreet.org/press-releases/j-street-welcomes-state-department-condemnation-of-settlement-expansion-urges-further-action/.

30 "President Biden Must Forcefully Oppose Netanyahu's Rafah Escalation Plans, Stress Unavoidable Consequences," J Street website, February 15, 2024, https://jstreet.org/press-releases/president-biden-must-forcefully-oppose-netanyahus-rafah-escalation-plans-stress-unavoidable-consequences/.

31 *The New York Times*, February 17, 2024, p. A9; Molly Redden, "Key Pro-Israel Group Reports Record Fundraising As It Targets The 'Squad,'" *Huffington Post*, February 1, 2024, https://www.huffpost.com/entry/aipac-fundraising-squad_n_65bbf3aee4b05c8779f860ad.

32 *The New York Times*, July 16, 2022, p. A15.

33 "J Street Dismayed By Vitriolic Attacks On New Human Rights Watch Report," J Street website, April 28, 2021, https://jstreet.org/press-releases/j-street-dismayed-by-vitriolic-attacks-on-new-human-rights-watch-report/#.Y_bnHuzMKBs.

34 Jeremy Ben-Ami, "J Street, Zionism And BDS," J Street website, September 3, 2022, https://jstreet.org/j-street-zionism-and-bds/#.Y_bbK-zMJDc; Ben-Ami, *A New Voice*, p. 159.

VII. Human Rights and Human Wrongs

1 US Department of Defense, *Law of War Manual*, June, 2015, https://dod.defense.gov/Portals/1/Documents/pubs/Law-of-War-Manual-june-2015.pdf.

2 Tim Lister, Clarissa Ward, and Sebastian Shukla, "Russian opposition leader Alexey Navalny dupes spy into revealing how he was poisoned," CNN, December 21, 2020, https://www.cnn.com/2020/12/21/europe/russia-navalny-poisoning-underpants-ward/index.html.

3 "Alexei Navalny: Report names 'Russian agents' in poisoning case," BBC, December 14, 2020, https://www.bbc.com/news/world-europe-55303703.

4 Guy Faulconbridge, "Russian opposition leader Navalny moved to high-security penal colony," Reuters, June 14, 2022, https://www.reuters.com/world/europe/jailed-kremlin-critic-navalny-transferred-unknown-location-2022-06-14/; *The New York Times*, March 3, 2024, p. 1.

5 Lucy Papachristou, "What we know about Alexei Navalny's death in Arctic prison," Reuters, February 19, 2024, https://www.reuters.com/world/europe/alexei-navalnys-death-what-do-we-know-2024-02-18/.

6 "Explainer: What Defines A Political Prisoner?," Radio Free Europe/Radio Liberty, January 23, 2013, https://www.rferl.org/a/explainer-political-prisoners/24881810.html.

7 "Prisoners of Conscience," Amnesty International USA, https://bidenhumanrightspriorities.amnestyusa.org/prisoners-of-conscience/.

8 Sarah Rainsford, "Amnesty strips Alexei Navalny of 'prisoner of conscience' status," *BBC*, February 24, 2021, https://www.bbc.com/news/world-europe-56181084.

9 "Amnesty International statement on Aleksei Navalny," Amnesty International, February 25, 2021, https://www.amnesty.org/en/latest/news/2021/02/aleksei-navalny-prisoner-of-conscience/; "Statement on Alexei Navalny's status as Prisoner of Conscience," Amnesty International, May 7, 2021, https://www.amnesty.org/en/latest/press-release/2021/05/statement-on-alexei-navalnys-status-as-prisoner-of-conscience/.

10 "Who We Are," Amnesty International, https://www.amnesty.org/en/about-us/.

Endnotes

11 Gerald M. Steinberg, "Abusing the Legacy of the Holocaust: The Role of NGOs in Exploiting Human Rights to Demonize Israel," *Jewish Political Studies Review* 16:3-4 (Fall 2004).

12 "Our Finances," Amnesty International, https://www.amnesty.org/en/about-us/finances-and-pay/.

13 "Our Finances," Amnesty.

14 "Financier Soros Gives $100 Million To Human Rights Watch," Radio Free Europe/Radio Liberty, September 08, 2010, https://www.rferl.org/a/Financer_Soros_Gives_100_Million_To_Human_Rights_Watch/2151959.html.

15 Benjamin Weinthal, "Human Rights Watch under fire for allegedly accepting millions in Qatar funds," i24 News, November 23, 2023, https://www.i24news.tv/en/news/middle-east/1700763578-human-rights-watch-under-fire-for-allegedly-accepting-millions-in-qatar-funds; Alex Emmon s, "Human Rights Watch Took Money From Saudi Businessman After Documenting His Coercive labor Practices," *The Intercept*, March 2, 2020, https://theintercept.com/2020/03/02/human-rights-watch-took-money-from-saudi-businessman-after-documenting-his-coercive-labor-practices/.

16 Hillel Neuer, "UN-Hijack Human Rights," in *Jewish Priorities: Sixty-Five Proposals for the Future of Our People*, ed. David Hazony, (Nashville: Post Hill Press, 2023), p. 252.

17 *The New York Times*, February 16, 1979, p. A27.

18 Amir Taheri, *The Spirit of Allah: Khomeini & the Islamic Revolution* (Bethesda: Adler & Adler, 1986), p. 117.

19 Hillel Neuer, "How the Human-Rights Industry Became Obsessed with Israel," *Tikvah* (Podcast), January 18, 2024, https://sites.libsyn.com/58385/hillel-neuer-on-how-the-human-rights-industry-became-obsessed-with-israel.

20 *The New York Times*, October 20, 2009, p. A31.

21 Steinberg, "Abusing the Legacy of the Holocaust: The Role of NGOs in Exploiting Human Rights to Demonize Israel."

22 Gerald Steinberg, "Foreign-Funded NGOs, Political Power, and Democratic Legitimacy," *Lawfare*, June 24, 2018, https://www.lawfaremedia.org/article/foreign-funded-ngos-political-power-and-democratic-legitimacy.

23 *Yediot Achronot, Hamosaf Leshabat*, November 24, 2017, p. 13.

24 Colleen Long, Zeke Miller, and Aamer Madhani, "Biden sanctions Israeli settlers accused of attacking Palestinians and peace activists in West Bank," AP News, February 1, 2024, https://apnews.com/article/biden-west-bank-israeli-settlers-palestinians-80f9e6be6f6a7bb75dc86360ac2fa6ce.

25 *Yediot Achronot, 7 Yamim*, June 28, 2024, p. 30.

26 Steinberg, "Foreign-Funded NGOs."

27 Amnesty International, Israel's Apartheid Against Palestinians: Cruel System of Domination and Crime Against Humanity (London: Amnesty International Ltd., 2022), p. 12.
28 Segal, *Sipuro Shel Hapolitika Hayisraelit*, p. 23.
29 Segal, *Sipuro Shel Hapolitika Hayisraelit*, pp. 18 and 32.
30 *Yediot Achronot, Hamosaf LeShabat*, December 6, 2002, p. 11.
31 *Yediot Achronot, Hamosaf LeShabat*, May 14, 2010, p. 6.
32 *Yediot Achronot, Hamosaf LeShabat*, February 20, 2009, p. 12.
33 Amnesty International, *Israel's Apartheid Against Palestinians*, p. 29.
34 Amnesty International, *Israel and The Occupied Territories/Palestinian Authority, The Right to Return: The Case of the Palestinians, Policy Statement*, March 2001, https://www.amnesty.org/en/wp-content/uploads/2021/06/mde150132001en.pdf.
35 Harrison E. Salisbury, *The 900 Days: The Siege of Leningrad*, (New York: Avon Books, 1969), pp. 366-367.
36 François-Xavier Nérard, "The siege of Leningrad (1941-1944)," Digital Encyclopedia Of European History, June 20, 2022, https://ehne.fr/en/node/12489.
37 "High Command Trial, The United States of America vs. Wilhelm von Leeb et al., US Military Tribunal Nuremberg, Judgment of 27 October 1948," *Trials of War Criminals Before the Nuremberg Military Tribunals, Vol. IX*, https://werle.rewi.hu-berlin.de/High%20Command%20Case.pdf, p.75.
38 Sir Arthur Harris, *Despatch on War Operations: 23rd February 1942 to 8th May 1945*, (London: Routledge, 1995), p. 44, https://a.co/d/8Fjk2EQ.
39 *United States v. Wilhem List, et al.*, Case 47, U.S. Military Tribunal, Nuremberg, 1948, p. 66.
40 Anya Wahal, "On International Treaties, the United States Refuses to Play Ball," Council on Foreign Relations blog, January 7, 2022, https://www.cfr.org/blog/international-treaties-united-states-refuses-play-ball.
41 *Protocol I of the Geneva Convention, Article 51(5)(b)*, https://ihl-databases.icrc.org/en/ihl-treaties/api-1977/article-51.
42 Final Report to the Prosecutor by the Committee Established to Review the NATO Bombing Campaign Against the Federal Republic of Yugoslavia, Sections 48 and 50.
43 Department of Defense Law of War Manual (2015), Sections 5.20.1 and 5.20.2.
44 Charlotte Alfred, "People Are Starving In An Iraqi City Surrounded By U.S.-Backed Forces," *Huffington Post*, April 29, 2016, https://www.huffpost.com/entry/fallujah-siege-starvation_n_57227a32e4b0b49df6aacbee.
45 Jeffrey Martini et al, *Operation Inherent Resolve*, Rand Corporation, October 17, 2022, p. 71.

46 Rand Corporation, *Operation Inherent Resolve*, p. 55.

47 Interview with Lieutenant Colonel Amos C. Fox.

48 Major Amos C. Fox, *The Mosul Study Group and the Lessons of the Battle of Mosul*, Land Warfare Paper 130, (The Association of the U.S. Army) (2020), pp. 7-8.

49 Rand Corporation, *Operation Inherent Resolve*, p. xiv.

50 Liam Collins and John Spencer, *Understanding Urban Warfare* (Hampshire: Howgate Publishing Ltd., 2022), p. 5.

51 Rand Corporation, *Operation Inherent Resolve*, p. 69.

52 Susannah George et al, "Mosul is a graveyard: Final IS battle kills 9,000 civilians," AP News, December 20, 2017, https://apnews.com/article/middle-east-only-on-ap-islamic-state-group-bbea7094fb954838a2fdc11278d65460.

53 Patrick Cockburn, "The massacre of Mosul: 40,000 feared dead in battle to take back city from Isis as scale of civilian casualties revealed," *The Independent*, July 19, 2017, https://www.independent.co.uk/news/world/middle-east/mosul-massacre-battle-isis-iraq-city-civilian-casualties-killed-deaths-fighting-forces-islamic-state-a7848781.html.

54 The Joint Doctrine & Concepts Center, Ministry of Defence, *The Joint Service Manual of the Law of Armed Conflict, JSP 383*, 2004, pp. 25-26, https://www.gov.uk/government/groups/development-concepts-and-doctrine-centre.

55 *The New York Times*, March 18, 2023, p. A5.

56 Congress.gov, "S.1610 – 107th Congress (2001-2002): American Servicemembers' Protection Act of 2001," November 1, 2001, https://www.congress.gov/bill/107th-congress/senate-bill/1610.

57 Gadi Bloom and Nir Hefez, *Haroeh, Sipur Chayav shel Ariel Sharon*, ("The Shepherd: The Life of Ariel Sharon"), (Rishon LeZion: Miskal—Yedioth Ahronoth Books, Tel Aviv: Chemed Books, 2005), p. 610.

58 Nahum Barnea, *Mas'otay im Pinkas*, ("My Travels with a Notebook"), (Rishon LeZion: Miskal—Yedioth Ahronoth Books and Tel Aviv: Chemed Books, 2008), p. 321.

59 Barnea, *Mas'otay im Pinkas*, p. 319. Secretary of Defense Jim Mattis, "Remarks at a Troop Event in Naval Base Kitsap, Washington," U.S. Department of Defense, August 9, 2017, https://www.defense.gov/News/Transcripts/Transcript/Article/1276693/remarks-by-secretary-mattis-at-a-troop-event-in-naval-base-kitsap-washington/.

60 *Jenin: IDF Military Operations: IX. Disproportionate and Indiscriminate Use Of Force Without Military Necessity By The IDF*, Human Rights Watch, May 2002, Vol. 14, No. 3 (E), https://www.hrw.org/reports/2002/israel3/israel0502-10.htm#P887_156446.

61 "Ukraine: Ukrainian fighting tactics endanger civilians," Amnesty International, August 4, 2022, https://www.amnesty.org/en/latest/news/2022/08/ukraine-ukrainian-fighting-tactics-endanger-civilians/.

62 Michael N. Schmitt, "The Expert Panel's Review of Amnesty International's Allegations of Ukrainian IHL Violations," The Lieber Institute for Law & Warfare at West Point, May 1, 2023, https://lieber.westpoint.edu/expert-panels-review-amnesty-internationals-ai-allegations-ukrainian-ihl-violations/.

63 Id.

64 The New York Times, April 28, 2023, p. A9.

VIII. Lies on The Prize: Mendacity and All Its Rewards

1 "The Nobel Peace Prize 1994," Press Release, Nobel Prize website, https://www.nobelprize.org/prizes/peace/1994/press-release/.

2 Bloomberg, Malkodet Oslo, p. 169.

3 Clyde Haberman, "Kidnapped soldier is killed as Israeli troops attempt rescue at captors' hideout," The New York Times, October 15, 1994, https://www.nytimes.com/1994/10/15/world/kidnapped-soldier-is-killed-as-israeli-troops-attempt-rescue-at-captors-hideout.html.

4 Jay Nordlinger, "The worst man ever to win the Nobel Peace Prize," The Times of Israel, March 31, 2012, https://www.timesofisrael.com/the-worst-man-ever-to-win-the-nobel-peace-prize/.

5 Dvora Waysman, "Kaare Kristiansen: A man of courage and conscience," The Jerusalem Post, September 14, 2021, https://www.jpost.com/international/kaare-kristiansen-a-man-of-courage-and-conscience-679475.

6 Bloomberg, Malkodet Oslo, p. 169.

7 Bloomberg, Malkodet Oslo, p. 314.

8 Waysman, "Kaare Kristiansen."

9 Thomas Friedman, From Beirut to Jerusalem (New York: Farrar Straus Giroux, 1989), p. 160.

10 The New York Times, September 26, 1982, p. 19.

11 Id.

12 The New York Times, September 20, 1982, p. 6.

13 The New York Times, September 26, 1982, p. 20.

14 "Thomas L. Friedman and Loren Jenkins of The New York Times and The Washington Post, (respectively)," The 1983 Pulitzer Prize Winner in International Reporting, The Pulitzer Prizes, https://www.pulitzer.org/winners/thomas-l-friedman-and-loren-jenkins.

15 "The George Polk Award: Past Winners," Long Island University, https://liu.edu/polk-awards/past-winners#1982.

16 Kahan Commission Report, Jewish Virtual Library, February 8, 1983, p. 2, https://www.jewishvirtuallibrary.org/the-kahan-commission-of-inquiry.

17 Kahan Commission Report, p. 46.

18 Kahan Commission Report, p. 43.

Endnotes

19 Robert D. McFadden, "William L. Calley Jr., Convicted in My Lai Massacre, Is Dead at 80," *The New York Times*, July 29, 2024, https://www.nytimes.com/2024/07/29/us/william-calley-dead.html?searchResultPosition=1; https://75.stripes.com/archives/my-lai-where-are-they-now

20 Friedman, *From Beirut to Jerusalem*, p. 163.

21 Weissglas, *Arik Sharon*, pp. 38-39.

22 Friedman *From Beirut to Jerusalem*, p. 164.

23 *Kahan Commission Report*, p. 45.

24 Weissglas, *Arik Sharon*, p. 39.

25 Friedman, *From Beirut to Jerusalem*, p. 391.

26 Michael Kinsley, *Please Don't Remain Calm* (New York: W.W. & Norton Company, 2008), pp. 180-183.

27 *The New York Times,* March 9, 2024, p. A1.

28 *Sharon v. Time, Inc.,* 599 F. Supp. 538, 543, (S.D.N.Y. 1984).

29 Sharon lost the libel case because he couldn't prove that *Time* ran the story with malice.

30 Richard Sandomir, "Ray Cave, Influential Time Magazine Editor, Is Dead at 91," *The New York Times*, August 21, 2020, https://www.nytimes.com/2020/08/21/business/media/ray-cave-dead.html.

31 David K. Shipler, *Arab and Jew: Wounded Spirits in a Promised Land* (New York: Times Books, 1986), p. 91.

32 Raphael Eitan, *Raful, Sipur shel Chayal* (Raful: A Soldier's Story) (Tel Aviv: Ma'ariv, 1985), pp. 163-164.

33 Shipler, *Arab and Jew*, p. 237.

34 "1987 Pulitzer Prizes—Journalism," The Pulitzer Prizes, https://www.pulitzer.org/prize-winners-by-year/1987.

35 "AI Awarded Nobel Peace Prize," *Amnesty International Newsletter*, November 1977, https://www.amnesty.org/fr/wp-content/uploads/2021/06/nws21011 1977en.pdf.

36 "Human Rights Watch Wins UN Prize," Human Rights Watch, November 26, 2008, https://www.hrw.org/news/2008/11/26/human-rights-watch-wins-un-prize.

37 "Israeli author David Grossman wins Man Booker International prize," *The Guardian*, June 14, 2017, https://www.theguardian.com/books/2017/jun/14/israeli-author-david-grossman-wins-man-booker-international-prize.

IX. Groucho Marx Journalism

1 *The New York Times,* March 27, 1964, p. 1.

2 Bloom and Hefetz, *Ha'Ro'eh*, pp. 717-723.

3 *Ma'ariv Sofshavua,* November 10, 2023, p. 35.

4 Weissglas, *Arik Sharon*, pp. 244-257.

5 Olmert, *B'Goof Rishon*, p. 619.

6 *Ma'ariv Mosaf Shabat*, January 14, 2005, p. 4.
7 Doron Sheffer, "Traveling to Gaza? Get a passport," *Ynet News*, September 21, 2005, https://www.ynetnews.com/articles/0,7340,L-3145224,00.html.
8 *Convention (IV) relative to the Protection of Civilian Persons in Time of War.*
9 *Convention (IV) respecting the Laws and Customs of War on Land and its annex: Regulations concerning the Laws and Customs of War on Land*, Article 42, The Hague, October 18, 1907, https://ihl-databases.icrc.org/en/ihl-treaties/hague-conv-iv-1907/regulations-art-42?activeTab=.
10 Weissglas, *Arik Sharon*, p. 225.
11 *The New York Times*, October 24, 2004, p. 11; Olmert, *B'Goof Rishon*, pp. 615-616.
12 Chris McGreal, "Israel hands settlements to Palestinians," *The Guardian*, September 11, 2005, https://www.theguardian.com/world/2005/sep/12/israel.
13 *The New York Times*, September 20, 2007, p. A12.
14 *The New York Times*, June 1, 2016, p. A6.
15 *The New York Times*, August 19, 2022, p. A7.
16 *The New York Times*, February 8, 2015, p. 6.
17 *The New York Times*, August 30, 2021, A6; see also *The New York Times*, February 24, 2021, p. A6.
18 *The New York Times*, June 5, 2022, p. A1.
19 *The New York Times*, March 19, 2019, p. A11; *The New York Times*, October 31, 2019, p. A8.
20 *The New York Times*, July 16, 2022, p. A8.
21 *The New York Times*, April 21, 2023, p. A4.
22 Interview on Israeli TV, author's notes.
23 *Yediot Achronot, Hamosaf LeShabat*, June 17, 2022, p. 22.
24 "Entrance of goods to Gaza via Kerem Shalom," Gisha website, December 26, 2023, https://gisha.org/en/entrance-of-goods-to-gaza-from-israel/.
25 *Hagar Shezaf*, "Israel Expands Number of Work Permits for Gazans," *Haaretz*, September 22, 2022, https://www.haaretz.com/israel-news/2022-09-22/ty-article/.premium/defense-ministry-expands-number-of-israeli-work-permits-for-gazans/00000183-6548-db87-a18f-67fc94e40000.
26 See, e.g., *The New York Times*, December 26, 2021, p. 4.
27 See, e.g., *The New York Times*, February 7, 2023, p. A5; October 26, 2022, p. A4.
28 *The New York Times*, December 26, 2021, p. 4.
29 "Hamas In Its Own Words," ADL website, January 10, 2024, https://www.adl.org/resources/blog/hamas-its-own-words.
30 Ambassador Mark A. Green, "Hamas: Words and Deeds...," The Wilson Center, October 24, 2023, https://www.wilsoncenter.org/blog-post/hamas-words-and-deeds.

Endnotes

31 "The Truth Is Hard" brand campaign for *New York Times*, Droga5, https://droga5.com/work/the-new-york-times-truth-is-worth-it/.

32 Alessandra Stanley, "A Terrorist, Plain-Spoken and Cold," *The New York Times*, April 18, 2010, https://www.nytimes.com/2010/04/19/arts/television/19mcveigh.html?searchResultPosition=5.

33 *The New York Times*, April 20, 2019, p. D6.

34 *The New York Times*, July 23, 2023, p. 8.

35 Jeremy Scahill et al, "Between the Hammer and the Anvil," *The Intercept*, February 28, 2024, https://theintercept.com/2024/02/28/new-york-times-anat-schwartz-october-7/.

36 Dionne Searcey, "They Ordered Her to Be a Suicide Bomber. She Had Another Idea," *The New York Times*, March 13, 2020, https://www.nytimes.com/2020/03/13/world/africa/Nigeria-Boko-Haram-bomber.html.

37 See, e.g., "U.S. Confirms Yemen Killing of Terrorist," *The New York Times*, February 7, 2020, p. A7.

38 "CNN anchor Amanpour apologizes for calling terror attack on Dee family a 'shootout,'" *The Times of Israel*, May 23, 2023, https://www.timesofisrael.com/cnn-anchor-amanpour-apologizes-for-calling-terror-attack-on-dee-family-a-shootout/.

39 Avnery, *Optimi II*, p. 64

40 Malin Fezehai, "The Disappeared Children of Israel," *The New York Times*, February 20, 2019, https://www.nytimes.com/2019/02/20/world/middleeast/israel-yemenite-children-affair.html?searchResultPosition=1.

41 See, e.g., *The Wall Street Journal*, April 16-17, 2022, p. A7.

42 Craig S. Smith, "Europeans Suggest Directing Aid to Abbas," *The New York Times*, February 24, 2006, https://www.nytimes.com/2006/02/24/world/europe/europeans-suggest-directing-aid-to-abbas.html.

43 Ross, *Missing Peace*, p. 624.

44 Olmert, *B'Guf Rishon*, pp. 833-834.

45 *The New York Times*, July 15, 2022, p. A16.

46 "Osama bin Laden v. the U.S.: Edicts and Statements," *PBS Frontline*, April 1995, https://www.pbs.org/wgbh/pages/frontline/shows/binladen/who/edicts.html.

47 *Ma'ariv Sofshavua*, January 5, 2024, p. 33.

48 *Ma'ariv Sofshavua*, March 17, 2023, p. 21.

49 *Yediot Achronot, Hamosaf LeShabat*, May 24, 2019, p. 13; *Yediot Achronot, Hamosaf LeShabat*, February 16, 2024, p. 15.

50 *Yediot Achronot, Hamosaf LeShabat*, May 24, 2019, p. 13on bar

51 Richard A. Posner, "Enlightened Despot," *The New Republic*, April 23, 2007, https://newrepublic.com/article/60919/enlightened-despot.

52 Segal, *Sipuro Shel Hapolitika Hayisraelit*, p. 148.

53 *Yediot Achronot, Hamosaf LeShabat*, April 28, 2023, p. 6.

54 *Ma'ariv Sofshavua*, October 27, 2023, p. 18.

55 *The New York Times*, March 9, 2023, p. A6.

56 *The New York Times*, March 9, 2023, p. A6.

57 *The New York Times*, January 15, 2023, p. 3.

58 *The New York Times*, January 13, 2023, p. A10.

59 *The New York Times*, July 31, 2023, p. A4.

60 *The New York Times*, December 18, 2022, p. 9.

61 *The New York Times*, April 26, 2023, p. A23.

62 *The New York Times*, February 21, 2023, p. A1.

63 *The New York Times*, February 21, 2023, p. A8.

64 *Ma'ariv Sofshavua*, March 17, 2023, p. 14.

65 "Quick to indict against ultra-Orthodox, not like the protesters against legal reform," *Walla*, https://news.walla.co.il/item/3592638.

66 *Ma'ariv Sofshavua*, March 10, 2023, p. 16.

67 *Ma Shekoreh*, July 21, 2024.

68 *Ma Shekoreh*, July 16, 2024.

69 *Yediot Achronot*, March 17, 2023, p. 4.

70 *Ma'ariv Sofshavua*, December 29, 2023, p. 20.

71 "Netanyahu criticizes reservist pilots' protests in new recordings," *The Jerusalem Post*, July 12, 2023, https://www.jpost.com/breaking-news/article-749810.

X. October Surprise

1 Golda Meir, *My Life* (New York: G.P. Putnam's Sons, 1975), p. 420.

2 Eitan Haver, *Hayom Tifrotz Milchama* ("Today War will Break Out") (Israel: Edanim, 1987), p. 98.

3 Ariel Sharon, *Warrior* (New York: Touchstone Books, 1989), p. 89.

4 Moshe Dayan, *Avnei Derech* ("Milestones") (Tel Aviv: Edanim & Dvir Publishers, 1976), p. 278.

5 David Ben-Gurion, *Israel: A Personal History* (New York: Funk & Wagnalls, Inc., 1971), p. 460; Sharon, *Warrior*, p. 87.

6 See N. Bar-Yaacov, *The Israel-Syria Armistice* (Tel Aviv: Magnes Press, 1967), p. 226.

7 United Nations Security Council (UNSC) S/3516, December 20, 1955.

8 Yehoshafat Harkabi, *Arab Strategies and Israel's Response* (New York: The Free Press, 1977), pp. 63-77.

9 Id. at 65.

10 Sharon, *Warrior*, p. 126; Dayan, *Avnei Derech*, p. 170.

11 Dayan, *Avnei Derech*, p. 142.

12 *Yediot Achronot Mosaf Leshabat*, October 20, 1989, pp. 4-5, 19.

13 Nissim Mishal, *V'Ayleh Shnot....50 L'Medinat Yisrael* ("And These were the Years....50 Years of the State of Israel") (Tel Aviv: Yediot Achronot, 1998), p. 212; *Yediot Achronot, Hamosaf Leshabat*, March 14, 2008, p. 14.

Endnotes

14 Eitan, *Raful, Sipur Shel Chayal*, p. 161.

15 *Ha'aretz*, August 21, 1987.

16 *Kahan Commission Report*, p. 11.

17 *Yediot Achronot*, June 12, 1983, p. 1.

18 Thomas L. Friedman, "Because We Could," *The New York Times*, June 4, 2003, https://www.nytimes.com/2003/06/04/opinion/because-we-could.html.

19 *Yediot Achronot, Hamosaf Leshabat*, August 3, 2007, p. 8.

20 *Ma'ariv, Sofshavua*, November 24, 2023, p. 14.

21 *Yediot Achronot, Hamosaf Leshabat*, August 3, 2007, p. 8.

22 Yehudah Schiff and Danny Dor, *Yisroel 50* ("Israel 50") (Israel: Galei Alpha, 1997), August 1968.

23 *Ma'ariv, Mosaf Shabat*, October 19, 2007, p. 5.

24 *Yediot Achronot, Hamosaf Leshabat*, June 27, 2008, p. 6

25 *Ma'ariv, Mosaf Shabat*, October 19, 2007, p. 5.

26 *Yediot Achronot, Hamosaf Leshabat*, p. 18.

27 *Ma'ariv, Mosaf Shabat*, March 20, 2009, p. 4.

28 *Yediot Achronot, Hamosaf Leshabat*, June 27, 2008, p. 7.

29 *Ma'ariv, Mosaf Shabbat*, October 19, 2007, p. 7.

30 Israel TV, July 4, 2011.

31 Olmert, *B'Goof Rishon*, p. 659.

32 Ronen Bergman, "Gilad Shalit and the Rising Price of an Israeli Life," *The New York Times*, November 9, 2011, https://www.nytimes.com/2011/11/13/magazine/gilad-shalit-and-the-cost-of-an-israeli-life.html.

33 *Yediot Achronot, 7 Yamim*, March 8, 2024, pp. 20-26.

34 *The Jewish Press*, October 21, 2011, p. 79.

35 Benjamin Netanyahu, *Terrorism: How the West Can Win* (New York: Farrar Straus & Giroux, 1986).

36 Netanyahu, *Bibi*, p. 481.

37 *Ma'ariv, Sofshavua*, February 16, 2024, p. 10.

38 *Yediot Achronot, 7 Yamim*, March 8, 2024, p. 22.

39 *Yediot Achronot, 7 Yamim*, June 6, 2005, p. 26; Zamir, p. 130.

40 *Ronen Bergman, "Operation Red Falcon," The Atavist Magazine, No. 47*, https://magazine.atavist.com/operation-red-falcon/.

41 *Ma'ariv, Sofshavua*, November 10, 2023, p. 13.

42 *Ma'ariv Sofshavua*, December 8, 2023, p. 24.

43 Author's notes.

44 *Ma'ariv, Sofshavua*, January 5, 2024, p. 21.

45 *Ha'aretz*, November 28, 2008, p. B2.

46 "Rocket & Mortar Attacks Against Israel by Date (2001-Present)," Jewish Virtual Library, https://www.jewishvirtuallibrary.org/palestinian-rocket-and-mortar-attacks-against-israel.

47 Olmert, *B'Goof Rishon,* p. 767.

48 Netanyahu, *Bibi,* pp. 492-493.

49 Netanyahu, *Bibi,* p. 521.

50 *Yediot Achronot, 7 Yamim,* December 8, 2023, p. 25.

51 Emanuel Fabian, "Israel okays 1,500 more entry permits for Gaza workers, bringing total to 17,000," *The Times of Israel*, September 22, 2022, https://www.timesofisrael.com/israel-okays-1500-more-entry-permits-for-gaza-workers-bringing-total-to-17000/.

52 Netanyahu, *Bibi,* pp. 492-493.

53 *Ma'ariv, Sofshavua,* December 22, 2023, pp. 24-25.

54 *Ma'ariv, Sofshavua,* October 20, 2023, p. 19.

55 *Yediot Achronot, 7 Yamim,* October 10, 2023, p. 18.

56 General Hayman talk in August 2023, *Mah Shekoreh,* January 25, 2024, video.

57 *Ma'ariv, Sofshavua,* September 29, 2023, p. 26.

58 Emanuel Fabian, "Israel okays 1,500 more entry permits," *The Times of Israel*, September 20, 2022, https://www.timesofisrael.com/israel-okays-1500-more-entry-permits-for-gaza-workers-bringing-total-to-17000/.

59 "Netanyahu announces advance in long-stalled plans to develop gas field off Gaza," *The Times of Israel*, June 18, 2023, https://www.timesofisrael.com/netanyahu-announces-advance-in-long-stalled-plans-to-develop-gas-field-off-gaza/.

60 *Ma'ariv, Sofshavua,* November 17, 2023, p. 13.

61 "Hamas Leader Abroad Khaled Mashal Rejects Accusations Of Transgressions Against Civilians On October 7 Attack," MEMRI TV, October 19, 2023, video, 6:02, https://www.memri.org/tv/hamas-leader-abroad-khaled-mashal-october-seven-israeli-civlians-no-apologies-hizbullah-arab-countries-do-more.

62 "Senior Hamas Official Ali Baraka: We Have Been Secretly Planning The Invasion For Two Years," MEMRI TV, October 11, 2023, video, 3:35, https://www.memri.org/reports/senior-hamas-official-ali-baraka-we-have-been-secretly-planning-invasion-two-years-russia.

63 *Ma'ariv, Sofshavua,* February 23, 2024, p. 11.

64 *Ma'ariv, Sofshavua,* February 23, 2024, p. 12.

65 *Yediot Achronot, 7 Yamim,* December 8, 2023, p. 24.

66 *Ma'ariv, Sofshavua,* March 8, 2024, p. 22.

67 *Yediot Achronot, Hamosaf Leshabat,* November 22, 2024, p. 7.

68 Lahav Harkov, "Analysis: Banning of Ben-Ari unprecedented and uneven," *The Jerusalem Post*, March 18, 2019, https://www.jpost.com/Israel-Elections/Analysis-Banning-of-Ben-Ari-unprecedented-and-uneven-583772.

69 "'Gaza is a bomb that will explode on us': Dr. Michael Ben Ari, predicted the attack in 2018 and was accused of racism," *Achshav 14*, October 24, 2023, YouTube video, 19:28, https://www.youtube.com/watch?v=MAiajn9AE-c.

Endnotes

70 Israel Channel 13 TV, February 25, 2024.

71 *Yediot Achronot, 7 Yamim,* December 8, 2023, p. 22.

72 *Ma'ariv, Sofshavua,* February 23, 2024, p. 13.

XI. The Gaza War

1 *Ma'ariv, Sofshavua,* February 23, 2024, p. 11.

2 Alistair Cooke, "Nixon, 'and the rest you know,'" in *Letter from America,* BBC Radio 4, August 9, 1974, 13:23, https://www.bbc.co.uk/sounds/play/p00ylk41.

3 Bill Hutchinson, "Israel-Hamas War: Timeline and key developments," ABC News, November 22, 2023, https://abcnews.go.com/International/time-line-surprise-rocket-attack-hamas-israel/story?id=103816006; "October 7: How Hamas Attacked Israel, Minute by Minute," *Haaretz,* https://www.haaretz.com/israel-news/2024-04-18/ty-article-static-ext/.premium/what-happened-on-oct-7/0000018e-c1b7-dc93-adce-eff753020000.

4 *Yediot Achronot, 7 Yamim,* March 1, 2024, p. 28.

5 *Yediot Achronot, 7 Yamim,* January 12, 2024, p. 46.

6 Roni Caryn Rabin, "Peace Activists Are Among the Israelis Missing and Killed," *The New York Times,* October 10, 2023, https://www.nytimes.com/2023/10/10/world/middleeast/peace-activists-killed-israel.html; "Canadian Israeli peace activist Vivian Silver, feared to be held hostage, confirmed killed in Hamas attacks," *CBC,* November 13, 2023, https://www.cbc.ca/news/canada/israel-gaza-vivian-silver-1.7027333; author's notes.

7 Yaniv Kubovich, "Israel Completes Vast, Billion-dollar Gaza Barrier," *Haaretz,* December 7, 2021, https://www.haaretz.com/israel-news/2021-12-07/ty-article/.premium/israel-completes-vast-billion-dollar-gaza-barrier/0000017f-ee2c-d4cd-af7f-ef7c25d40000.

8 Shira Silkoff, "Gaza fence was not designed to prevent mass assault on its own, builder said in 2018," *The Times of Israel,* October 19, 2023, https://www.timesofisrael.com/gaza-fence-was-not-designed-to-prevent-mass-assault-on-its-own-builder-said-in-2018/; *Yediot Achronot, 7 Yamim,* October 20, 2023, p. 16.

9 *Yediot Achronot, Hamosaf Leshabat,* March 1, 2024, p. 11.

10 Silkoff, "Gaza fence was not designed."

11 *Ma'ariv, Sofshavua,* November 10, 2023, p. 13; *Yediot Achronot, 7 Yamim,* December 1, 2023, p. 20.

12 *Yediot Achronot, 7 Yamim,* January 12, 2024, p. 24.

13 *Yediot Achronot, 7 Yamim,* October 20, 2023, pp. 17 and 19.

14 *Ma'ariv, Sofshavua,* November 17, 2023, p. 13.

15 *Yediot Achronot, 7 Yamim,* October 20, 2023, pp. 16-17.

16 *Yediot Achronot, 7 Yamim,* February 2, 2024, p. 26.

17 *Ma'ariv, Sofshavua,* January 19, 2024, p. 10.

18 *Ma'ariv, Sofshavua*, December 1, 2023, p. 7; Israel Channel 13 TV, October 13, 2024.

19 Israel Channel 13 TV, March 19, 2024.

20 Emanuel Fabian, "IDF says head of Israeli brigade on Gaza border was killed Oct 7, body held by Hamas," *The Times of Israel*, December 2, 2023, https://www.timesofisrael.com/idf-says-a-gaza-brigade-chief-was-killed-on-october-7-body-held-by-hamas/.

21 *Yediot Achronot, 7 Yamim*, October 20, 2023, p. 16.

22 *Yediot Achronot, 7 Yamim*, April 12, 2024, pp. 44-48.

23 Hans M. Kristensen and Matt Korda, *Israeli Nuclear Weapons, 2022, Bulletin of the Atomic Scientists*, 2022, Vol. 78, No. 1, p. 46, https://thebulletin.org/premium/2022-01/nuclear-notebook-israeli-nuclear-weapons-2022/.

24 "Israel social security data reveals true picture of Oct 7 deaths," *France 24*, December 15, 2023, https://www.france24.com/en/live-news/20231215-israel-social-security-data-reveals-true-picture-of-oct-7-deaths.

25 *Yediot Achronot, 7 Yamim*, March 15, 2024, p. 22.

26 *Yediot Achronot, 7 Yamim*, November 24, 2023, p. 24.

27 *The New York Times*, October 29, 2023, p. 21.

28 *The New York Times*, January 29, 2024, pp. 1 and 4.

29 "Rep. Elise Stefanik (R-NY) Questions University Presidents on Antisemitism," CSPAN, December 8, 2023, YouTube video, 3:34, https://www.youtube.com/watch?v=5VtAZBvmzcQ.

30 *Ma'ariv, Sofshavua*, November 10, 2023, p. 26.

31 *The New York Times*, October 11, 2023, p. A22.

32 "Israel: Palestinian armed groups must be held accountable for deliberate civilian killings, abductions and indiscriminate attacks," Amnesty International, October 12, 2023, https://www.amnesty.org/en/latest/news/2023/10/israel-palestinian-armed-groups-must-be-held-accountable-for-deliberate-civilian-killings-abductions-and-indiscriminate-attacks/.

33 "Israel/OPT: Urgent call for an immediate ceasefire by all parties to end unprecedented civilian suffering," Amnesty International, October 26, 2023, https://www.amnesty.org/en/latest/news/2023/10/israel-opt-urgent-call-for-an-immediate-ceasefire-by-all-parties-to-end-unprecedented-civilian-suffering/.

34 "Israel/Palestine: Devastating Civilian Toll as Parties Flout Legal Obligations," Human Rights Watch, October 9, 2023, https://www.hrw.org/news/2023/10/09/israel/palestine-devastating-civilian-toll-parties-flout-legal-obligations.

35 *Yediot Achronot, Hamosaf Leshabat*, March 8, 2024, p. 34.

36 "Me Too Unless You're a Jew," UN Watch, https://unwatch.org/un-women-looks-the-other-way-when-the-victims-are-israel/.

37 "Call for submissions on gender-based crimes since 7 October 2023,"
United Nations Human Rights Council, https://www.ohchr.org/en/
hr-bodies/hrc/co-israel/call-submissions-gender-based-crimes-7-Oc-
tober-2023; Macarena Sáez, "Investigating Sexual and Gender-Based
Violence in Conflict," Human Rights Watch, December 12, 2023, https://
www.hrw.org/news/2023/12/12/investigating-sexual-and-gender-based-
violence-conflict.

38 *Ma'ariv, Sofshavua,* March 29, 2024, p. 6; Emanuel Fabian, "In interro-
gation clip, captured terrorist confesses to raping Israeli woman on Oct.
7," *The Times of Israel,* March 28, 2024, https://www.timesofisrael.com/
in-interrogation-clip-captured-terrorist-confesses-to-raping-israeli-
woman-on-oct-7/.

39 *Mission report: Official visit of the Office of the SRSG-SVC to Israel and the
occupied West Bank,* Office of the Special Representative of the Secretary
General on Sexual Violence in Conflict, January 29–February 14, 2024,
https://www.un.org/sexualviolenceinconflict/wp-content/uploads/2024/
03/report/mission-report-official-visit-of-the-office-of-the-srsg-svc-
to-israel-and-the-occupied-west-bank-29-january-14-february-2024/
20240304-Israel-oWB-CRSV-report.pdf; *Yediot Achronot, Hamosaf Leshabat,* November 15, 2024, p. 14.

40 Search on "Rape" in Amnesty International reports, https://www.amnesty.
org/en/search/Rape/page/3/.

41 "Israel/OPT: Horrifying cases of torture and degrading treatment of Palestinian detainees amid spike in arbitrary arrests," Amnesty International,
November 8, 2023, https://www.amnesty.org/en/latest/news/2023/11/
israel-opt-horrifying-cases-of-torture-and-degrading-treatment-of-pales-
tinian-detainees-amid-spike-in-arbitrary-arrests/.

42 Jeffrey Gettleman, Adam Sella, and Anat Schwartz, "What We Know
About Sexual Violence During the Oct. 7 Attacks on Israel," *The New
York Times,* December 4, 2023, https://www.nytimes.com/2023/12/04/
world/middleeast/oct-7-attacks-israel-hamas-sexual-violence.html?
searchResultPosition=1.

43 Scahill, "Between the Hammer and the Anvil"; David Folkenflik, "Newsroom at 'New York Times' fractures over story on Hamas attacks,"
NPR, March 6, 2024, https://www.npr.org/2024/03/06/1236130609/
new-york-times-hamas-attacks-israel-palestine.

44 *The New York Times,* March 30, 2024, p. A6.

45 "Netanyahu: Israel wants to stave off 'humanitarian collapse' in Gaza,"
The Times of Israel, June 4, 2018, https://www.timesofisrael.com/netan-
yahu-israel-wants-to-stave-off-humanitarian-collapse-in-gaza/; *Ma'ariv,
Sofshavua,* March 22, 2024, p. 14.

46 *Yediot Achronot, Hamosaf Leshabat,* December 12, 2022, p. 5.

47 Mark Mazzetti and Ronan Bergman, "'Buying Quiet': Inside the Israeli Plan That Propped Up Hamas," *The New York Times*, December 10, 2023, https://www.nytimes.com/2023/12/10/world/middleeast/israel-qatar-money-prop-up-hamas.html?searchResultPosition=2; *The New York Times*, December 17, 2023, p. 1.
48 *Ma'ariv Sofshavua*, November 29, 2024, p. 29.
49 *Ma'ariv, Sofshavua*, January 5, 2024, p. 26.
50 Barak Ravid, "Scoop: Marine Corps 3-star general advising Israeli military on Gaza ground operation," *Axios*, Oct 23, 2023, https://www.axios.com/2023/10/23/israel-gaza-war-marine-general-ground-operation?stream=politics.
51 *Yediot Achronot, Hamosaf Leshabat*, February 16, 2024, p. 6.
52 *Ma'ariv, Sofshavua*, March 15, 2024, p. 12.
53 *Yediot Achronot, Hamosaf Leshabat*, March 29, 2024, p. 7.
54 *Yediot Achronot, 7 Yamim*, January 19, 2024, p. 18.
55 Israel Channel 13 TV, October 13, 2023.
56 *Ma'ariv, Sofshavua*, March 15, 2024, p. 21.
57 *Yediot Achronot, Mamone Shishi*, January 5, 2024, p. 6.
58 *Yediot Achronot, 7 Yamim*, March 15, 2024, p. 34.
59 MEMRI TV, Al-Aqsa TV (Hamas/Gaza), February 29, 2008.
60 Nan Jacques Zilberdik, "Hamas leader: 'We need the blood of the children, women, and elderly,'" Palestinian Media Watch, video, 1:10, December 11, 2023, https://palwatch.org/page/34835.
61 "Israel accuses Hamas of using over 100 women and children as human shields in Gaza," *The Times of Israel*, November 2, 2023, https://www.timesofisrael.com/israel-accuses-hamas-of-using-over-100-women-and-children-as-human-shields-in-gaza/.
62 *Ma'ariv*, April 21, 1996, p. 14; *Ma'ariv*, April 19, 1996, p. 2.
63 David Greene, "Caught on Tape: Bush's Blunt Diplomacy," Reporter's Notebook, NPR, July 18, 2006, https://www.npr.org/2006/07/18/5566122/caught-on-tape-bushs-blunt-diplomacy.
64 Abraham Wyner, "How the Gaza Ministry of Health Fakes Casualty Numbers," *Tablet*, March 6, 2024, https://www.tabletmag.com/sections/news/articles/how-gaza-health-ministry-fakes-casualty-numbers; Merlyn Thomas, "Israel Gaza: What Gaza's death toll says about the war, *BBC*, December 20, 2023, https://www.bbc.com/news/world-middle-east-67764664.
65 Samia Nakhoul, Jonathan Saul, and Humeyra Pamuk, "Rafah attack: How Israel plans to hit Hamas and scale back war," *Reuters*, February 19, 2024, https://www.reuters.com/world/middle-east/israels-six-week-drive-hit-hamas-rafah-scale-back-war-2024-02-19/; "Hamas Admits 600-700 of Its Men Were Killed in Cast Lead," *Haaretz*, November 9, 2010, https://www.haaretz.com/2010-11-09/ty-article/hamas-admits-600-700-of-its-men-were-killed-in-cast-lead/0000017f-ee02-ddba-a37f-ee6edc3f0000.

Endnotes

66 Wafaa Shurafa and Samy Magdy, "More than 29,000 Palestinians have been killed in Israel-Hamas war, Gaza Health Ministry says," AP News, February 19, 2024, https://apnews.com/article/israel-hamas-war-news-02-19-2024-81c2d362340b611a98e4b929b4b5d0a4.

67 Jane Prinsley, "BBC admits Hamas 'civilian' death reporting was inaccurate," *The Jewish Chronicle*, April 26, 2024, https://www.thejc.com/news/uk/bbc-admits-hamas-civilian-death-reporting-was-inaccurate-v5ol1jek.

68 BBC presenter Lucy Hockings to Nir Barkat, "Lawyers around the world want to put Israel in front of the Hague," *Middle East Eye*, November 25, 2023, YouTube video, 1:26, https://www.youtube.com/watch?v=96eFBD7ByZA.

69 Kayla Guo, "On Israel's War Against Hamas, Sanders Faces a Backlash From the Left, *The New York Times*, November 30, 2023, https://www.nytimes.com/2023/11/30/us/politics/bernie-sanders-israel-cease-fire.html.

70 Amanpour & Company, Channel 13 Television, July 3, 2024.

71 *The New York Times*, March 24, 2024, p. 25; "Fact Sheet: South Africa, Hamas, and the ICJ 'genocide' case against Israel," The Australia/Israel & Jewish Affairs Council, February 6, 2024, https://aijac.org.au/fact-sheets/factsheet-south-africa-hamas-and-the-icj-genocide-case-against-israel/.

72 Camilla Turner, "Britain's statistics watchdog to examine Hamas's Gaza death toll figures," *The Telegraph*, April 20, 2024, https://www.telegraph.co.uk/news/2024/04/20/statistics-watchdog-examine-hamas-gaza-death-toll-figures/; "Hamas-Run Gaza Health Ministry Admits to Flaws in Casualty Data," Foundation for Defense of Democracies, April 9, 2024, https://www.fdd.org/analysis/2024/04/09/hamas-run-gaza-health-ministry-admits-to-flaws-in-casualty-data/; David Adesnik, "Gaza Health Ministry Cannot Provide Names for More Than 10,000 It Says Have Died," Foundation for Defense of Democracies, May 2, 2024, https://www.fdd.org/analysis/2024/05/02/gaza-health-ministry-cannot-provide-names-for-more-than-10000-it-says-have-died/.

73 United Nations, "Daily Press Briefing by the Office of the Spokesperson for the Secretary-General," United Nations website, May 13, 2024, https://press.un.org/en/2024/db240513.doc.htm.

74 Abeer Salman et al, "UN says total number of deaths in Gaza remains unchanged after controversy over revised data," CNN, May 14, 2024, https://www.cnn.com/2024/05/13/middleeast/death-toll-gaza-fatalities-un-intl-latam/index.html.

75 Cheryl Levi, "What Rashida Tlaib knows, or how to win when you're losing," *The Times of Israel*, July 1, 2024, https://blogs.timesofisrael.com/drama-in-congress/.

76 Julian E. Barnes et al, "The Stark Reality of Israel's Fight in Gaza," *The New York Times*, April 22, 2024, https://www.nytimes.com/2024/04/22/us/politics/israel-gaza-hamas-war.html.

77 Katie Robertson, "*The New York Times* Wins 3 Polk Awards," *The New York Times*, February 19, 2024, https://www.nytimes.com/2024/02/19/business/media/polk-award-winners.html; "Israel decries top US award for Gazan NYT photographer, alleging he has Hamas ties," *The Times of Israel*, February 24, 2024, https://www.timesofisrael.com/israel-decries-top-us-award-for-gazan-nyt-photographer-with-alleged-hamas-ties/.

78 Israel Channel 13 TV, November 24, 2023; the story of the little girl was reported by Clarissa Ward on CBS Television on November 28, 2023.

79 Israel Channel 13 TV, November 23, 2023.

80 *The New York Times*, March 1, 2024, p. A18.

81 *Maariv Sofshavua*, May 17, 2024, p. 22.

82 Israel Channel 13 TV, March 22, 2024.

83 Israel Channel 13 TV, March 27, 2024.

84 *PBS News Hour*, November 13, 2023.

85 U.S. Central Command, "Coalition Strikes Mosul Hospital," December 8, 2016, https://www.centcom.mil/MEDIA/PRESS-RELEASES/Press-Release-View/Article/1023962/coalition-strikes-mosul-hospital/.

86 Barak Ravid, "Scoop: U.S. put a hold on an ammunition shipment to Israel," *Axios*, May 5, 2024, https://www.axios.com/2024/05/05/israel-us-ammunition-shipment-hold; Alon Ben-David, speaking on Israel Channel 13 Television, May 3, 2024.

87 Rachel Scott et al, "Harris says US has not ruled out 'consequences' if Israel invades Rafah," ABC News, March 24, 2024, https://abcnews.go.com/Politics/harris-us-ruled-consequences-israel-invades-rafah/story?id=108431225.

88 United Nations Security Council (UNSC) Res 2728 (March 25, 2024) UN Doc S/RES/2728.

89 Natalie Andrews, "Schumer Calls for End of Netanyahu-Led Government in Israel," *The Wall Street Journal*, March 14, 2024, https://www.wsj.com/politics/policy/schumer-calls-for-end-of-netanyahu-led-government-in-israel-ebcb15c1.

90 Yasmeen Abutaleb, "U.S. Cites Intelligence, offers Israel supplies to limit Rafah operation," *The Washington Post*, May 11, 2024, https://www.washingtonpost.com/politics/2024/05/11/us-israel-rafah-invasion-palestinians-evacuation/.

91 *The New York Times*, April 28, 2024, p. 5.

92 *The New York Times*, April 3, 2024, p. A7.

93 *Reuters*, April 8, 2024; Kelly Garrity, "Elizabeth Warren says she believes Israel's war in Gaza will legally be considered a genocide," *Politico*, April 8, 2024, https://www.politico.com/news/2024/04/08/israel-gaza-war-elizabeth-warren-00151120.

94 *The New York Times*, April 5, 2024, p. A1.

Endnotes

95 Chris Johnston, "MSF Afghanistan hospital airstrike death toll reaches 42," *The Guardian*, December 12, 2015, https://www.theguardian.com/world/2015/dec/12/msf-afghanistan-hospital-airstrike-death-toll-42.

96 Alissa J. Rubin, "Airstrike Hits Doctors Without Borders Hospital in Afghanistan," *The New York Times*, October 3, 2015, https://www.nytimes.com/2015/10/04/world/asia/afghanistan-bombing-hospital-doctors-without-borders-kunduz.html.

97 *The New York Times*, April 3, 2024, p. A1.

98 *The New York Times*, May 7, 2024, p. B6.

99 "May 6: Israel rejects Hamas truce terms but sending team to Cairo for fresh talks," *The Times of Israel*, May 6, 2024, https://www.timesofisrael.com/liveblog-may-6-2024/.

100 Israel Channel 13 TV, May 17, 2024.

101 *Ma'ariv Sofshavua*, June 21, 2024, p. 24.

102 Kat Lonsdorf, "Fact checking Netanyahu's claim that Rafah civilian casualties are 'practically none,'" NPR, July 25, 2024, https://www.npr.org/2024/07/25/nx-s1-5051749/fact-checking-netanyahus-claim-that-rafah-civilian-casualties-are-practically-none.

103 Emanuel Fabian, "IDF says 'increasing signs' indicate Hamas's Muhammad Deif was killed in Gaza strike," *The Times of Israel*, July 19, 2024, https://www.timesofisrael.com/idf-says-increasing-signs-indicate-hamass-muhammad-deif-was-killed-in-gaza-strike/.

104 *Yediot Achronot, Hamosaf Leshabat*, June 28, 2024, p. 4.

105 Julia Frankel And Drew Callister, "Israel's Netanyahu blames Biden for withholding weapons. US officials say that's not the whole story," AP News, June 18, 2024, https://apnews.com/article/israel-palestinians-hamas-war-news-06-18-2024-2a7aeb71867150c5a9d84ae57e2e7bf2.

106 "Netanyahu reiterates claim about U.S. withholding weapon shipments as Democrats grapple with attending his Congress address," CBS News, June 23, 2024, https://www.cbsnews.com/news/israel-prime-minister-benjamin-netanyahu-us-weapons-democrats-congress/.

107 Barak Ravid, "Scoop: U.S. to release part of suspended bomb shipment to Israel," *Axios*, June 27, 2024, https://www.axios.com/2024/06/27/us-israel-bombs-release-shipment-biden.

108 Israel Channel 14 TV, January 26, 2025.

109 Jeremy Ben-Ami, "Senators: As Friends of Israel, Vote To Disapprove What The Gaza War Has Become," Substack, November 17, 2024, https://jeremybenami.substack.com/p/disapproval.

110 "VP Kamala Harris makes public statement on Israel-Palestine conflict during Benjamin Netanyahu visit," WFAA, July 25, 2024, YouTube video, 6:07, https://www.youtube.com/watch?v=65LhA1APWZQ&list=RDNS65LhA1APWZQ&start_radio=1; Rebecca Shabad, Kelly

O'Donnell, and Zoë Richards, "Harris describes suffering in Gaza and need for a cease-fire deal after meeting with Netanyahu," NBC News, July 25, 2024, https://www.nbcnews.com/politics/white-house/biden-harris-meet-separately-netanyahu-white-house-rcna163590.

111 "Hamas said to reject proposal for hostage-ceasefire deal before receiving it," *The Times of Israel*, July 26, 2024, https://www.timesofisrael.com/hamas-said-to-reject-proposal-for-hostage-ceasefire-deal-before-receiving-it/.

112 "Bill Clinton talks war in Middle East," MLive, October 30, 2024, YouTube video, 1:24, https://www.youtube.com/watch?v=IPmO2PBlxkE.

113 Sanjana Karanth, "Bill Clinton Justifies The Mass Killings Of Palestinians In Racist Michigan Speech," HuffPost, November 1, 2024, https://www.yahoo.com/news/bill-clinton-justifies-mass-killings-000813500.html?guccounter=1.

114 Edith Olmsted, "Even Leon Panetta Says Israel's Pager Attack Is 'Terrorism,'" *The New Republic*, September 23, 2024, https://newrepublic.com/post/186244/leon-panetta-israel-lebanon-pagers-terrorism.

115 *Yediot Achronot*, September 20, 2024, p. 2.

116 Israel Channel 14 TV, December 8, 2024.

117 Ben Hubbard, "Yahya Sinwar, Leader of Hamas, Is Dead," *The New York Times*, October 17, 2024, https://www.nytimes.com/2024/10/17/world/middleeast/yahya-sinwar-dead.html?searchResultPosition=8.

118 "Trump says there will be 'all hell to pay' if Israeli hostages are not released by January," CBS Mornings, December 3, 2024, YouTube video, 0:59, https://www.youtube.com/watch?v=XCTPYslCJik.

XII. Coda

1 Ray Takeyh, Reuel Marc Gerecht, and Clifford D. May, "Iran's Road from Monarchy to Islamist Theocracy and Empire," *Foundation for Defense of Democracies* (podcast), February 11, 2021, https://www.fdd.org/podcasts/2021/02/11/irans-road-from-monarchy-to-islamist-theocracy-and-empire/.

2 Lily Ford, "Eurovision Analysis: The Takeaways From Voting Results as Chaos Lingers," *The Hollywood Reporter*, May 14, 2024, https://www.hollywoodreporter.com/news/music-news/eurovision-2024-voting-results-analysis-switzerland-croatia-israel-1235897378/.

3 *Real Time With Bill Maher*, HBO, March 10, 2024.

4 Takeyh, Gerecht, and May, "Iran's Road from Monarchy to Islamist Theocracy."

5 Taheri, *The Spirit of Allah*, pp. 32-35.

6 Taheri, *The Spirit of Allah*, p. 131.

7 Taheri, *The Spirit of Allah*, pp. 75 and 91.

Endnotes

8 Vali Nasr, *The Shia Revival* (New York: W.W. Norton & Company, 2006), p. 137.

9 Nasr, *The Shia Revival*, p. 120.

10 Nasr, *The Shia Revival*, p. 134.

11 A. William Samii, "Iranian Attitudes toward the Kosovo Crisis," The Washington Institute for Near East Policy, April 23, 1999, https://www.washingtoninstitute.org/policy-analysis/iranian-attitudes-toward-kosovo-crisis.

12 "Firas Tlass—Son of the former Syrian Defense Minister Interview Part 1," *Al Arabiya English*, March 25, 2021, YouTube video, 34:28, https://www.youtube.com/watch?v=rVT1uEweuVU&t=243s.

13 *The New York Times*, July 31, 2024, p. A4.

14 *Yediot Achronot, Hamosaf Leshabat*, July 5, 2024, p. 5.

15 *The New York Times*, July 11, 2024, p. A5.

16 Senator Tom Cotton, "Speech On Senate Floor Condemning The Biden Administration's Inadequate Response To Attacks By Iran And Its Proxies On American Troops," November 14, 2023, https://www.cotton.senate.gov/news/speeches/senator-cotton-speech-on-senate-floor-condemning-the-biden-administrations-inadequate-response-to-attacks-by-iran-and-its-proxies-on-american-troops.

17 Zeke Miller and Lolita C. Baldor, "Biden says US 'shall respond' after drone strike by Iran-backed group kills 3 US troops in Jordan," AP News, January 29, 2024, https://apnews.com/article/biden-american-service-members-killed-jordan-iran-5cb774fd835a558d840ae91263037489.

18 Alexandra Hutzler, Jon Haworth, and Nadine El-Bawab, "US retaliatory airstrikes updates: White House vows to take 'more action,'" ABC News, February 4, 2024, https://abcnews.go.com/International/live-updates/us-airstrikes-iran-militias/?id=106747137; *The Wall Street Journal*, July 20-21, 2024, p. A13.

19 President Barack Obama, "Remarks by the President on the Iran Nuclear Deal," White House website, August 05, 2015, https://obamawhitehouse.archives.gov/the-press-office/2015/08/05/remarks-president-iran-nuclear-deal.

20 Itay Stern, "A pollster sheds light on Palestinian attitudes toward the U.S., Israel and Hamas," NPR, July 26, 2024, https://www.npr.org/2024/07/26/g-s1-12949/khalil-shikaki-palestinian-polling-israel-gaza-hamas.

21 *Mah Shekoreh*, April 10, 2024, and August 2, 2024.

22 *Call Me Back—with Dan Senor* (podcast), July 25, 2024, https://podcasts.apple.com/us/podcast/call-me-back-with-dan-senor/id1539292794; *On Brand with Donny Deutsch* (podcast), July 31, 2024, https://podcasts.apple.com/us/podcast/on-brand-with-donny-deutsch/id1565200309.

23 Parisa Hafezi, "Supreme Leader Khamenei says U.S. is Iran's 'number one enemy,'" Reuters, November 2, 2017, https://www.reuters.com/article/world/supreme-leader-khamenei-says-us-is-irans-number-one-enemy-idUSKBN1D211H/.

24 Andrew Solender, "Around half of Congress' Democrats skip Netanyahu speech," Axios, July 24, 2024, https://www.axios.com/2024/07/24/half-house-senate-democrats-boycott-netanyahu.

25 New York Times, February 8, 1979, p. A4.

26 Savannah Kuchar, "'Right side of history': Iran Supreme Leader thanks campus protesters, calls them 'The Resistance,'" USA Today, May 30, 2024, https://www.usatoday.com/story/news/world/2024/05/30/iran-supreme-leader-sayyed-ali-khamenei-letter-college-protests/73904227007/.

27 Nick Robertson, "Pelosi says Netanyahu gave 'the worst' speech to Congress from any foreign leader," The Hill, July 24, 2024, https://thehill.com/homenews/house/4790348-pelosi-netanyahu-worst-speech-congress/.

28 Stephanie Haines, "4 in 5 Americans support Israel over Hamas in Gaza war: Poll," News Nation, May 1, 2024 https://www.newsnationnow.com/world/war-in-israel/most-americans-support-israel-over-hamas-poll/.

29 Melanie Phillips, "On the British Election and the Jews," Tikvah (podcast), July 11, 2024, 54:00, https://sites.libsyn.com/58385/melanie-phillips-on-the-british-election-and-the-jews.

Acknowledgments

This is my second book. And like the first one, writing the Acknowledgments reminds me of the proverb, "It takes a village."

This book, like the last one, would never have happened without the advice and support of my agent, Mel Berger.

The editing of Tony Daniel and Judith Weiss made this book what it is. This is a little book that covers a lot of history, so mistakes are bound to happen. Those that might have slipped through are mine and mine alone.

No book of mine would be complete without the input, friendship, and support of Steven Schwell.

To my courageous publisher, Al Regnery, for taking on the subjects that others would rather ignore.

And finally, to my wife, Esther, and our four children, without whom I wouldn't be having all this fun.

About the Author

Uri Kaufman is the author of *Eighteen Days in October: The Yom Kippur War and How it Created the Modern Middle East* (St. Martin's, 2023), selected by The Financial Times in 2023 as one of the year's best history books. His work has appeared in *Foreign Affairs, Newsweek, The Jerusalem Post*, and numerous other publications. Kaufman lives in Lawrence, New York, with his wife and four children.

www.ingramcontent.com/pod-product-compliance
Lightning Source LLC
Chambersburg PA
CBHW011745020426
42333CB00022B/2716